"*Aces?* How about *Aced?* This colorful account of Hudson, Mulder, and Zito takes the reader through their final season together in Oakland, which was as stormy as it was stirring. Along the way, Urban provides some wild anecdotes from what he witnessed and what they told him in his exclusive interviews. Who else could give never-before-told insight into the pitchers' achievements on the mound as well as a revealing look into their personal lives, including a memorable night at the Pussycat Club? From the speedy rise of the Big Three to their stunning breakup, Urban's book says it all."

—John Shea, national baseball writer, *San Francisco Chronicle*

"Every baseball fan knows that the Oakland Athletics have beaten the odds by winning a lot of baseball games in this era of big payrolls and high-priced free agents. You ask: Didn't someone already write a book about that? Sure. But while *Moneyball* is about Oakland's baseball philosophy, Mychael Urban's *Aces* tells the fun and real story about the three great and very different pitchers who actually won the games on the field. Sadly, Tim Hudson, Mark Mulder, and Barry Zito have been split up now—that's how baseball goes. But the aces live and breathe in these pages."

—Joe Posnanski, columnist, *Kansas City Star*

Aces

The Last Season on the Mound with the Oakland A's Big
Three: Tim Hudson, Mark Mulder, and Barry Zito

MYCHAEL URBAN
Foreword by Billy Beane

WILEY
John Wiley & Sons, Inc.

Copyright © 2005 by Mychael Urban. All rights reserved

Published by John Wiley & Sons, Inc., Hoboken, New Jersey
Published simultaneously in Canada

Photo credits: pages iii, 18, 21, 38, 44, 45, 72, 92, 95, 97, 102, 115, 117, 118, 135, 146, 152, 166, 185, 186, 199, 250, 261, and 265 copyright Michael Zagaris; pages 14 and 201 copyright Barry Zito.

Design and composition by Navta Associates, Inc.

For general information about our other products and services, please contact our Customer Care Department within the United States at (800) 762-2974, outside the United States at (317) 572-3993 or fax (317) 572-4002.

Wiley also publishes its books in a variety of electronic formats. Some content that appears in print may not be available in electronic books. For more information about Wiley products, visit our web site at www.wiley.com.

Library of Congress Cataloging-in-Publication Data:

Urban, Mychael.
    Aces : the last season on the mound with the Oakland A's Big Three : Tim Hudson, Mark Mulder, and Barry Zito / Mychael Urban ; foreword by Billy Beane.
        p. cm.
    Includes bibliographical references.
    ISBN-13 978-0-471-67502-0 (cloth)
    ISBN-13 978-0-471-76316-1 (paper)
    1. Oakland Athletics (Baseball team) 2. Pitchers (Baseball)—United States.
    I. Title.
    GV875.O24U73 2005
    796.357'64'0979466—dc22
                                                                    2004027097

10 9 8 7 6 5 4 3 2 1

For Kelli and Grama,
my angels on earth

CONTENTS

FOREWORD

On June 8, 1999, Tim Hudson took the mound against the Padres in San Diego and ushered in a new era for the Oakland Athletics. The organization had spent much of the 1990s mired in mediocrity, the low point being 1997, when we lost ninety-seven games and finished with the worst record in major league baseball. As every fan knows, to win in baseball you need strong pitching, and that was one thing we didn't possess for a good long time. In fact, our pitching staff was among the very worst in baseball for several years, the low point again being 1997, when the team ERA was 5.49, the highest in the American League.

To say we had poor pitching was probably an understatement.

Particularly poor was the starting rotation, where over the lean years we trotted out some truly forgettable names, and we had only ourselves to blame. Bad decisions and bad luck both played a part. In 1990, we had four first-round picks in the June amateur draft, and we used them to select four highly regarded starting pitchers, the most notable being right-handed high school phenom Todd Van Poppel. Before we knew it, these kids were dubbed the "Four Aces" by *Baseball America*. Well, I don't think much more needs to be said. Only Van Poppel went on to have a big-league career, and even his was below everyone's expectations.

Perhaps our biggest miscalculation came in 1995, when in the eleventh hour we decided to select Cuban right-hander Ariel Prieto, instead of University of Tennessee first baseman Todd Helton. This was against the advice of our scouting department, and Helton went on to a fantastic career. Prieto won all of fifteen games for us in five years. It was a lesson learned the hard way, and one we wouldn't forget. At the time, we were so desperate for starting pitching in Oakland that we became undisciplined with our decision making. It seemed that every choice we made was the wrong one, and if it was right, as was the case with Kirk Dressendorfer, the player was lost to injury. Meanwhile, the local press was taking note of the fact that the A's hadn't developed a major league starting pitcher since Curt Young, who'd made his debut all the way back in 1983. Internally, we had a private joke that we had developed more major league groundskeepers than we had starting pitchers in the last fifteen or so years, and maybe that was our niche.

It was frustrating for an organization that had seen the likes of Catfish Hunter, Ken Holtzman, Dave Stewart, and Vida Blue in its starting rotations. There had been a time when the A's were regularly among the top pitching staffs in the American League, but that era seemed a lifetime ago, as we endured year after year of inflated ERAs and draft busts. Thankfully, all of that changed on that June day in San Diego when Hudson took the mound. After five innings and eleven strikeouts, we knew that the drought had ended.

The year after Hudson's debut was equally important in the recent history of the franchise. In 2000, Mark Mulder and Barry Zito joined Hudson in the big leagues. After nearly a decade and a half of trying to make do with mostly back-of-the-rotation talent, we had not one but three potential number one starters. Three aces. The Big Three.

Their talent and impact were apparent almost immediately, particularly with Tim and Barry, who hit the ground running as big-leaguers. Mark, after jumping directly from college to triple-A, spent less time in the minors than the other two did and subsequently went through a trial-by-fire rookie year, but he soon joined Tim and Barry as perennial Cy Young Award candidates for the next several years. The achievements and the accolades that followed were historic for pitchers at such an early stage in their careers, and possibly most amazing is the fact that they each won twenty games before their twenty-fifth birthdays. By 2002, they had a Cy Young Award and two runner-ups among them.

You could go on and on talking about what they've done, both as a group and as individuals, and you could talk just as long about their importance to the franchise. But as great as they are on the field, they're even more special off it—three amazing athletic talents, with their own distinct personalities, from completely different backgrounds. To admire their exploits is a good thing. To know them is even better.

First is Tim Hudson, the "Gunslinger," from Auburn University in Alabama. A tremendous athlete who, when he wasn't pitching in college, played centerfield and hit over .400. In fact, in addition to striking out eleven in that first major league game of his, he singled and just missed hitting a homer off Adam Eaton, no slouch of a big-league pitcher.

Tim was the only one of the three who wasn't a first-round draft pick; because of his size and—at the time—less than overpowering fastball, he lasted until the sixth round in 1997. But that he's where he is now, throwing in the low- to mid-90s, speaks to his tenacity and work ethic. Tim reminds me of James West from the old television show *The Wild, Wild West*. He's supremely self-confident in an old-South sort of way and the kind of guy who walks away from every card game with more chips than everyone else. He's a competitor and a team leader out of the mold of Stewart, who was the heart and soul of some truly great teams with us. Also, Tim is the only family man of the Big Three, with two beautiful daughters and a lovely wife, Kim, who also happens to be an attorney.

Second to make the scene was Mark Mulder, the "Golden Child," as we affectionately call him. Everything always seems so easy for Mark, whether it's playing scratch golf or hitting a homer with his first professional swing in spring training of 1999. But don't let the apparent effortlessness fool you. Mark works as hard as anyone else at his craft.

If you were going to build a major league starting pitcher, he'd look like Mark—six foot six, with the grace of an NBA small forward. Out of Michigan State University, he hit fourth on his college team and was drafted out of high school as a first baseman by the Detroit Tigers. With good looks and an easygoing, always-in-control air, Mark gives you the feeling that he would be just as happy working as a lifeguard at a Southern California beach as he would being a major league baseball star.

Last, but certainly not least, is Barry Zito, or "Z," as he is known. Six foot four, out of the University of Southern California, Barry is probably the most misunderstood of the three. Eccentric, yes. Flaky, no. A great talent on the field, as well as off. Well-read and an accomplished musician, Barry is the clubhouse Renaissance man. Every spring, I look forward to hearing about his newest passion, whether it be surfing, photography, acting, or Nietzsche.

What is sometimes lost in the portrayal of Barry as a man of many interests, though, is his absolute obsession with being the best major league pitcher in the game. On any given day, you can catch him studying his delivery on video or reading about psychocybernetics, and I've yet to meet a professional athlete this side of Jerry Rice with his dedication.

In the following pages, you'll get a chance to know these three special talents as I do through Mychael Urban, who started covering the A's as a beat writer in 2001. As a big-league general manager, I, like the rest of my colleagues, have a great many demands on my time, and it's been a long time since I've written anything as lengthy—or as formal—as a foreword. I even complained of having writer's block to Mychael. But I agreed to do this because I like and respect Mychael, both personally and professionally. A former left-handed pitcher at the University of San Francisco, he's joked to me that he's the only 6-foot-6 lefty in major-college history to go undrafted. And to be honest, that could very well be true. But the fact that he played at all at such a high level of baseball sets him apart from most sportswriters. Not once have I felt the need to razz him about something he's written in relation to the team, mostly because he "gets it." In addition to being an outstanding writer and an entertaining storyteller, he understands the game. He knows how much pressure is involved. And, most important, he knows how difficult it is to play.

It's these unique sensibilities and sensitivities, not to mention his sense of humor, which seem to have been honed by many hours in a dugout somewhere, that helped Mychael forge a unique relationship with the Big Three. Tim, Mark, and Barry obviously like, respect, and trust him, as do I. As a result, they've opened up to him in ways they probably wouldn't have with any other writer. They've given him access that few outsiders could obtain. And in return, Mychael, in the following pages, is able to provide insights

into their personal and professional personalities, while chroni-
cling what was ultimately a disappointing season for all of us in the
organization but an entertaining year from start to finish.

Talented, different, dedicated, and colorful, the Big Three are
unique. And there's no doubt in my mind that you'll enjoy getting
to know them as much as we have here in Oakland.

—Billy Beane
General Manager, Oakland Athletics

INTRODUCTION

Heading into the 2004 season, it seemed that Tim Hudson was an elite pitcher because he was so utterly determined to be one. Mark Mulder was an elite pitcher because it was almost predetermined. Was Barry Zito an elite pitcher, or was he simply a good pitcher who had one mind-blowing year? Well, that was yet to be determined.

Now that the season is over, all of the above still apply but to a slightly lesser degree. Hudson, despite an ability to exert his iron will over most situations, was powerless against an injury he had spent the entire off-season determined to avoid. Mulder, for the first time in his life, had to deal with the same demons that haunt athletes everywhere, and, suddenly, after a dominant first half, the game wasn't so easy for him. And Zito, after doing little to quiet the talk of his demise as an elite pitcher throughout the first half of the season, rallied after the All-Star break to remind everyone that yes, he's still a star-quality starter.

But as the season unfolded, I heard a version of the same question over and over: *Does this hurt your book?* As Zito struggled with inconsistency in his quest to find the form that made him the 2002 American League (AL) Cy Young Award winner, I heard the question. As Hudson went on the disabled list, interrupting what was shaping up to be his best season yet, I heard the question. And as Mulder slid from Cy Young front-runner in the first half to just another guy fighting himself mentally in the second half, I heard the question again. *Does this hurt your book?*

My answer every time was, "No. It makes it more interesting." Often, that answer was met with puzzled looks. The assumption most people made was that the ideal season in which to write a book about Hudson, Mulder, and Zito, who as a trio had been the one constant as the Oakland A's made four consecutive playoff appearances, despite a payroll well below the league average, was one in which they all put up acelike numbers and pitched the A's deep into the postseason. World Series or bust. Even I felt that way as recently as spring training 2004. But the more things went in the opposite direction, the more I became convinced that it was making for a better story.

Why? Because had Hudson, Mulder, and Zito all enjoyed wildly successful seasons, this would have been a book dominated by the nuts and bolts of pitching. It would have been all about *ball*. Cutters, sliders, sinkers, pitch counts, wins, and losses. And that's not really the book I wanted to write. I wanted to illustrate how different Hudson, Mulder, and Zito are, not just as pitchers but as people, and the fact that all three went through a very different drama over the course of the 2004 season helped me do that in ways that three 19–7 records and 2.86 ERAs couldn't possibly have done.

As you turn to the first chapter, it's important that you understand one thing: this book isn't about the A's, per se. In fact, when I first started pitching the project to publishers, it wasn't going to be about the A's at all. It was going to be a three-headed biography of sorts. It was going to feature the life stories of three young men, brought together by various twists of fate, who happen to be extremely good at what they do but who go about what they do in extremely different ways. Thanks to the foresight of Stephen Power, the editor who convinced John Wiley & Sons to take a chance on the idea, it became so much more—and a little bit less—than that.

Stephen wanted a glimpse of the Big Three with a single season as the backdrop, and as a result, we had to sacrifice some of the detail that goes into telling someone's life story. So you won't find Hudson's third-grade teacher talking about what a tough little kid he was. You won't find Mulder's high school coach recounting the ease with which he mowed down hitters as a sixteen-year-old. And you won't find any of Zito's ex-girlfriends detailing the various ways in which he freaked them out with his intense desire to hear their innermost thoughts.

Nor will you find a detailed account of A's shortstop Bobby Crosby's-award-winning rookie year. You won't find blow-by-blow accounts of the breakout seasons enjoyed by center fielder Mark Kotsay and designated hitter Erubiel Durazo. And you won't find Jermaine Dye lamenting the injury that curtailed what was shaping up to be a brilliant comeback. For this is not a book about the 2004 A's as a whole. Rather, it's about the 2004 A's season as experienced by Hudson, Mulder, and Zito, and it's a story told largely in their own words.

They are, of course, star pitchers. That's why the book exists, and you'll still find plenty of nuts and bolts related to the craft of pitching. Hudson, for instance, explains how in the world his catcher keeps track of his nine different pitches. Mulder tells you why he, unlike many pitchers, doesn't like to rely too much on videotape. And Zito gives you an idea of what it's like to face a free-swinger like New York Yankees star Gary Sheffield.

But there's more. Hudson vents some of his growing aggravation at Oakland's owners for letting star after star depart as free agents, putting more and more pressure on the Big Three to be perfect. Mulder exposes a side of his personality that few people have seen, as he discusses the sudden crisis of confidence that came out of nowhere to derail a dream season. And Zito, in his wonderfully unique way, explains how a little time spent at the mercy of the ocean can do a mind, a body, and a career some serious good.

By now, you know that the 2004 A's didn't make the playoffs. The Big Three did not dominate all year. And then they were torn apart. Does this hurt the book? Ultimately, that's your decision. I say no. It turns a baseball book, written as the season was being played out, into a book about coping with frailty, frustration, and failure, while under the unforgiving microscope of fame. It's a book about three guys who are just as human—and just as prone to the highs and lows of life—as the rest of us.

They just have better fastballs and bigger paychecks.

1

GREEN + GOLD = BLUE

Few things in big-league baseball are more beautiful than Oakland A's lefty Barry Zito at the top of his game. Granted, the sight of Seattle's Ichiro Suzuki gliding from first to third on a single to center is certainly impressive. It's like watching someone running on one of those moving airport walkways—only much, much faster and without the wobbling wheeled luggage awkwardly in tow. Similarly freakish and fascinating is the sight of Angels outfielder Vladimir Guerrero unleashing the beast that is his right arm. Let's see . . . 385 feet from the right-field corner to home plate? Not a problem. Here's a laser-guided strike to beat the runner with enough time for the catcher to brace for the blow that typically comes when a runner is so comically beaten. Oh, and do you want it on one hop or a line? Alex Sanchez of the Detroit Tigers can blow you away, too—with a bunt. It matters not that everyone in the park knows he's going to drop one down. He drops it down anyway, and, far more often than not, he drops it where nobody can possibly stop him from turning it into a single.

As memorable as these moments are, though, they come and go in a matter of seconds. They are riveting solos in the middle of a rock concert, the blurred fingers of Jimmy Page at the end of "Stairway to Heaven." Zito, at his absolute best, is more like the conductor of a symphony. As a starting pitcher, he controls the show's pace, tempo, and rhythm, giving you ample time to soak it all in. And for more than an hour on October 6, 2003, at Oakland's Network Associates Coliseum in game five of the best-of-five American League Division Series (ALDS), Zito was in complete control. Of his stuff, of the game, of the record-breaking Boston Red Sox offense, and, most important as far as the A's were concerned, of the label certain to be affixed to them were they to lose this game.

It's the worst label in sports: CHOKER. And as the media's coverage of sports continues to grow with the explosion of the Internet, the omnipresence of sports-talk radio, and the quick-to-judge nature of television's talking heads, the label has gotten uglier and uglier— and more unfair.

It used to be that only something truly shocking, such as blowing a massive late lead or failing to execute the most fundamental play under crunch-time pressure, warranted the use of the dreaded C word. Think the 1964 Philadelphia Phillies, who gagged away a 6½-game lead in the National League (NL) East by losing 10 games in a row down the stretch. Or the 1975 Pittsburgh Penguins, who won the first three games of a best-of-seven NHL playoff series against the New York Islanders before melting down with four straight losses. Or Jana Novotna, coughing up a 4–1, third-set lead to Steffi Graf in the 1993 Wimbledon women's final, then sobbing on the Duchess of Kent's shoulder. Or Nick Anderson of the Orlando Magic missing four free throws late in game one of the 1995 NBA Finals, when any one of those freebies would have sealed a win. Or poor Jean Van de Velde, needing only a double-bogey 6 at the eighteenth hole on Sunday to win the 1999 British Open, absolutely imploding—mentally and physically—on the way to a 32-ounce-Slurpee-straight-to-the-head brain freeze of a triple-bogey 6.

And, of course, there's the guy who is, and probably always will be, the unfortunate poster boy for sport's least fortunate. That would be Bill Buckner, who proved in game six of the 1986 World Series that it is indeed impossible to field an easy ground ball with both hands wrapped around your own throat. It's ironically delicious that the team equivalent of Buckner is now the 2004 Yankees, who will be forever infamous for blowing a three-game lead in the American League Championship Series (ALCS) to the rival Red Sox.

These were all classic choke jobs, truly deserving of the Heimlich-themed mockery they've induced over the years. Yet every now and then, one media outlet or another will come up with a list of All-Time Chokers, and the list invariably includes the names of athletes or teams who, upon more thoughtful reflection, appear most undeserving of the infamy.

The Buffalo Bills of Jim Kelly, Thurman Thomas, and Bruce Smith, for instance, are always taken to task because they lost four consecutive Super Bowls in the early 1990s. For the glass-half-empty set, which, unfortunately, encompasses the majority of those in the increasingly cynical society of sport, that's considered choking. If you care to see the glass as half-full, however, you'll see those Bills for what they *really* are: the only team in NFL history to win four consecutive conference championships.

Golf's Phil Mickelson used to take a beating on such lists, too, mainly because his immense talent, until a breakthrough win at the 2004 Masters, wasn't translating to success in the game's four majors championships. Dig a little deeper, though, and you'll find that heading into 2004, he'd won more than twenty times on the PGA Tour. That he was a three-time NCAA Champion and Player of the Year. That he shares, along with Jack Nicklaus and only one other golfer in history, the distinction of having won the U.S. Amateur and an NCAA title in the same year. The other golfer, by the way, is one Tiger Woods. Mickelson has the misfortune of being in his prime at the same general place and time as this mind-blowing majors magnet.

The lesson here, apparently, is that in this day and age, to win on a regular basis is to create your own candidacy for a seat on the council of Choke City. Winning's great and all, but if, heaven forbid, you fail to win the proverbial big one once in a while, you're a choker.

This, in a sense, is the weight Barry Zito bore on his back as he took the mound for game five at Oakland in 2003. The A's, a wildly successful team by most reasonable measures, were in danger of failing to advance out of the first round of the playoffs for a fourth consecutive season.

The A's surprised the baseball world in 2000 by winning their division on the last day of the regular season—Tim Hudson beat the Rangers, 3–0, for his twentieth win of the year—before pushing the defending world champion New York Yankees to the limit in the ALDS. But because they'd needed to pull out all the stops just to get *into* the playoffs, they had to send journeyman Gil Heredia out for a game five at home that was all but over by the second inning. In 2001, while they were still seen as the Cute Little Team That Could, the A's pulled off an even bigger surprise as a wild card team, beating the again-defending champion Yankees twice at Yankee Stadium to open the ALDS. But the now-famous play in Oakland by New York shortstop Derek Jeter—*Slide, Jeremy, Slide!*—rendered meaningless a brilliant night by Zito, who allowed a run on two hits over eight innings, and started a downward spiral that led to three straight losses and another early exit.

In 2002 the A's finally got to see what it felt like to be a favorite in the ALDS, but that didn't work out so well, either. They were up two games to one on the Minnesota Twins but lost game four at the Metrodome and game five at home. And here, in 2003, they'd beaten the Red Sox in Oakland in the first two games, only to drop both games in Boston to send everyone back across the country for yet another game five one day later.

Eight times over four years, the A's had worked themselves to within a single victory from clinching their first ALCS since 1992. Eight times they'd lost. "It's not something we think about a lot," Hudson said before the 2003 playoffs started. "But when it's brought up, you're kind of like, 'Man, that is pretty bad, isn't it? We need to get that fixed.'"

Hudson was the starting pitcher in clinch game number eight, which the A's lost 5–4. Zito had the ball for number nine.

Part of what makes Zito's act so entertaining is that it's difficult to define in traditional pitching terms. Most pitchers generally fall into one of two major categories: power or finesse. Power pitchers—Randy Johnson and Roger Clemens are two contemporary prototypes—win on the strength of a dominant fastball. They've got exceptional setup pitches, of course. Not even Nolan Ryan lived by fastball alone; his curveball was devastating. But power pitchers instill fear, command respect, and make big money by blowing balls past guys at between 95 and 100 miles per hour. At the other end of the spectrum are the finesse pitchers—see Jamie Moyer or Greg Maddux—who often don't throw any harder than a good high school hurler. What allows them to thrive is pinpoint accuracy and an ability to adeptly change speeds with four to six different pitches. They keep hitters frustrated and off balance.

Between those two extremes is a very small subset of "gimmick pitchers," such as Boston's own Tim Wakefield, whose knuckleball appears to stagger like a teenager after his first encounter with Jack Daniels. Throw ageless lefty Jesse Orosco into that lot as well, if for no other reason than, as the only pitcher in modern big-league history to possess a glove autographed by Moses, he seems to have accomplished what Ponce de Leon could not.

And then there is Zito, a free-spirited southpaw who is in something of a category all his own. He definitely isn't a power pitcher; his fastball barely tops 90 mph. He isn't a finesse pitcher, either; his control is good but not pinpoint. And while his curveball is so good that it's something most people can throw only with the help of a PlayStation joystick, it's no gimmick. It's a classic over-the-top, noon-to-six bender that generally starts at the hitter's eye level and drops—two-thirds of the way to the plate—below the knees. But because of that big curveball, which many baseball people consider the best in the game, Zito at his best is a power pitcher and a finesse pitcher at the same time. He doesn't always throw the big breaker for strikes, but he does so often enough that hitters have to be on the lookout for it. And when they're looking for a 72-mph curveball and get an 89-mph fastball instead, even the best hitters can look hapless. "That's when it looks like he's throwing about 120," said Yankees first baseman Jason Giambi, who played with Zito in Oakland during the 2000 and 2001 seasons. "But if you're looking for the fastball, that's when he freezes you by dropping that cartoon hammer on you for strike three. That's when he makes you look like an idiot."

And when Zito freezes someone in that situation with two out in an inning, it's a priceless bit of theater. Why? Because often he's already taken a few steps off the mound toward the A's dugout by the time the umpire lets the hitter know he's been had. So sure is Zito of the pitch he's just released that he doesn't even bother to check out the aftermath. He just *knows*. "I don't mean to show anyone up when I do that," Zito insists. "And I don't do it on purpose at all; I didn't even really know I did that. But when you know, you know. You know?" Yankees catcher Jorge Posada knew, during a playoff game in which Zito froze him for a called third strike to end an inning, and he didn't take even the slightest umbrage when Zito prematurely pimped off the mound without so much as a glance back at the plate. Instead, Posada, shaking his head in amazement, actually burst out laughing. "That's ridiculous," he could be seen saying to nobody in particular, and he wasn't talking about Zito's confident walk off the hill. He was talking about the manner in which he'd just been tooled by a master craftsman.

—   —   —

Here was Zito again, on October 6, 2003, tooling the powerful Red Sox for five shutout innings. Boston set a slew of big-league records during the regular season, breaking the slugging percentage record set by the fabled 1927 Bronx Bombers along the way, but they weren't doing any slugging on this day. Zito was perfect through the first three frames, quickly dispatching the first nine batters he faced, and through five innings he'd allowed two hits. One was an infield single by speedy Johnny Damon, who had left the low-budget A's as a free agent the previous off-season, and the other was a clean single to center by Kevin Millar, who was thrown out by center fielder Chris Singleton trying to stretch it into a double. The first two times Most Valuable Player (MVP) candidate Manny Ramirez came to the plate, Zito sat him down on strikes. "He was dominating us," Millar would say later. "Again."

"Again" was a reference to game two of the series, in which Zito, the 2002 AL Cy Young Award winner, earned himself a measure of redemption for a substandard—by *his* standards, anyway—regular season. A day after lead-footed catcher Ramon Hernandez had given the A's a victory in the series opener by way of a gorgeously stunning bases-loaded bunt single with two out in the bottom of the twelfth inning, Zito led the A's to within a game of the

ALCS—again—by striking out nine, including five in a row at one point. He scattered five hits over seven innings, and Oakland's 5–1 win upped his career postseason record to 3–1, while lowering his career postseason ERA to 2.03. "All you can say when Barry's on like that is, 'Wow!'" Hernandez said after the game. "I'm just glad I don't have to face him when he's like that."

— — —

The starting pitcher for day games after night games is often allowed to leave the night game early to get extra rest, and on the night of game one, it ended up being a particularly good idea. Hernandez's heroics ended the longest playoff game in Oakland history—four hours, thirty-seven minutes—just before midnight, and by then, Zito was already in bed at his spartan San Francisco flat. But he wasn't asleep. He was listening to the game on the radio, and when he arrived at the ballpark the next day, he couldn't help himself. He sneaked into the tiny Oakland video room to take a quick peek at what he'd missed. "Just from listening, I think I pictured [game one] pretty well," Zito said. "But I still came into the clubhouse and watched the tape of the last couple of guys, just to make it real and get me fired up for my start." He needed no such devices to get the juices flowing for game five. It was what first-year A's manager Ken Macha called an "everything game," and everything about it reeked of drama.

For one thing, Zito was working on short rest for the first time in his brief-but-brilliant career. A slave to the carefully choreographed between-starts routine crafted by then–pitching coach Rick Peterson, whose attention to detail borders on maniacal, Zito had made every one of his previous 123 starts since reaching the big leagues in 2000 on at least four days of rest. Now, in the biggest start of his life, he was going on three days. That means the routine had changed, and instead of his standard two sessions in the bullpen between starts, he got one. "It's going to be interesting if we go to game five," Zito said before the series started. "You want to think that your mind can will your body to do whatever you want it to do, but until you're out there, you just don't know."

Making Zito's task all the more daunting was that opposite him on the mound for Boston was one of the most feared big-game pitchers of his time. Red Sox righty Pedro Martinez was the run-away winner when, in an informal poll conducted by MLB.com late in the 2003 season, ninety-five big leaguers were asked which pitcher they'd most like on their side with the season on the line. "Pedro's the toughest pitcher out there," said shortstop David Eckstein of the 2002 world champion Anaheim Angels. "He throws from so many angles and can do so much with the baseball. He can make it cut, he can back it up, he throws the slider, then the changeup. He has so many different pitches that he can rely on at any time." What's more, Martinez would be taking the mound with a bit of a chip on his shoulder. He was knocked out of his only regular-season start of 2003 in Oakland after just five innings, thoroughly outpitched by Hudson in the process, and despite pitching well in game one of the ALDS, he was long gone by the time Hernandez's bunt won it in the twelfth.

There was this little subplot, too: Martinez, who won the NL Cy Young Award in 1997 and the AL Cy Young in 1999 and 2000, privately fumed when Zito edged him for the 2002 AL award, suggesting that race and image were factors in the vote. A rumor swirled that he had derisively called Zito, a handsome budding musician whose acquaintances include singer/songwriters Dave Matthews, Ben Folds, John Mayer, and Ari Hest, a "cute little white boy with a guitar." Zito tried to take the high road, but he was surprised and disappointed by the alleged swipe. "I didn't hear him say it myself, so I'm not going to worry about it," he said. "But if he did say that, that's pretty weak. That's punk shit right there." Now Zito and Martinez were facing each other in game five, marking the first time in baseball history that two former Cy Young winners were to square off in a series-deciding game. An "everything game."

When, exactly, everything started to unravel for the 2003 A's is open to interpretation. A great many people point to game three at Boston's Fenway Park, where Oakland tied a playoff record by making four errors—three came in one inning, including two by third baseman Eric Chavez, a four-time Gold Glove winner—and cost themselves two runs with base-running blunders. On one play, Eric Byrnes failed to touch home plate with what would have been the game-tying run and was tagged out on his way to the A's dugout. Not long after that, Boston shortstop Nomar Garciaparra mishandled a ground ball that allowed the A's to tie the game at 1–1, but Oakland's former MVP shortstop, Miguel Tejada, bumped into Boston third baseman Bill Mueller while running from second to third, then stopped between third and home, thinking that umpire Bill Welke had called interference and ruled the play dead. Tejada thought wrong, and after he, too, was tagged out, Boston went on to win 3–1 on Trot Nixon's eleventh-inning homer to keep the series alive.

It was in the morgue of Oakland's postgame clubhouse that Chavez, whose brutal, often-unsolicited honesty is equal parts refreshing and disarming, verbalized the doubt that had to be setting up camp in the minds of many A's. "If we don't win tomorrow, we're gonna lose this thing," Chavez blurted. "Because they've got Pedro ready for game five, and I just don't see Boston losing two games that he starts in a row." Two days after the mental mistakes of Byrnes and Tejada, Chavez was proven prophetic. And that's why there are others who look at the night *before* game three, when Zito and Hudson made the mental mistake of showing their faces in a downtown Boston bar, as the beginning of the end for Oakland.

Considering Beantown's well-documented passion for the Red Sox and the fact that the A's held a 2–0 series lead when Zito and Hudson popped into a popular nightspot, the result was fairly predictable. Hudson got into a dust-up with a fan that, depending on whose version you believe, was either mostly verbal or intensely physical. Either way, it was ugly, and when Hudson had to leave game four with a strained oblique (side/hip) muscle after throwing just nine pitches, it opened the door to all kinds of speculation— addressed in detail later—as to whether he'd been injured in that bar. "Y'all got me made out to be a bare-knuckle champion," Hudson said before game five. "It was just a small verbal altercation that resulted in a little bit of finger-pointin' and a couple of shoves. . . . But the fact that it happened to Tim Hudson blew it up to a scale where everybody thinks I was bear-rasslin' the bouncers and handling eight men."

Although sidelined with a leg injury during the 2003 ALDS against
Boston, Mark Mulder traveled with the team to Fenway Park to
continue rehabbing in hopes of making his return for the ALCS.

Still another theory on the origins of Oakland's latest playoff
demise centered on August 19. That's the day lefty Mark Mulder,
who was among the league leaders in wins (15) and ERAs (3.13) at
the time, had to leave a start—in Boston, no less—after three
innings with what was later determined to be a stress fracture in his
right femur, just below the hip. Mulder did not pitch again in 2003,
and his absence is what forced the A's to send Hudson and Zito out
for games four and five on short rest. "It couldn't have been worse
timing," Mulder moped, upon hearing his prognosis. "It's different
from any other injury, and nobody knows what caused it. I was surprised. It really caught me off guard." As did the sixth inning of
game five, when Boston finally broke through against Zito and
started pounding the final nails in Oakland's newest October coffin.

The trouble actually started in the fifth inning. Zito, nursing a 1–0
lead, got out of it without allowing a run, but early in the frame
there were telltale signs of the doom to come. He fell behind to

David Ortiz, three balls and a strike, before getting him to ground out to second base on what probably would have been ball four. Then he made a mistake on a two-strike pitch to Millar, who drilled it into center field before getting thrown out at second. Then, after getting ahead of Mueller, the AL batting champ, 1-and-2, he walked him with three balls in a row. Ortiz's lack of plate discipline, Millar's poor judgment, and an inning-ending ground out by Nixon allowed Zito to get away with the unsteady inning, but his aura of invincibility was gone. He was bouncing pitches in the dirt. He was missing his spots. He was laboring. From the time he had joined the professional ranks, his body had been conditioned to respond and perform every fifth day. This was day four, and Zito looked like he was running out of gas. "I didn't *feel* like I was," he said later. "But maybe I was. I don't know. I felt fine."

Jason Varitek led off the sixth, and Zito started him with three balls. Two pitches later the count was full, and a pitch after that, the game was tied. Varitek's homer to left opened the floodgates. Zito walked Damon, and with one out, he hit Todd Walker with a pitch. That's when Ramirez exacted revenge for his two strike-outs—one looking, one swinging—by guessing right that he'd be seeing one of those 89-mph fastballs and bashing it into the seats for a 4–1 lead. The A's cut into the lead with a run in the bottom of the sixth and chased Martinez with a run in the eighth, but Boston's bullpen survived a dicey bottom of the ninth to earn an ALCS date with the rival Yankees. Clinch game number nine was over for Oakland, and the result was more painful than the previous eight.

For Mulder, who'd also missed the 2000 playoffs, with a back injury, it was especially painful because he'd been working like hell to get back into shape. As trainers put him through drills during late September and early October, the A's downplayed the notion that Mulder was trying to get ready for the ALCS, but a month after the 2003 playoffs ended, he came clean. "I was definitely going to pitch against the Yankees," Mulder said. "There was no other reason to be working out."

For Hudson, one of Oakland's most intense and respected players, there was the pain of letting his teammates down. Dating back to the 2002 series against the Twins, he was winless in his last four playoff starts. "It's getting old now," he said, as he packed his things up for the winter the day after game five. "It's a team game, but when you don't get your own job done, it makes it tougher on everyone else."

And for Zito, who prides himself on being every bit the big-game pitcher that Martinez is, there was the pain of knowing he'd failed to come through when the stakes were as high as they'd ever been for this young core of A's. "It leaves a really bad taste in my mouth, because I was the one that could have put an end to all that talk about us being chokers," he said. "I don't buy into that, anyway, because getting to the playoffs four years in a row is pretty hard to do, but that's what people are going to say."

And they did. Winning a ton of games every year doesn't mean much, remember? Even if you're a low-payroll team who loses marquee free agents every winter the way trees lose leaves. Just getting to the postseason isn't good enough. Unless you do something once you're there, you might as well have not gone at all. You get *that label*. So until the 2004 playoffs at the earliest, Hudson, Mulder, and Zito knew they'd have to live with the fact that in addition to being the anchors of one of the best young teams in baseball, they were members of what the glass-half-empty set was now calling the *Chokeland* A's.

2

THREE OF A KIND (SORT OF)

Is a great pitcher born, built, or both? It's a question that takes some time to answer, and it probably isn't even a question for which there is one definitive answer. Physiology, psychology, biomechanics, and other similarly complicated topics are all part of the equation, and different people have different theories as to the importance of each factor. But at the surface level, as the question applies to Oakland's Tim Hudson, Mark Mulder, and Barry Zito, it's safe to say that there are three different answers. And as simple as it sounds, you need only to know a little about each man while watching the trio take batting practice to see which answer applies to whom. As American League pitchers, Hudson, Mulder, and Zito don't get to hit very often, but for about a month each summer they're in the cage preparing for interleague play.

Witness the ease with which Mulder, the MVP of the Michigan State University baseball team in 1997 and 1998 as a pitcher/first baseman, uses a long, fluid swing to effortlessly lift balls deep into the outfield and often over the fence. A similar version of that sweet stroke is what makes Mulder the longest and best golfer on the A's; he says he'd be trying to make a living on the PGA Tour if not for

Mulder, here talking with Ken Macha in the dugout at Pac Bell Park during his rookie season of 2000, batted cleanup and played first base when
he wasn't pitching at Michigan State University. He never imagined
being a big-league pitcher while he was growing up. He wanted to hit.

baseball, and tales such as the one about his 5-wood out of the sand,
over water, from 250 feet out to 5 feet from the pin suggest that it's
not an overly ambitious notion. But baseball called first dibs, and
Mulder is a natural in every aspect of it. In fact, there doesn't seem
to be much that *doesn't* come natural to him. Through the 2003 season, there'd always been an effortlessness about Mulder, both on
and off the field, and even he'd admit that life hadn't exactly been
a grind thus far. It had pretty much been a breeze, and that's
reflected in the way he goes about his work. A 6-foot-6, 210-pound
picture of athletic grace, he has the perfect body for a pitcher, and
he always seems to have a preternatural calm about him under the
stress of competition. Mark Mulder was born for the big leagues.

Now watch Zito take a few hacks, if you can stand it. His body
type—6 foot 4, 215—is very similar to Mulder's, but his swing is
most definitely not. Imagine a flamingo, hypnotized into thinking

it's a frog, trying to catch flies through a screen door. Now take away the flamingo's equilibrium and one of its legs. That's Zito with a bat in his hands, struggling to get anything airborne. Drafted out of the University of Southern California, he's the only one of Oakland's aces who wasn't also a full-time hitter in college, and after watching him flail at just a few pitches, it's easy to see why. Put a baseball in his hand on top of a slab of rubber stationed 60½ feet from home plate, though, and everything makes sense. Always has, really. From the time his father, Joe, noticed him bouncing a ball off the wall from his crib, Zito has been urged to explore every aspect of what Barry calls "the process" of pitching. His dad, who built a mound in the family backyard, never played the game and knew nothing of it when Barry was born, but as his son got older, he'd read books on the game at night and teach Barry what he'd learned the next day. And when books weren't enough, Joe brought in former Cy Young Award–winner Randy Jones to give the boy lessons. That's not to say Zito isn't a good athlete. He is. He's an excellent surfer, and he's good enough on guitar to play in his sister's band—two disciplines that require a fair share of physical dexterity. But it's his discipline when it comes to his day job that helps set him apart. He studies. He analyzes. He computes. These are things you don't have a lot of time for in the batter's box, but on the mound it's another story. Barry Zito is a man-made pitcher, built from the ground up.

Hudson? When he's in the cage, he's spraying line drives all over the field—and telling anyone within earshot all about it. "Ain't a park that can hold me!" he shouts, as a line drive clears the left-field wall. Hudson's swing isn't as pretty as Mulder's, but it's better. It's the swing of a real hitter, and it's essentially wasted in the American League. "If Huddy played in the National League, he might hit .300," former A's batting coach Thad Bosley once said. "He knows what he's doing in there. He's got an idea. And he'll ask questions, too." Hudson always has been something of a jack-of-all-trades on the diamond. When he wasn't carving through Southeast Conference (SEC) lineups as Auburn University's stud pitcher, he was roaming center field for the Tigers. As a senior he went 15–2 on the mound and hit .396 with eighteen homers and a school-record ninety-five RBIs—breaking future Hall of Fame candidate Frank Thomas's mark—while earning SEC Player of the Year and

All-America honors as a utilityman. So it's obvious that Hudson wasn't shortchanged when it comes to athletic ability. But he's had to work hard for everything. Listed at 6 foot 1 and 165 pounds, which is small for a big-league pitcher as it is, he's actually shorter than that. Closer to 5 foot 10. But he complements his natural talent with unshakable determination and a willingness to learn that allows him to make adjustments on the fly, whether it's to a batting-practice fastball tailing back into him or to the sudden flattening of his beloved sinking fastball. He can flat-out improvise. So was Tim Hudson born to be a great pitcher, or was he built into one? The answer is . . . yes.

Being young and ridiculously gifted is only part of what makes Hudson, Mulder, and Zito so intriguing as a trio. Hudson was the 2000 AL Cy Young Award runner-up at age twenty-five. Mulder was the 2001 Cy Young runner-up at twenty-four. And some eight months after Hudson jokingly predicted that Zito would keep the "bridesmaid streak" alive by becoming the 2002 Cy Young runner-up, Zito broke through and became, at twenty-four, the youngest winner of the award in fourteen years. But most people already know that. What they don't know is that despite having developed almost simultaneously into three of the brightest stars in the baseball galaxy, they essentially come from different planets. Hudson, Mulder, and Zito have been shaped by sharply contrasting experiences, yet they arrived smack-dab in the center of their sport's spotlight—together—after following strikingly similar professional paths. How much of that has been coincidence? How much of it has been Oakland's good luck? How much of it science, scouting, and plain old-fashioned smarts? To answer those questions, you need to know more.

You need to know that Hudson grew up small in small-town Phenix City, Alabama, giving him an underdog—make that *bulldog*—mentality and a maturity, offset by perfectly placed playfulness, that make him a popular clubhouse presence. You need to know that Mulder's fairly idyllic upbringing in suburban Chicago (South Holland, Illinois) helps to explain his unflappable presence—be it with runners on the corners and nobody out, or with two hot blondes eyeing him from the corner of a hotel bar. And you need to know that Zito was every bit the maverick as a mullet-haired Little Leaguer that he became as an occasionally blue-haired big leaguer. Baseball is the backdrop, but it's a collection of people stories that helps to explain how three incredibly different young men ended up as the three aces in one of baseball's toughest hands to beat. Some of the stories are analytical, some are biographical, and some, because the pace of baseball's long season lends itself to great humor and drama, are simply anecdotal. But they are all connected, just as much of what's happened in the private lives of the three men is connected to what they do for a very public living.

Zito, Mulder, and Hudson are often written about, talked about, and judged as one. All three were drafted out of major colleges as All-Americans, all three ripped through the minor leagues in less than three years, and all three became bona-fide stars within their first two years in the big leagues. Collectively, they've been the dominant force that keeps the A's competitive, marketable, and on the national radar. But they're even more interesting individually, mainly because they're every bit as colorful as their collective nickname—"the Big Three"—is not.

Zito, Hudson, and Mulder have a brotherly bond, and they can often be found joking with one another in the A's dugout.

Hudson, the oldest of the A's trio but the youngest of three Hudson brothers, is the lone right-hander. He's the only husband, the only father, and the only one who needs to stand on his stool in the clubhouse to reach something at the back of the top shelf in his locker. The 6 foot 1 he's listed at? "Must've been wearin' them stripper heels the day they took that measurement," he says with his infectious Southern twang. Hudson also is the only one of Oakland's aces for whom hair is not particularly important. Mulder often doesn't wear a hat in the dugout when he's not pitching, and he makes sure his coiffure—think Ryan Seacrest meets Chuck Woolery—is always matinee-idol perfect. Zito works to make sure his 'do looks combed-with-a-rock stylish. Hudson simply shaves and shines his head to mask premature balding. "I'd be the world's ugliest Chia Pet if I didn't shave my head," he says. Hudson has been among the smallest players on the field for most of his life, and he's by far the most demonstrably competitive of Oakland's aces. He also has the quickest wit and the easiest manner, making him the most roundly liked by teammates, and his intensity on the field gives him cachet as one of Oakland's few true team leaders. A family man with a seemingly endless supply of energy and one-liners, Hudson is like the next-door neighbor you so desperately want to like you. And because he has a far better handle on diplomacy than most major leaguers do, you'd never know it if he didn't.

Mulder, the A's trio's "middle brother" in age but the oldest of three brothers in the Mulder family, is the carefree playboy of the group. Literally. Life has been good to Mulder, who's always been among the biggest, most gifted players on the field, and he's rarely faced adversity. After injuring his left forearm early in the 2002 season, for example, he said, "I'm not really used to bad things happening to me." He lives the kind of life you might expect a young millionaire to live. In the first several years of his career, he spent the bulk of his time on baseball, golf, video games, and women, and he is the most outwardly confident of the three. But somehow he's also the least comfortable socially, the least likely to fill a reporter's notebook, and he can come off as aloof or even arrogant. He's admitted to all of this and has said it's in part by design, because while he loves most of the perks that come with being a star baseball player, such as free golf at the nation's top country clubs and attractive, interested women, he doesn't want any part of the media circus that comes with being an A-list celebrity. Or so he says. With each passing year, he becomes more at ease with what he calls "the drill" of dealing with fame, to the point where he actually seems to enjoy it from time to time.

Zito, the youngest of the trio, has two older sisters and is the anti-Mulder when it comes to fame. Zito has A-list written all over him, and he wears it with pride. Born in Las Vegas, he lives in the Hollywood Hills during the off-season and spent the winter after winning the 2002 Cy Young Award playing guitar with his sister's band, surfing Fiji with big-league buddies, and exploring his options as an actor. He's appeared in Showtime's *The Chris Isaak Show*, HBO's *Arli$$*, and the CBS military drama *J.A.G.* His parents met while touring with the great Nat King Cole—his father as a composer, his mother as a singer—so entertainment is in Zito's blood, and he's one of the most entertaining interview subjects a sportswriter is likely to find. He's been chronicled as having traveled with a satin pillow and scented candles. He has stuffed animals in his locker. He dyes his hair. He practices yoga. He meditates. And with regular trips to thrift shops while the A's are on the road, he has a wardrobe—butterfly collars and all tight-fitting things polyester—that makes you wonder when Tom Jones is going to call and ask for his closet back. But while he's a fan and media darling as much for his eccentricities as for his electric talent, he chafes at the common perception that he's a flake. Intensely devoted to perfection, he's extremely serious about baseball and is probably the most disciplined, thoughtful, and ambitious of the trio.

Simply put, Hudson, Mulder, and Zito are a baseball anomaly, in that they've arrived at the same place at the same time and, at least initially, enjoyed roughly the same level of success. But their respective routes—and roots—present a remarkable study of contrasts.

∿   ∿   ∿

About 12.5 seconds after the Florida Marlins punctuated their improbable wild card run of 2003 by beating the heavily favored Yankees in the World Series, the gun-jumpers of the game went to work. They looked at Florida's gifted young staff of starting pitchers and proclaimed it one of the best in the business. Anchoring the rotation was right-hander Josh Beckett, a cocksure twenty-three-year-old Texan who got better as his second full season in the big leagues wore on and who capped a sensational postseason with a five-hit shutout—on three days of rest—in game six at Yankee Stadium. Beckett was named the MVP of the series, but the award could have just as easily gone to twenty-five-year-old righty Brad Penny, who allowed a total of four runs in winning his two starts. Righty Carl Pavano, twenty-seven, was no slouch himself in the series, allowing a run over eight innings of work. And while the babe of the bunch, twenty-one-year-old Dontrelle Willis, was moved to the bullpen for the Fall Classic to give the Marlins a reliable lefty in relief, it was his sensational season as a starter that won him the 2003 National League Rookie of the Year Award. And Beckett, still soaking in champagne a good ninety minutes after his title-clinching game six, reminded anyone and everyone in his drenched corner of the clubhouse that Florida did what it did without twenty-six-year-old A. J. Burnett, a classic power pitcher whose season had ended with April elbow surgery. "If A. J. comes back healthy, who's better than us?" Beckett boomed, as yet another beer made its way down his gullet. "I don't know, man. I don't see anyone out there that we can't match up with."

At first glance, it didn't seem such a reach. The Marlins, after all, had proved themselves on the grandest of stages—even more so than the other young guns getting a load of attention late in 2003. Before the Florida staff stole the spotlight, it was trained squarely on a quartet of Cubs. Chicago's twenty-three-year-old Mark Prior and twenty-six-year-old Kerry Wood were the headliners of a rotation that included Carlos Zambrano, a twenty-two-year-old with explosive stuff and seemingly limitless potential, and Matt Clement, a late bloomer who appeared to have finally figured things out at age twenty-nine. But then the Marlins beat Prior and Wood in consecutive games at Wrigley Field to snatch the 2003 NL Championship Series and outlasted a Yankees team loaded with big, expensive names on the mound. In full what-have-you-done-for-me-lately froth, the gun-jumpers eagerly embraced Florida as the staff to beat for 2004. That's what winning in the playoffs does for you.

Now for a quick history lesson, courtesy of Hudson. "Don't get me wrong. They're great," he says of the Marlins and the Cubs pitchers. "But I think they've got a ways to go before people start putting them up on that pedestal." Indeed, if any collection of arms belongs on that pedestal, it's probably the unique collection swathed in green and gold. Hudson, Mulder, and Zito aren't just the most accomplished trio of young pitchers in big-league baseball these days. They are one of the most accomplished trios of young pitchers *in the history of the game.*

Example: One of the common benchmarks for single-season greatness on the mound is twenty wins, and Hudson reached it in 2000 at age twenty-five. Mulder reached it in 2001 at age twenty-four. And when Zito, then twenty-four, reached it in 2002, it marked the first time in *102 years* that a team had three different twenty-game winners under age twenty-five in consecutive seasons, and the third time since 1900 that the same team had three different pitchers lead the league in wins in consecutive seasons. The Cubs and the Marlins? Going into 2004, Prior's career high in victories was eighteen, and none of the other young pitchers on either team had won more than fourteen games in a year. Hudson had won at least fourteen games four times, Mulder and Zito three each.

More proof: in only seven seasons since 1920 has a team had three starters under age twenty-eight with at least fifteen wins and an ERA 20 percent better than the league average. Hudson, Mulder, and Zito gave the A's two such seasons, in 2001 and 2002. "I hope people realize how special these three guys are," says Art Howe, who managed the A's from 1996 to 2002 before taking over with the New York Mets. "Fifty years from now, people are going to be telling their grandkids, 'I was there when those three guys were teammates, and now they're all in the Hall of Fame.'" Asked during the 2003 off-season to compare the Marlins and the Cubs to the A's of Hudson, Mulder, and Zito, Howe laughed and echoed Hudson's sentiment. "It's not even close," Howe said. "Talk to me in a few years if you want to know what I think of those other guys. Those kids in Oakland have already proven themselves."

Thirty minutes or so after pinch hitter Terrence Long was caught looking at the called third strike from Boston's Derek Lowe that ended the 2003 ALDS, the A's clubhouse was a cauldron of emotion. Off in an area closed to the media, general manager (GM) Billy Beane was trying to keep Tejada, his star shortstop, from blowing a gasket. Actually, he was trying to repair the gasket Tejada had already blown. Perhaps the most passionate player on Oakland's roster, Tejada had taken serious offense when Lowe punctuated his punchout of Long with a gesture that Tejada interpreted as being an effort to show the A's up on their own turf. What Tejada had seen was Lowe, turned toward Oakland's dugout, doing something of a karate chop to the crotch area, and he took it as Lowe suggesting something along the lines of, "Take a suck on *that!*" So as soon as the clubhouse was opened to the media after the game, Tejada, a Dominican Republic native whose improving-but-still-balky command of the English language leaves some of his comments open to translation, let loose with an uncharacteristically profane tirade that left little doubt as to how he felt. "He's going to pay for that sign he made!" Tejada yelled of Lowe. "I'm a fucking man! I'm a fucking professional. You don't *do* that shit! . . . That's bullshit, man. Bullshit! . . . I have my kid up in the stands, dammit! He's going to fucking pay for that!"

Beane quickly stepped in to usher Tejada into the shower area, but an unmistakable sense of frustration was in the air, and Tejada's frustration was as understandable as anyone's. Signed by the A's as a dirt-poor, skinny seventeen-year-old, he'd confirmed his ascendancy into the ranks of the game's elite players by winning the 2002 American League MVP, but 2003, the last year of his current contract, was a major disappointment. It started with A's co-owner Steve Schott, in an astoundingly poor public relations move, announcing during spring training that perennially cash-strapped Oakland, for fear of insulting Tejada with an under-market offer, wasn't going to make even a token effort to re-sign him. Schott backed off that stance after several weeks of backlash in the Bay Area and beyond, but the damage had been done. Tejada, who hit a career-high .308 the previous season, went into a funk that saw him hit .161 in the first month of the season, and he entered the All-Star break still mired at a mediocre .245. He bounced back with a strong second half, hitting .326 after vowing to stop putting so much pressure on himself to live up to the MVP standards he had set, but when the pressure of the playoffs arrived, Tejada's funk returned. He had two hits in twenty-three at-bats for an ugly .087 average to go with his brain cramp on the bases in that series-turning game three.

Had he known for certain that he'd be back in Oakland for 2004, Tejada might not have reacted so angrily after game five. The truth is that Lowe wasn't showing anyone up at all, and more than a few A's acknowledged that. The truth is that the cold reality of the business of baseball was setting in for Tejada, who, like Beane, knew that the best shortstop in Oakland history very likely had just seen the disappearance of his last shot at glory with the team who discovered him. "I feel really sorry for my fans," Tejada said, after his cooling-off session. Added Beane, "It's very, very difficult. Not just professionally but personally. Miguel's more than just our shortstop. He's an incredible personality. He represents the organization."

Not far from Tejada's locker sat Long, representing himself. The season had been disappointing in other ways for Long, whose relationship with first-year manager Ken Macha was chilly in the best of times and Lambeau Field–frozen in the worst of times. This was the worst of times, and Long let loose. "Fuck him," he said of Macha. "After the game, he shook every motherfucker on the team's hand and walked right past me. So if that's how it is, I don't need to be here. Let me go. I don't need this shit. Get me out of here." That would prove easier said than done, though, for there's never been much of a market for disgruntled outfielders coming off consecutive seasons of hitting .245 or less and due to make $8 million for the next two years. Throw in the unsavory reputation that came with the rant against Macha—"Maybe what's needed here is a mirror; I think his comments are way off base," Beane said—and the GM's hands appeared tied. But like the front-office magician he's reputed to be, Beane managed to get rid of Long's contract and strengthen Oakland's outfield for 2004 in the same deal. There was a steep price to pay, though. In sending Long to the San Diego Padres in a November 2003 trade that brought center fielder Mark Kotsay, whom Beane had long admired, the A's had to say good-bye to yet another player they had signed as a seventeen-year-old and developed into an All-Star. Catcher Ramon Hernandez, who made his big-league debut in the same season that Hudson became the first of Oakland's aces to make it to the Show, went to the Padres in the swap as well. "Wow," Hudson said, upon hearing the news of Hernandez's departure. "Nothing Billy does should surprise me by now, but I gotta admit it: this one's a shocker." Zito's initial reaction was one of shock, too. "I'm still trying to figure this one out. Ramon was such a huge part of our staff," he said. Added Mulder: "It's gonna be weird not throwing to Ramon. He's the guy we've been working with since we got here." The same could be said of another casualty of a typically tumultuous Oakland off-season. Not long before Hernandez was sent packing, pitching coach Rick Peterson was allowed to end his six-year association with the A's by reuniting with Howe as the pitching coach of the New York Mets.

So as Hudson, Mulder, and Zito headed into the winter of 2003, here's what they knew of the challenge that would be 2004: likely without Tejada, the team's most productive offensive player and a dynamic defender up the middle, and definitely without two men who played a big part in shaping their rapid rise to pitching prominence, the A's would be leaning on the Big Three more than ever to carry them to the promised land. Oh, and closer Keith Foulke, who led the AL with forty-three saves, would probably be gone, too. "Ain't that somethin'?" Hudson mused. "No pressure at all, boys. It's all on you now. Go get 'em."

3

THE BIG STORY

The ways in which Hudson, Mulder, and Zito differ in personality are evident everywhere they go and in virtually everything they do. In interviews, on the mound, and off the field, they are as dissimilar as dawn, noon, and dusk. And two nights before A's pitchers and catchers are to officially report for spring training in Phoenix, those differences are on full display as they hang out with one another and a few teammates and friends in the VIP section of the Pussycat Lounge, a popular hangout in Scottsdale, Arizona. Twelve of major league baseball's thirty teams get ready for the regular season in the dry heat of Arizona, most of them at complexes either in or within a short drive of Phoenix. But if Phoenix is where so many big leaguers go to work every spring, Scottsdale is, for various reasons, where they go to play.

"I don't know what's hotter here: the women or the weather," A's infielder Frank Menechino says to nobody in particular, as one of the Pussycat Lounge's gorgeous waitresses drops off a tray of drinks that resembles the Manhatttan skyline. And heat is probably reason number one behind Scottsdale's popularity with athletes. Packed with beautiful women, an inordinate number of whom are trim, tan, silicone-enhanced, and single, Scottsdale allows players to be *players*, and Mark Mulder, when he doesn't have a girlfriend, as is the case when spring training begins, is nothing if not a player—in every sense of the word. So there he sits on a couch behind the velvet ropes of the Pussycat Lounge, flanked by a pair of women who look like they just stepped out of the pages of *Playboy*.

Not far from where Mulder sits is Hudson, on his feet, a drink in one hand, as the other hand flies about while he excitedly tells a friend about the due date of his second daughter. Hudson and his wife, Kim, are expecting sometime in early May, and the plan is to induce labor on May 4, the day after Hudson and the A's return to Oakland from a trip through New York and Tampa Bay. Hudson, a Southern Baptist who attends chapel every Sunday on the road and places family above all, is beaming as he talks about Kim, their first daughter, Kennedie, now two years old, and the little girl on the way. But the second that hip-hop artist 50 Cent's omnipresent party anthem "In Da Club" starts thumping from nearby speakers, Hudson's eyes pop wide open and he stops speaking to break into a dance that's every bit as silly as the song to which he's dancing. His shaved head gleaming and his temporary Fu Manchu moustache forming a furry "M" above his pursed lips, Hudson is, for the moment, oblivious to everything around him. Dancing solo, for the apparent amusement only of his good friend Menechino, Tim Hudson is as happy as a man has a right to be, and it shows.

If Zito is happy at the moment, it does not show. But that doesn't mean he's not happy. He's an amazing dancer and can play the life-of-the-party role with the best of them, but right now he's simply engrossed in what appears to be a very deep conversation with someone *outside* the velvet ropes, and that says a little something about Zito's approach to life in general. While Mulder sits on the couch in what Zito once called Mulder's "Johnny Ballplayer Mode," and as Hudson entertains himself with one of his big-league buddies, Zito is content to quietly converse on the fringes, talking with someone who isn't even part of the party. Mulder is an intelligent young man, but he really *is* Johnny Ballplayer most of the time, and Johnny's conversations don't often get deep. Hudson is bright, too, but he'll admit to a certain simplicity. He's usually talking about baseball—either the business of it, the playing of it, or the strange things that go on around it. Zito, on the other hand, wants to talk about anything *but* baseball. "I don't want to get locked into that space where I'm defined by what I do," he says. "I mean, I love being a baseball player, don't get me wrong. It's what I've wanted to do my whole life. But playing baseball is what I do. It's not who I am. And I want people to know that, so if someone wants to talk to me about whatever, if I have the time, I'm usually game." On this night at the Pussycat Lounge, Barry Zito obviously has the time.

In two days, Hudson, Mulder, and Zito will report to Papago Park, Oakland's multifield complex in Phoenix, to start the necessary evil that is the tedious but important process of preparing for the season. It will be their fourth full season as teammates—and possibly their last. All three are under contract through 2005, and the A's have no-brainer club options to keep Mulder and Zito in the mix through 2006, but baseball is a business, first and foremost. None of the three have a no-trade clause in their deal, none of them have the trade-veto power that's granted a "five-and-ten" player (ten years in the majors, five with the same team), and, just as important, they play for the Oakland A's. They're all aware that there's a chance that the tight-fisted ownership team of Steve Schott and Ken Hoffman could very well order one or more of them moved in exchange for younger, cheaper talent. "Hey, this is the same team that traded Mark McGwire," says Hudson, referring to the 1997 deal in which the A's sent one of the game's legendary sluggers to St. Louis for the baseball equivalent of a tuna sandwich and a six-pack of Schlitz malt liquor. "If Big Mac can get traded, anyone can get traded." That's exactly what Eric Chavez was thinking as he pondered his future with the A's and a possible life without the Big Three.

Every year, at every big-league camp, someone is designated the Big Story. And this year, for Oakland, Eric Chavez is the Big Story. As expected, the A's lost Tejada to free agency when he signed a six-year, $72-million deal with the Baltimore Orioles in mid-December. They also lost closer Foulke when the Boston Red Sox—*Want a little salt in that playoff wound, boys?*—outbid them with a four-year, $26.5-million offer. And while Oakland's replacements at those positions, as well as the new catcher, center fielder, and pitching coach, are certain to get their fair share of attention during the course of camp, nobody's arrival is anticipated quite like that of Chavez.

Replacing Tejada is rookie Bobby Crosby, a first-round draft pick from 2001 whose monster season at triple-A Sacramento (.308, 20 homers, 90 RBIs) in 2003 convinced Oakland's brass that he was, at twenty-four, ready for prime time. Replacing Foulke is Arthur Rhodes, who had spent exactly none of his previous thirteen years in the majors as a closer but, at thirty-four, was given $9.2 million over three years to become the A's fourth closer in four years, raising eyebrows throughout the game. Replacing catcher Ramon Hernandez is another thirty-four-year-old, Damian Miller, who in the previous two seasons alone had proved more than capable of working with elite pitchers; he handled Randy Johnson and Curt Schilling in Arizona and Mark Prior and Kerry Wood in Chicago. Replacing the hole in center field occupied at various times by Long and Singleton, among others, is Mark Kotsay, a career .281 hitter with lingering questions about a bad back, who is coming off the worst of his six full seasons in the majors. And replacing Rick Peterson as pitching coach is Curt Young, who pitched in the big leagues for twelve years but has never coached beyond triple-A. Juicy stories, all. But not the Big Story.

Like Tejada the spring before, Chavez is going into his "walk year"—the last year of his current contract. Unlike Tejada, whose real age was always something of a running joke in Oakland because he's from the Dominican Republic, where the birth records of baseball players have been famously fudged for years, Chavez is just now entering his prime. Drafted in 1996 out of the same San Diego high school at which A's GM Beane starred, Chavez spent one full year in the minors before making his big-league debut with Oakland at age twenty and quickly served notice that he was among the most promising young players in the game. It didn't take long for him to deliver on that promise, either. The A's always knew Chavez would be a great power hitter, and from 2000 to 2003 he averaged more than thirty home runs and one hundred RBIs. They did not know, when moving him from shortstop to third base after drafting him, that he'd be as good on defense as he was at the plate. In fact, the knock on Chavez when he came up to Oakland was that he was a butcher on defense. But through countless hours of hard work with A's infield coach Ron Washington, Chavez shed the butcher label and, starting in 2001, won four consecutive Gold Gloves as the AL's best at the hot corner. All of this—not to mention Chavez's unique character, which prompted him to thank Washington by giving the coach his third Gold Glove trophy—is what has the A's determined to do what they refused to do with Tejada: invest in the future.

Chavez knows he's the Big Story. That much is clear when he's surrounded by reporters the moment he steps into the crowded clubhouse at Papago Park. And if he's looking to escape the spotlight, he doesn't do himself any favors when he announces that he's taking a new mental approach into the season. "Mentally, I've prepared myself to be more of a badass," he says. "I mean, this is going to be my sixth year. I guess I'm just starting to believe the hype. I think up to now, I've been doing it all on ability. Now I need to step it up mentally and go beyond what I've been doing. . . . Miguel's not here anymore, so I need to do more." Anyone who has known Chavez for a while knows that he means what he's saying, because his next lie will probably be his first. And his willingness to take on more responsibility in the wake of Tejada's departure is admirable. But his general message seems to get lost. Nobody can get past the "badass" line. Why? Because Chavez, known as "Chavvy" to just about everyone, has established himself as the most approachable and ego-free player on a roster loaded with genuinely good guys. Eric Chavez is to badass what Barry Bonds is to cuddly. "He said, 'badass'?" Mulder says with a laugh. "That's pretty funny. Chavvy's about as badass as a kitten."

Throughout the following weeks of negotiations between his agent (former A's pitching great Dave Stewart) and Beane, Chavez remains unbothered by it all. Even when the talks bog down, stopping altogether for more than a week, he appears about as concerned as Donald Trump with a parking ticket in hand. "I mean, really, how much better can my life be?" he says. "New deal, no deal, whatever. I'm still incredibly lucky to be in my situation, right?" It's just that kind of perspective that prompts the A's to give Chavez, at $66 million over the next six years (with a club option for 2011), the richest contract in franchise history.

"If you're going to invest in a baseball player, you want to invest in the highest quality of human being, and that's certainly the case here with Eric," Beane says at the March 18 press conference announcing the deal. A's co-owner Schott, cast as a penny-pinching villain by many, as star free agents such as Giambi, Damon, Jason Isringhausen, Tejada, and Foulke took their leave, wears the look of a conquering hero. "Everybody in this room couldn't wait for this day," Schott says. "It is a fantastic day for the Oakland A's franchise, and it shows a true commitment to the fans of Oakland." Stewart tells the gathering that his client took less than market value to stay in Oakland, but to Chavez, less is relative. To him, less in this situation is actually more. He's the star the A's decided to keep, and he's hoping it means they'll keep more. Like the Big Three. "Considering all the guys who've left, it's pretty unbelievable that I'm the one sitting here," he says. "Maybe this is the start of a new way of doing things here." Just in case it isn't and the A's eventually decide to deal him, Chavez has what's called a limited no-trade clause in his deal. If the A's decide they need to dump Chavez's contract, they can send him packing but not to one of seven teams Chavez sees as having less than a great chance at sustained success over the life of his new deal: the Cleveland Indians, the Florida Marlins, the Milwaukee Brewers, the Minnesota Twins, the Montreal Expos, the New York Mets, the Tampa Bay Devil Rays, and the Toronto Blue Jays. "So it's really not that big of a risk for me," Chavez says. "One way or another, I'm probably going to be with a contender."

Hudson will be the Big Story in spring 2005. That's the last year of *his* deal, and unless the A's break form and start discussing an extension for him during the 2004 season, he'll be in Chavez's shoes next spring. And had Chavez not been signed, he'd already have one foot out the door, and he'd expect Mulder and Zito to follow. "The signing of Chavvy definitely sent things in the right direction," Hudson says in the empty clubhouse at Phoenix Municipal Stadium. "I know that had they not signed Chavvy, signing any of the three of us would probably be tough. I think signing

Chavvy sent a statement to the other players. In the past, it's been something that's been up in the air as far as free agents go, but it looks like we want to do something now. It was tough to see great players like Giambi and Tejada take off, but Billy Beane's a lot smarter than I am, and I'm sure him and ownership have been thinking about who they want to keep for a long time now, so maybe it's just that the guys they want to keep are still here."

Hudson shakes his head. "At least, I hope that's the case," he says. "Chavvy had the biggest decision of anybody, man. He's going on blind faith right now. He was the first one to sign. He's hoping that they're going to be able to sign our three top starting pitchers. He's hoping that he's not going to be the one marquee guy in this lineup for the next six years. He took the big step. And the free agents after him, like myself, Zito, Mulder . . . we have to respect that. You have to understand that he made that commitment to us."

The notion that the A's won't be able to afford to re-sign all three of their aces has been floating around for a while. Beane, in fact, has done nothing to make anyone think otherwise. "The economic realities of being the Oakland A's says that keeping them all will be very, very difficult," he's said a number of times. And the truth is, the economic realities of 80 to 90 percent of the teams in baseball would probably prevent Hudson, Mulder, and Zito from being together for too long. Part of Beane's brilliance in building the A's into contenders was in getting young, on-the-rise stars such as Giambi, Tejada, Chavez, Hudson, Mulder, and Zito to sign fairly modest multiyear deals before they—to borrow a phrase from the MTV generation—"blew up." Once the expected explosion occurs, though, the market value of these players skyrockets, making extensions for more than a couple of them all but impossible. And because premium pitching is so pricey, most owners not named Steinbrenner couldn't even *entertain* the notion of paying three aces in their prime.

How valuable are Hudson, Mulder, and Zito? Josh Suchon, a reporter for the *Oakland Tribune* who covered the Giants from 2000 to 2003 but was put on the A's beat for 2004, explored that question during spring training. The idea, he says, came when he recalled an episode from the 2002 season in which Shawon Dunston, a Giants veteran, polled his teammates as to whether they would make the following trade: Hudson, Mulder, and Zito for then-Giants pitchers Livan Hernandez, Kirk Rueter, and Ryan Jensen, plus $20 million in cash. "All of his teammates said they'd take 'the Big Three,'" Suchon says. Then he adds with a laugh, "Rueter was so pissed he didn't talk to Dunston for a couple of weeks, if not a month. He was absolutely furious." Emboldened by the support from his other teammates, Dunston went to Giants GM Brian Sabean and asked if he'd make the trade. According to Suchon, Sabean said, "I'd throw in another $10 million, just so they don't change their minds." Intrigued, Suchon conducted a series of interviews with scouts, executives, players, and coaches, all of whom were granted anonymity in exchange for the kind of candor that baseball's tampering rules prevent. The consensus: placing a value on the Big Three collectively might be impossible. How valuable is invaluable, anyway?

"There's nothing you could offer for all three," said one GM. Said another executive, "If I could, I'd trade my ballpark for those three guys." And it's amusing to no end picturing Schott and baseball commissioner Bud Selig, who have said the A's can't survive if they don't soon get out of the spacious coliseum they share with the NFL's Oakland Raiders and into something shiny, taking in the following words from yet another GM: "They are far more valuable than any new stadium." That's pretty heady stuff, given the fact that new stadiums cost more than $250 million these days. But the comments underscore the many meanings of the word *value*. It's about far more than money.

The 2003 Yankees spent $31.6 million on their three aces: Mike Mussina, Roger Clemens, and Andy Pettitte. Hudson, Mulder, and Zito made $6.2 million total. That certainly didn't make them less valuable than the Yankees' pitchers. It just made Beane look that much better. And that's why, a couple of weeks before spring training, Beane laughed heartily when asked if he'd consider trading not all, but even one, of the aces he was holding. "Let me see," he said. "They're just now entering their prime, they're relatively cheap, and they're all under contract for at least two more years. What you're asking me, basically, is, 'Would I trade my brain?' Because that's what I'd be doing. As long as these guys are here, I'm smart. Why would I trade that?"

The rest of spring training is fairly uneventful for the A's. Mulder suffers some back spasms that sideline him for a few days early in camp, and starting second baseman Mark Ellis is knocked out for the season in the last week when he tears his labrum in a freak collision with Crosby, but the rest of the time passes without major incident. Rhodes is more or less coddled as the new closer, pitching in low-stress situations for most of the spring as he adapts to his new role. Miller and Young draw praise from the pitchers for their handling of the staff. Kotsay, whose acquisition didn't set well with most A's fans, is healthy and looking like the impact player Beane hoped to be getting. And Crosby, the untested rookie, is a revelation, making all the plays and pounding balls all over the yard. "Every new guy was brought in for a specific reason," says Macha, now entering his second season as Oakland's manager. "And so far, there hasn't been anything I've seen that makes me think they weren't all the right moves. It's been a quietly productive camp, and a quiet camp is a good camp, as far as I'm concerned. Everybody reported in shape, and they're only getting better."

Back in the old days, players spent the bulk of the off-season getting out of shape and used camp to work back into it. Today's players, who have considerably more money, resources, and information at their disposal, use the off-season to build their bodies back up after the long grind of the season. "Before free agency, guys had to get jobs in the off-season," says Ray Fosse, a former All-Star catcher who won world titles with the A's in 1973 and 1974 and has been the team's radio and TV analyst for the last nineteen years. Fosse spent one winter selling real estate in Cleveland, another working in the Indians' public relations department. "Now, with all this money, all they have to worry about is staying in shape." So, rare is the slacker who reports to spring training twenty pounds overweight and needs a month or so in the sun to find his form. The norm is someone like Mulder, who started working out earlier than usual and spent the winter making sure that by the time camp opened, the only part of his body that he really needed to get into game shape was his left arm. "I usually take a month off when the season ends, just to get away from baseball for a while," he says.

"But as long as I'm healthy, I'll start lifting weights, stretching, light work like that, in November. Then once December first hits, I start playing catch, probably every two days, three days. And come January, you start letting it go. Like, *really* letting it go. This year I was on the mound probably on January twentieth, twenty-fifth."

Mulder, who lives in golf-happy Arizona in the off-season, had the luxury of getting most of his winter work done in the privacy of the club complex at Papago Park, under the supervision of A's strength and conditioning coach Clarence Cockrell. A couple of years ago, he tried the public approach and quickly found it wanting. "Joining a gym and walking around, having people stare at you and interrupt your workouts, was brutal," he says. "Me and Clarence and Ellis joined 24-Hour Fitness just so we didn't have to drive all the way to the complex, but it got to be a pain. Clarence is there trying to work us out, and then the guys working there, the trainers there, are getting pissed because he's working us out and he's not supposed to be. So he kind of had to work out with us so it looked like it was, you know, just buddies working out together. So it was stupid. It got to be . . . it was just annoying, put it that

Spring training can be tedious, but Zito, stretching here during a February 2004 workout at the A's minor league facility in Phoenix, Arizona, thrives on routine and is meticulous in his preparation.

way." As was the sudden disappearance of Mulder's golf game. "I don't know what happened, but I just lost it," he says with a shrug and a slight chuckle. "It's crazy. All of a sudden I just sucked. I stopped playing, it got so bad. I didn't want to hurt anyone."

Hudson, who owns a home in Tampa, splits his off-season between Florida and Alabama. "My parents live in Auburn, and Kim's parents live in Fort Myers," he says. "We pretty much spent a lot of the off-season going up to Auburn to see my folks, going to Auburn football games, and then going down to see her family. Between my family coming down and her family coming up, it's pretty busy." Zito stayed close to home, too. He has a house high up in the Hollywood Hills that, when he bought it, would have allowed him to sneak a peek, with the help of a telescope, at Britney Spears sunbathing. "Never got around to buying that telescope, though," he says, shaking his head as if to lament the lost opportunity. Zito, like Hudson, does most of his off-season work on his own, and he incorporates yoga into his regimen, but in general their routines and schedules are about the same as Mulder's. A month or so off before weights and stretching, then light throwing, then mound work a few weeks before camp. "It's pretty basic stuff," Hudson says. "The only thing different for me this year was that as far as stretching and weights and stuff, pretty much everything I did was designed to attack that side where I had the injury. We just wanted to make sure that gets taken care of so it never happens again."

As of late March, so far, so good. Zito has the best spring of the Big Three, going 3–1 with a 2.30 ERA in six starts to quiet concerns about his pedestrian 2003 season. And while Hudson and Mulder take their share of lumps, each finishing with an ERA over 6.00, neither is concerned. Mulder's leg and back are fine, and so is that troublesome muscle in Hudson's left side. "You know, some guys go into spring training games wanting to just shove it up the other team's ass," Mulder says. "But I don't *care*. I don't *care* if I get lit up in spring training. I'm working on pitches, I'm working on this and that. I just can't get pumped up for a spring training game. I just can't. It's not my demeanor. I'd love to. I just can't. But you know what? When they put you on the mound in a big-league stadium, under the lights, you're ready to go. I don't care what's going on. Adrenaline is that powerful."

4

"RING THE BELL"

In professional football, basketball, and hockey, it's widely accepted that defense wins championships. That simple axiom applies to baseball, too, but in baseball you can whittle it down some. More specifically, pitching wins championships. Pitching is where defense starts, and it can mask all kinds of weaknesses. Think about it. What was the primary strength of the 2001 Arizona Diamondbacks? It was the two-headed monster on the mound that was Randy Johnson and Curt Schilling. What keyed the 2002 Anaheim Angels' run to the title? Without the late-season addition of twenty-year-old righty reliever Francisco Rodriguez, who quickly earned the nickname "K-Rod," in homage to his propensity for making established hitters look feeble, the AL's wild card winners don't even get to the World Series, much less win it. The 2003 Marlins? Nothing like sending a young horse like Beckett out for a clincher at hallowed Yankee Stadium and having him shove the bats down the Bronx Bombers' throats.

Try to come up with a recent world champion of baseball that didn't dominate in some way on the mound. It's impossible, because while you obviously need some semblance of an offense, big bats tend to shrink in the cold of October. Extremely rare is the team who bludgeons its way to a playoff series win. Playoff teams are too tough on the mound. It's the teams who can scratch and claw for enough runs to support their studs on the mound—to wit: the 2001 Diamondbacks, the 2002 Angels, and the 2003 Marlins— that get to taste that wonderfully nasty blend of champagne and beer after the last out of the last game of the year is recorded. "You can have all the hitters you want, but it's all about those twenty-seven outs in a ball game, and who can get them fast enough," Angels manager Mike Scioscia said in the aftermath of his team's 2002 title. And that's why Arte Moreno, a Phoenix businessman who turned billboards into billions and bought the Angels from the Disney Corporation for $183.5 million in cash early in the 2003 season, spent the 2003 off-season committing about $145 million more to free agents.

Anaheim's surprise signing of the biggest offensive name on the market—Vladimir Guerrero—to a five-year, $70 million deal got the most attention. Guerrero, who had previously toiled in the vacuum of obscurity that was the muddled future of the Montreal Expos, is a difference-maker with his arm and his bat. And the two-year, $6 million deal the Angels gave Jose Guillen, who batted .455 for the A's in the 2003 ALDS with a broken hand, was one of the best bargains of the off-season. But in committing $51 million over four years to right-hander Bartolo Colon—the biggest, in size and stature, pitcher available—and $18.75 million over three years to righty Kelvim Escobar, Anaheim took a huge step toward closing the talent gap between its starting rotation and Oakland's. Still, Ken Macha sounds less than impressed when discussing Moreno's moneyed moves, while chomping on fried ravioli in early March at Frasher's Smokehouse and Lounge in Scottsdale. "We beat Colon in his only start against us last year," Macha says as his friend, A's first-base coach Brad Fischer, nods in agreement. "And Escobar's got a nice arm, but we've done pretty well against him, too."

Indeed, the A's were 2–0 against Colon and Escobar in 2003. And they absolutely crushed Escobar, scoring nine runs on ten hits over 5⅓ innings. But the consensus among baseball insiders heading into the 2004 season is that the addition of Colon and Escobar to a starting staff that already had a couple of young horses in John

Lackey and Jarrod Washburn, plus the addition of Guerrero and Guillen to an offense that already had plenty of pop in Garret Anderson and Troy Glaus, made the Angels, who already had one of the best bullpens in baseball, the favorites to unseat the A's as the two-time defending champs of the AL West. The Seattle Mariners are seen as a possible contender, but they're going to be relying on a core of stars that includes the past-their-prime pack of first baseman John Olerud (age 34 on opening day), second baseman Bret Boone (34), designated hitter Edgar Martinez (41), and ace lefty Jamie Moyer (41). The Texas Rangers, who finished in last place in the division the previous four years with Alex Rodriguez, traded A-Rod in the off-season and did next to nothing significant in an effort to improve their woeful pitching, so they're seen as less of a factor in the AL West than Pauly Shore is in Hollywood. According to most experts, the AL West is going to be a two-horse race between the free-spending Angels and the penny-pinching—but starting pitching–rich—Oakland A's.

"Look," Macha says, after washing a bite down with his favorite drink, an ice-cold Budweiser. "Signing free agents and making headlines and all that stuff is great, and obviously the Angels did some major upgrading in the off-season; they look great on paper, especially with that bullpen of theirs. But we don't play the games on paper in January. It's what you do on the field that matters, and when they ring the bell in April and we get out there, all this stuff you're reading about who's the favorite to win our division and this and that isn't going to matter, is it? I'll put our starters up against anyone out there and take my chances from there." Two weeks later, Macha reveals the worst-kept secret of Oakland's spring training: Hudson, in kicking off his fifth full season in the big leagues, is going to ring the bell on opening day for the A's for the third time in his career.

The way Zito sees it, the process by which the A's selected their starting pitcher for opening night in 2004 was the same one used to determine their starting pitcher for opening night in 2003. "Everyone says with me and Mulder and Huddy, you could flip a coin and not go wrong, but I think the guy who had the best year the season before should get that first start," Zito says, while flipping through a guitar magazine in the home clubhouse a few hours before the A's

Zito, here roaming the streets of the Presidio district, is the only member of the A's to make his in-season home on the "other" side of the bay, in San Francisco. He picks a different district in which to live—and explore—each year.

open their season with the first of three games against the visiting Texas Rangers. "And in my opinion, that's been Huddy both times, so I'm fine with it." In saying that, Zito is being modest. The truth is that he, not Hudson, was originally scheduled to start Oakland's first game of 2003—in Japan, against the Mariners. That trip was canceled in the wake of the United States' war in Iraq, and the revamped schedule, combined with the throwing schedule the A's had mapped out for their aces weeks in advance, put Hudson in line to start opening day. But modesty aside, Zito also was reiterating something he'd said not long after accepting the 2002 AL Cy Young Award: Hudson might have been just as deserving of that award.

"Look at the numbers," Zito says. "*All* of the numbers. Not just wins and losses. Huddy was awesome in 2002, and he was even better last year. Check it out, dude. You'll see."

Many pitchers have long decried the emphasis put on their win-loss records, and Zito has always been particularly vocal about his displeasure with what he sees as the media's unfair focus. Wins and losses, goes the argument, aren't a true indicator of a pitcher's success. Too many uncontrollable variables are in play with wins and losses—primarily, run support and the efficiency of a team's defense and bullpen. The numbers that provide a more accurate reflection of what's really going on out there on the mound are those controlled almost exclusively by the person standing atop it.

By winning the 2002 American League Cy Young Award, Zito created a lofty set of expectations early in his career, and he's struggled at various times to live up to them.

"I'd say number one is the opponent's batting average against you," Zito says. "That's straight-up yours. The number of innings you pitch is big, too, because there's so much value in a guy that takes every turn and gets you into the seventh inning or deeper in most of his games. And then there's ERA. That's pretty much yours, too." On his way to winning the 2002 Cy Young, Zito held opponents to a batting average of .218, fourth-best in the AL. He pitched 229⅓ innings, fifth-best in the league, and averaged more than 6 innings per outing over a league-high thirty-five starts. His ERA of 2.75 was the third-best in the league. But the number that prompted the Baseball Writers Association of America (BBWAA) to bestow upon Zito the top pitching honor in the American League was twenty-three—his league-leading number of wins. "There's no doubt in my mind that if I'd had those exact same numbers but only sixteen or seventeen wins, somebody else would have won the Cy Young," he says. "Don't get me wrong. I was so honored and humbled and proud and stoked and all that to win it. It's a dream come true. But if I had all those numbers without all the wins and *didn't* get the award, I'd have been just as happy about my season." In urging his examination of "*all* of the numbers" while supporting Hudson's assignment as the opening night starter, however, Zito isn't just pointing to the numbers he views as the best barometers for a pitcher. He's most pointedly referring to the startling number of times that Hudson, in 2002 and 2003, had pitched well enough to get one of those media-friendly wins but didn't. "No-decisions have just crushed the guy," Zito says.

There are three scenarios that lead to a pitcher getting a no-decision, the most pleasant being when he leaves the game with his team trailing and his team comes back to at least tie the game. The kiss-your-sister kind comes when he leaves with the game tied. The most damaging one—both for a pitcher's record and, potentially, for a clubhouse's cohesion—is the kind that Hudson suffered most often in 2002. He posted what was then a career-best 2.98 ERA that year but won only fifteen games. He was hit with ten no-decisions, and in eight of those, he'd left the game with a lead, only to see Oakland's bullpen blow his win-in-waiting. Had those eight saves been converted, Hudson would have matched Zito's twenty-three wins. A year later, while setting a new career low with the second-best ERA (2.70) in the league, holding opponents to the third-lowest batting average (.223), and ranking third in the AL with a career-high 240 innings for an average of more than 7 innings per start, Hudson had eleven no-decisions, including four of the blown-save variety. With those four extra wins, he'd have had twenty. "It's unbelievable," Zito says with a shake of his head. "With just a little luck, the guy might have *two* Cy Youngs by now." Instead he has none. In 2002, he finished out of the top ten in the BBWAA's Cy Young voting. In 2003, he finished fourth. In 2000, when Hudson won twenty games despite a 4.14 ERA, which remains the highest of his career, he was the Cy Young runner-up. "My point *exactly*," Zito says. "It's a total chafe. Everything's wins, wins, wins. But wins don't tell the whole story. It's kind of a joke."

Later that night, Hudson does what great pitchers do: he survives without his best stuff. He battles. He grinds. He gets out of jams. And when the A's score a run in the bottom of the fifth inning to take a 3–2 lead, Macha decides Hudson's 106 pitches to that point are enough for the night. Five innings is well below Hudson's standards—"When I don't go seven, I'm pretty much disappointed in myself," he says—but he's on track to pick up the win . . . until lefty reliever Chris Hammond coughs up a couple of runs in the seventh to put the A's in a 4–3 hole. Pinch hitter Eric Byrnes's two-run, two-out double in the eighth inning helps Oakland escape with a victory that's saved by Rhodes, the new closer, but the win doesn't go to Hudson. Instead, he gets his twenty-second no-decision since the start of 2002, and in part because he's pissed off at himself for not getting deeper into the game, he doesn't show even a trace of frustration over his lousy luck— thirteen blown saves—over the last two-plus years. "Hammond shouldn't *have* to pitch the sixth and seventh inning," he says. "That's my job, the way I see it. So how can I be mad? I mean, we won the game, and that's all that matters."

As Hudson talks with the media after his latest no-decision, Mulder, whose locker is separated from Hudson's only by an open locker that's used to store memorabilia, fan mail, and extra game gear, watches the scene with a smile on his face. "Wear it, Huddy," he chirps. "Wear it" is part of the colorfully caustic language unique to baseball clubhouses, and it's the same as saying, "Deal with it," or, "Better you than me." An eager fan corners you into a conversation that you'd rather not have? Wear it. You're left out on the mound in a blowout loss because the bullpen is taxed? Wear it. Struck out four times? Wear it. Someone got a bigger chicken breast off the postgame spread? Wear it. Mulder loves this phrase, and now he's applying it to Hudson having to deal with a swarm of reporters clamoring for his theories on why he didn't look razor-sharp. But a night later, after beating the Rangers in a game that essentially sets the tone for his season, Mulder is the one wearing it. He was *very* sharp in picking up his MLB-leading fifty-sixth win since the start of the 2001 season, scattering five hits and a walk over seven innings, but he trailed 1–0 through five. The A's rallied for three runs in the sixth, two of them coming on Jermaine Dye's first homer of the year, and after working a perfect seventh inning, Mulder watches reliever Jim Mecir's perfect eighth and Rhodes's perfect ninth.

"My arm felt great," Mulder says, while nursing a bottled water after the game. "Like I told Curt [Young] before the season started, 'I've never had all of my pitches working this early in the season.' Granted, my last couple outings in spring training weren't good, but that's just because my delivery got a little screwed up. Now that's pretty much fixed, so, hopefully, I can keep it going." It's a typically bland batch of comments from Mulder, who takes to group interviews only slightly better than the manner in which cats take to hot tubs, but after most of the reporters move on to their next subject, Mulder exhales and further reflects on the night. Only four runners had gotten past first base, and only when the Rangers scored their lone run in the fifth did Mulder face anything resembling a jam. Told that he makes it look easy at times, he rolls his eyes. "It ain't easy, believe me," he says. "I don't care who you're facing—it's not easy. But the Rangers, man. They can mash. They're gonna be better than a lot of people think. Yeah, they lost A-Rod, but they've got Michael Young, [Hank] Blalock, [Alfonso] Soriano, [Mark] Teixeira. Those guys can hit." The ensuing months will confirm Mulder's suspicions about Texas's top guns, but on this night Young, Blalock, Soriano, and Teixeira—batting 1-2-3-4 in the order—have gone a combined 1-for-10 against Mulder. Teixeira is particularly inept, going 0-for-3 with three of Mulder's four strikeouts. "To tell you the truth, my mechanics still don't feel that great," Mulder confides. "I'm not worried about it or anything, 'cause I know I'll find it. But it's hard to explain. When everything is right, everything feels smooth. I'm just not there yet."

Zito, on the other hand, is exactly where he wants to be in his first start of the year. Kind of. Through eight innings he allows seven hits, none of them for extra bases, and one of the two runs the Rangers score off him is created by a broken-bat single. The other is the product of back-to-back walks to start the fourth inning. "I thought Barry was outstanding," Macha says in his office after the game. "He just lost it a little bit for two hitters." And because he lost it for those two hitters, he lost to the Rangers for the first time in eighteen career starts. The extent of Oakland's offense against Texas starter Colby Lewis was Dye's second homer of the season, and three Rangers relievers combined on 3⅔ perfect innings to stick the A's with a tough 2–1 loss. "Their bullpen did well today and Lewis had a great outing," Zito tells reporters. "I thought I gave us a pretty good chance to win, at least, and my goal for this season is to average seven innings a start, so I feel good about that part of it, too."

But nobody feels good after a loss, and privately, Zito admits that he *really* wanted to start the year with a win. "That first one is big," he says. "If for no other reason than to totally put last year behind you and feel like you're off to a fresh, clean start. But instead of 1–0, I'm 0–1, and I feel like I pitched a really good game. But all anyone's gonna see the next time I pitch is 'Barry Zito, 0–1.' It'll be, 'Oh, what's wrong with Barry?' So that's kinda shitty." The game perfectly underscores Zito's contention that wins and losses are hugely overrated when used to evaluate a pitcher. Remember, run support is one of the variables not under a pitcher's control. Nor is the quality of the stuff the opposing pitcher— in this case, Lewis—brings to the mound. "What can you do, though?" Zito asks. "All I can do is make my pitches and do my job." As soon as those words escape Zito's mouth, a mental governor seems to kick in. The last thing he wants to do is gripe about run support, so he catches himself and reverses field. "Like I said, Lewis did a great job today. Sometimes you just get beat," he says. "This game is so weird sometimes, man. Next time I'm out there I could pitch like ass and get a win because the offense just goes off."

Five days later, this time in Texas, Zito pitches like ass. He gives up six runs—only four are earned, but it's his own throwing error that leads to the unearned runs—on eleven hits and two walks. He throws 107 pitches over just five innings. But the offense goes off. Dye hits his third homer of the year and doubles in a run to lead Oakland's sixteen-hit attack. And when Texas's comeback falls short, Zito gets the win, 10–9. "Must be nice," Mulder says, as he strolls past Zito in the clubhouse, obviously referring to the run support. "Wear it," Zito shoots back.

The trip to Texas is the first of three for the A's this season, and the first trip of any season is important to a club. From the outside, it might seem as if placing too much emphasis on any early-April games is a tad dramatic. After all, whatever ground you might lose in the first month of the season can be made up over the five months that follow. The Oakland A's, however, have recently developed two distinct regular-season reputations. The first is that of a team who struggles to get things going early on, and Chavez is the poster boy for that rep. Through 2003, he was a .256 career hitter in the first half of the season and a .301 hitter in the second half. "That's my main goal this year: to get off to a good start," Chavez had said during spring training. "I need to pull some weight early so we don't get into too big of a hole."

The A's are no strangers to big holes. In 2000, they were seven games out of first place on August 11 and ended up winning the division by a half-game. In 2001, when the A's won the wild card berth, they were 8–18 on May 1 before becoming the seventh team in big-league history to make the playoffs after falling ten games under .500. In 2002, they trailed Seattle by ten games on May 30 and won the division by four games, becoming the ninth team in history to win a race after trailing by 10 or more games. And in 2003, the A's were seven games out of first place on July 8. They won the division by three. That's why their other regular-season rep is that of second-half monsters. In storming into the playoffs the past four years, they went 196–97 after the All-Star break. Their .669 winning percentage over that span was the best in baseball by more than eleven games. "I don't know what it is about us in the second half," Mulder says. "Maybe it's because we're a pretty young team and we don't wear down like some of the more veteran clubs. It just seems like we know when it's time to really pick it up."

Hudson, talking the day before his second start of the season and three days before the first road trip, would like to see the A's ditch all of their reputations this year, including the one that tags them as postseason chokers. "Championship clubs are consistent," he says. "It's nice to know that we have the ability to make up ground in a hurry, and we've needed to do that the past few years. But if we play consistent baseball, we don't have to put that kind of pressure on ourselves late in the year. And if that happens . . . I don't know, maybe we're fresher for when the playoffs come around. It'd be nice to just get it all going early and stay on top of things all year for once."

The next day Hudson does his part by beating the Mariners 2–1 with a four-hitter, but he endures a slow start of his own. Seattle touches him for three hits and a run in the first inning, and his counterpart, Gil Meche, shuts out the A's through six innings. "Everyone knows I'm an aggressive pitcher. I like to pound the strike zone," Hudson says. "They just came out swinging the bats early in the count, so I had to adjust to that and nibble a little more with my first couple pitches to each guy." Once the nibbling starts, Hudson is virtually untouchable, facing the minimum of twenty-four batters over the last eight frames. He retires ten in a row before Rich Aurilia reaches on an error to open the fifth, and a double-play grounder quickly takes care of that. Ichiro Suzuki slaps an infield single to open the sixth, but he, too, is erased by a double-play ball. The A's scratch out two runs in the bottom of the seventh, and Hudson expresses his gratitude by retiring the final six Mariners on harmless ground balls. "That," says Macha, "was as dominant as I've ever seen Huddy." Asked if he'd given any thought, as Meche was stifling the A's, to the possibility of another no-decision, or even a loss, Hudson smiles. "I can see why you'd ask that, but I honestly didn't think about it at all," he insists. "Maybe if we hadn't scored in the seventh I would have, and maybe more in the eighth, but we're talkin' 'bout a 1–0 game through six. There's a whole third of the game left for us to get one run, and with the kind of groove I was in—my sinker was pretty nasty today—I just knew they wasn't gonna get any more runs off me. I was pretty sure we were gonna pull this one out. I really was." He was equally sure that he wasn't going to hand the ball over to the bullpen. His gem required all of eighty-six pitches, the fewest by an Oakland starter in a complete game since Mulder threw eighty-six in beating the Devil Rays on September 2, 2001. Told of this, Hudson rolls his eyes and busts out laughing. "The Devil Rays?" he says with mock indignation. "Great, Mulder does it to the Devil Rays in September, when they're a thousand games back and playing seventeen-year-olds from A-ball. These are the Mariners I just carved up, man. Ichiro, Bret Boone, John Olerud, Edgar Martinez. Tell Mulder I win."

Mulder is long gone by now, though. He's starting Sunday, and after Sunday's game, on April 11, he's in no mood for jokes. The A's gave him a 3–0 lead in the first inning, Chavez's first homer of the year gave him a 4–0 lead in the fifth, and Mulder left the game after seven sturdy innings of work with a 4–2 lead. But Rhodes, who was perfect in his first three save chances of the year, had given up two runs to his former teammates in the ninth, Hammond had given up five runs in the tenth, and Mulder gets a no-decision as the A's fall to 4–2, heading to Texas. "Arthur's been getting the job done," Mulder says. "The bullpen in general has been getting it done. We just didn't get it done today. Shit happens." He has no idea.

5

BEFORE THE STORM

The comparisons are inevitable for Rich Harden. As a young and extremely talented pitcher with the A's, he simply cannot avoid being hailed as an ace in the making. Like Hudson, Mulder, and Zito, Harden quickly proved to all that the minor leagues were no match for him. He started 2003, his third year in the Oakland organization, at double-A Midland and earned an immediate promotion by throwing 13 consecutive perfect innings—39 up, 39 down—over his first two starts. The streak stretched to 47 up, 47 down in his first start for triple-A Sacramento, and in fact that had stretched it to 57 because he'd retired the final ten batters he faced for Midland in 2002. At Sacramento, Harden made fourteen starts, going 9–4 with a 3.15 ERA, and by July 17 the A's had seen all they'd needed to see. Harden was called up to Oakland, and on July 21 he made his big-league debut at Kansas City.

The buzz had been building about Harden for months, much of it centering around a fastball that's been clocked as high as 100 miles per hour, and he did nothing to quiet it against the Royals. At age twenty-one, he was the youngest A's pitcher to start a game in more than ten years—Hudson was twenty-three when he came up in 1999, Mulder and Zito were twenty-two when they came up in 2000—and he carved through the Kansas City lineup for six spectacular innings, allowing a run on four hits. He got stuck with a no-decision (shocker) that night, but five days later he picked up his first win by holding the host Angels to a run over seven innings. In his first four starts with the A's, he went 3–0 with a 1.33 ERA. He lost his fifth start, but there was no shame in that. He was beaten by Esteban Loaiza of the White Sox, who'd started the All-Star game for the AL, and Harden had allowed just two runs over six innings. He was the talk of baseball, and all of this sent the already-out-of-control hype into overdrive. Five starts into his big-league career, Harden was the subject of a column that appeared on ESPN.com that all but anointed him the second coming of Roger Clemens.

"Where once the A's could boast of a Big Three (Mulder, Zito and Hudson)," wrote special contributor Sean McAdam, "Harden, just 21, has transformed the Oakland rotation into the Fab Four." The quote that followed this bold proclamation further illustrated the sizzle of Harden's story. "It used to be bad enough to go into a series thinking about beating one of those guys (Mulder, Zito and Hudson). That's pretty tough," an AL general manager said. "But now, when you think about playing them in a four-game series, that's downright scary. Or about a five-game playoff series—who are you going to beat three times out of that group?" A few paragraphs later came this from a big-league scout: "It was like giving [the A's] a vitamin shot, or a shot of adrenaline. The timing was excellent. The way he started out, some organizations wouldn't have been as patient. They would have brought the guy up in late April. But they stayed close [in the division race], and all of sudden, they've got a guy from within their own organization to help them." And then more from McAdam: "Beyond Harden's obvious talent is how well he complements the rest of the rotation," he wrote. "The Fab Four now offers perfect balance: two lefties and two righties. Each possesses a singular style: Zito wins with a big, slow curve; Hudson changes release points and arm angles and buries his pitches at the knees; Mulder is the prototypical power lefty, and Harden, though smaller in stature, is his mirror image from the right side."

The point here is not to discredit or mock McAdam. He is a sportswriter, and all of us are, to varying degrees, classic overreactors.

Observes Hudson, "It's like everybody wants to jump on the band-wagon as early as possible, just so, if the guy does happen to end up being some kinda superstar, they want to tell people, 'See? I knew this guy was gonna be awesome. I called it four starts into his career. Can I judge me some talent, or what?' It's like a little race to discover someone." And what was particularly interesting about the Harden hype is that Billy Beane, the A's GM who likes to chide the press for such overreactions, seemed to buy into it. Beane is typically the type to reserve judgment on players until there's a large sample size of performance. For instance, when Carlos Peña, then a rookie with the A's, was enduring a horrific slump during spring training 2002, Beane told reporters, "Anybody who makes evaluations based on spring training is an idiot." Spring training, though, is six weeks. Harden hadn't been with the A's that long when Beane himself jumped behind the wheel of the bandwagon. "When a kid comes in," Beane says in the column, "you worry about what's going to happen after his second or third start, whether there'll be a dip in his performance once other teams get a look at him or get scouting reports. But he's followed up every one of his good outings, and he's done it with different styles. Some games he won by getting two or three double plays, and some he's won by blowing guys away."

Harden appeared in eleven games after the column appeared and went 2–4 with a 6.23 ERA. Apparently, it took other teams' scouts just a touch longer to get a read on Harden, but get a read they did. The "book" on him was out. And on April 15, in Harden's first start of 2004 after opening the season at triple-A because the A's didn't need a number five starter in the first week, the Texas Rangers take him to school to the tune of six runs on eleven hits before sending him to the showers with nobody out in the fifth inning. "Rich still has a lot to learn about pitching at this level," Macha says after the game. Adds Hudson, "So now what? Every-body's gonna start sayin' he's a flash in the pan."

Left-hander Mark Redman was part of Oakland's annual off-season overhaul, brought in to be the number four starter in the wake of a trade that sent the team's number four starter in 2003, Ted Lilly, to

Toronto for outfielder Bobby Kielty. Redman came with impressive credentials, having won fourteen games with a regular-season ERA of 3.59 for the 2003 world champion Marlins, but he came with questions, too. The A's would be his fourth organization in four years, and that's not something any player wants on his résumé. The general thinking is that guys who bounce around the league do so for a reason, and the reason is usually that they're not all that good. Redman's performance under the pressure of the 2003 play-offs wasn't anything to write home about, either. He beat the San Francisco Giants with 6 strong innings in the National League Division Series (NLDS), but in two National League Championship Series (NLCS) starts against the Chicago Cubs, he gave up thirteen hits and seven runs over 9⅔ innings for an ERA of 6.52. And when the New York Yankees knocked him out of game two of the World Series with four runs on five hits over 2⅓ innings, Redman was dropped from the Marlins rotation.

"Redman's a nice pitcher," says a veteran American League scout, "but he's the kind of guy I can see playing for six or seven teams before he's done. He's a lefty who throws strikes, so he's always going to find work, but he a complementary guy at best. I don't think he's someone you want to count on when the chips are down." Nonetheless, there was predictable optimism from Beane, who said he originally planned to sign Redman for two years, when he announced that the A's had signed Redman, thirty, to a three-year, $11-million contract. "Quite frankly, we're pleased it's a three-year deal because having Mark around for three years gives us some stability." Behind Hudson, Mulder, and Zito, there was little stability in the rotation for the three full years (2001–2003) they spent together in the big leagues. Fourth and fifth starters came and went, with Cory Lidle's two seasons (2001 and 2002) at number four setting the standard for back-of-the-rotation longevity over that span. Now, at least, with Hudson signed through 2005; Mulder, Zito, and Redman under club control through 2006; and Harden not eligible for free agency until 2010, the A's, if they decided to keep them all, would have the same five starting pitchers for at least two full seasons.

Redman had pitched well in his first start, leaving with a 4–2 lead over the Mariners after six innings, but the bullpen turned the game into a slugfest, so Redman got stuck with a no-decision—sensing a pattern here yet?—in an 8–6 A's victory. And here in Texas, the night after Zito's first win and the night before Harden would take his lumps, Redman gives Oakland another strong six and picks up his first win of the year, 9–4. His outing is overshadowed, though, by Jermaine Dye's fourth and fifth home runs of the year.

Dye, who drove in fifty-nine runs in sixty-one games after Beane picked him up at the trade deadline in 2001, signed what was then a club-record contract for $32 million over three years after that season, and the deal caused some head scratching around the league because Dye had suffered a broken left shin when he fouled a ball off it in the A's 2001 playoff loss to the Yankees. As a result, Dye missed all of spring training 2002 and opened the season on the disabled list. When he returned to the team, he was a shell of the player who'd been such a huge part of the 2001 playoff push, batting .241 with six homers and thirty-three RBIs in sixty-one games before the All-Star break. He bounced back to belt eighteen homers and drive in fifty-three runs over seventy games in the second half, and his 8-for-20 (.400) showing in the 2002 playoffs against the Twins seemed to signal his return to health, but his 2003 season was nothing short of a disaster. In late April, he tore cartilage in his right knee, requiring surgery, and missed more than a month of action. He went back on the shelf—this time for nearly two months—with a separated shoulder suffered when he tried to dislodge the ball from Angels catcher Bengie Molina's grasp in a nasty collision at home plate. Hitless in his first fifteen at-bats after returning to action again September 1, Dye finished the regular season with the kind of numbers you see from backup middle infielders, not $11-million-a-year corner outfielders. In sixty-five games, he batted .172 with four homers and twenty RBIs. So the heat is on for Dye in 2004. It's the last year of his huge contract—the team holds the option of bringing him back for 2005 at *more* than $11 million but almost certainly won't—and the A's are counting on him to join Chavez in helping to pick up some of the production lost when Miguel Tejada left town. "Everyone just tells me to forget last year, so that's what I'm going to do," he said, upon reporting to spring training 2004. "It's like I was in rehab the whole time, so that's the way I have to look at it. It was a lost year. But now I'm healthy and can concentrate on playing baseball instead of just tying to get healthy."

There's no disputing Dye's health in Oakland's eighth game of the season. His pair of homers—number five gives him one more than all of 2003, remember—drive in four runs, leaving him just eight RBIs short of his 2003 total. He's hit in all eight games, going 11-for-32, and he leads the AL in homers and RBIs. "When you're locked in, you're locked in," he says, and from Dye such words are rare. This is a man who spouts so many clichés in interviews—"I'm just trying to have fun and taking it one day at a time" is a standard—that he should consider passing out No-Doz before he starts talking. Like Mulder, he's admitted that he's boring on purpose at times. Only when you get him talking about something other than his on-field performances, such as his work to enhance inner-city youth baseball programs or his love of the Negro Leagues Museum in Kansas City, do you get a glimpse of his obvious intelligence. But now he's borderline bubbly, and Redman, who isn't big on attention, either, doesn't mind taking the backseat to Dye one bit. "It's nice," Redman says. "People are expecting a lot out of Jermaine this year, and right now he's living up to it."

Having taken two of three from the Rangers to improve to 6–3 on the year, the A's roll into Anaheim on April 16 for their first look at the new-and-much-improved Angels. As AL West rivals, these teams will play nineteen times during the regular season—including a three-game, season-ending series in Oakland that a lot of people expect to crown the division winner. And ninety minutes before his third start of the year, Hudson is pumped. An unwritten rule in baseball says that the day's starting pitcher is off-limits to the media before the game, so Hudson is left alone. But he's got a feeling about tonight, and he can't help sharing it. With his teammates on the field for batting practice, Hudson stops abruptly while walking from the locker area of the near-empty visitor's clubhouse at Angels Stadium to the trainers' room, looks around with a mischievous smile, and makes an announcement: "Strap yourself in, man. Tonight's gonna be a good one. I can feel it in my bones."

Vladimir Guerrero, the Angels' prized off-season acquisition, is new to the rivalry between Oakland and Anaheim, and Hudson has never faced him. So with two out and the bases empty in the first inning, Hudson takes it upon himself to offer a little introduction. The first pitch to Guerrero is a 94-mile-per-hour fastball, high, hard, and tight, sending Guerrero spinning out of the way. Surrounded by reporters after the game, Hudson is unconvincing when asked if the pitch was his way of welcoming Guerrero to the AL West. "I was just trying to pitch him in," he says with the kind of smile a three-year-old sports when he's been busted with his hand in the cookie jar. "That first one got away from me a little bit." But not more than five minutes later, after the reporters have dispersed, Hudson comes clean. "I was *kinda* tellin' the truth," he says. "It wasn't, 'Welcome to the AL West.' It was more like, 'Welcome to *me*, motherfucker.'" Guerrero, it should be noted, didn't quite seem intimidated by the greeting. The at-bat ended five pitches later with an absolute rocket of a line drive to second baseman Marco Scutaro for the third out of the inning. "Well, yeah, he definitely smoked that ball," Hudson says. "If that gets over 'Scoot,' it's a double to the wall. So I guess that was his way of saying, 'Welcome to me right back, bitch.'" Nevertheless, with that first pitch to Guerrero, the tone that Hudson so relishes in setting had indeed been set. "When you buzz a guy like that, it's not even really somethin' you do to intimidate a guy," Hudson says. "I mean, if you're a big-league hitter, you shouldn't be intimidated by a whole lot—'specially a little pipsqueak like me. So what that pitch does more than anything is establishes the fact that 'Look, that's *my* plate down there. Not yours. So don't get too comfortable in there, 'cuz I'm gonna be bustin' you inside all night long.'"

Hudson does indeed work inside for most of the night, humming his ever-moving heat in on the hands of nearly every batter he faces. Coming off that brilliant start against Seattle, he nearly matches it by going right after the Angels' vaunted offense. The home team doesn't get their first hit until the fourth inning, and by the time Hudson walks off the mound for the last time, with one out in the eighth inning, he does so as the soon-to-be winner of his duel with another of Anaheim's prime pickups, Bartolo Colon. Hudson allows six hits without a walk, Dye hits one of three solo homers by the A's, and Macha makes all the right moves in a 3–0 victory. "Pretty close to perfect," Hudson says.

Even Lady Luck, who hasn't made herself available to Hudson very often over the last few years, makes an appearance. The Angels hit several balls on the nose, but a sliding catch by Dye in the first inning, a diving stop by first baseman Scott Hatteberg in the third, and Crosby's spinning play in the seventh help keep the shutout intact. In another memorable confrontation, with a runner at second and two out in the sixth, Guerrero vaporizes a line drive that disappears in Chavez's glove. "You're not going to go through a lineup like that and just dominate them all night," Hudson says. "It just so happened that when they squared the ball up, it went right at someone and we made some plays."

The defense was great, yes. But Hudson was better, justifying his pregame claim. As is always the case when he's on top of his game, he spends most of the night making the Angels beat the ball into the ground with a heavy sinker and a jumpy four-seam fastball. "There's no secret to what he does," says Angels outfielder Garret Anderson. "He's just really good at it." Adds Angels second baseman Adam Kennedy, "That was typical Hudson. You don't hit that many balls hard off him, and when they're making the plays behind him, it's that much tougher. He has good movement on all his pitches and knows each hitter and what they do in situations. It's not easy."

The late innings are never easy in Anaheim, where the Angels have made a killing with comebacks. And in the bottom of the eighth, out comes the symbol for those comebacks—the Rally Monkey, bouncing around on the big screen to the strains of House of Pain's "Jump Around." And *justlikethat*, the Angels chase Hudson by loading the bases with one out. "Was I thinking about another no-decision?" Hudson says. "No, man. I was pissed at that fuckin' monkey." But with series of clutch relief performances, the A's put the primate down. Macha turns to lefty Ricardo Rincon, who strikes out Darin Erstad on three nasty pitches. Then on comes righty Jim Mecir, setting up one more dramatic moment for Guerrero, and one more big groan for the sellout crowd of 43,657. After working the count in his favor at 3–1, Guerrero takes a fastball on the inside half for strike two and whiffs on a wicked screwball for strike three. "Bases loaded, Vlad Guerrero up there in a three-run game; that's why the man came here," says Macha. "But Jimmy did a great job."

Now it's Rhodes's turn, and he closes out the near-perfect night for Oakland by nailing down his fifth save in six chances with a 1-2-3 ninth. "Everyone did their job tonight," Hudson says, before leaving the clubhouse. "That's a big-time win right there."

Baseball often makes less sense than Paris Hilton's growing celebrity, so don't even try to figure it out. For a game so driven by numbers, it can be maddeningly untrue to those numbers more often than not. Mulder's third start of the year is a perfect example. Angels starter Jarrod Washburn enters the game with an 8.44 ERA, struggles with his command, and needs 107 pitches to get through five innings. Mulder goes in with a 1.93 ERA and gets through seven innings on 102 tosses. So what happens? Angels 6, A's 3. Washburn, who leads the league in run support, gets the win. Mulder gets the loss.

Along the way, Mulder makes his first error since August of 2001, failing to touch first base after taking a feed from first baseman Eric Karros on Anderson's leadoff grounder in the second inning. Later in the inning, Chavez, the perennial Gold Glover, makes a two-run throwing error with the bases loaded. After the game, Chavez and Mulder, who were in-season housemates for three years (2000–2002), try to absolve each other of the blame. Mulder: "If I touch first, it's a completely different ball game." Chavez: "If I make that play, this game's a whole different story." Baseball people often say that hitting is contagious. Are errors? "I don't think so," says Mulder. "If they were, you'd see a lot more than one or two a night, right?"

Also along the way, Guerrero finally hits a ball where nobody can reach it. Mulder had spent some time before the game talking to Hudson about how he'd handled Guerrero the night before and to catcher Damian Miller, who'd had to deal with Guerrero for several years when they were both in the National League. But with nobody out in the third inning, Guerrero hammers a line drive to center field that crashes into a wall about fifteen feet behind the outfield fence about 2.2 seconds after it left the bat. Had the wall not been there, the ball might have ended up in nearby Riverside

County. "I kind of had an idea of how to pitch to him. I just made a mistake," Mulder says with a shrug. "And Vlad did what Vlad does. He crushed it."

If Mulder is disturbed by the loss, which drops his record to 1–1 and raises his ERA to 2.14, he doesn't look or sound it. "Today was just one of those days where weird things happen," he says. "And now it's over. I'm not going to look at videotape. I'm not going to sit here and dwell on, 'Oh, I should have done this, or I should have done that.' I'm just going to go home, get some sleep, and tomorrow I start preparing for my next start in Seattle." This is classic Mulder. Unbothered, unbowed, confidence very much intact.

Confidence for Zito, on the other hand, can be fleeting. Whereas Mulder makes a point to avoid thinking about why things happen, Zito can't help it. He's insatiably curious about everything. So after going 14–12 in 2003 on the heels of his 2002 Cy Young Award season, he set about discovering the source of the drop-off, and one conclusion he came to was that he wasn't getting deep enough into games. He led the majors in 2003 with 3,747 pitches, and that, he decided, just wouldn't do. "My pitch counts were pretty high last year, and that's why I want to average seven innings per start," he said during spring training. "Because think about it: if I'm still in there in the seventh, that probably means I'm pitching pretty well and we've got a good chance to win."

Zito is not still on the mound in the seventh inning of the series finale against the Angels. He throws 103 pitches before leaving after the sixth inning. He doesn't get a 1-2-3 inning until the fourth and has only two such innings all night. There's constant motion on the bases throughout, as the Angels steal three bags in three tries to add to the headaches. "It definitely wasn't the cleanest game I've ever thrown," Zito says later. But it's one of his gutsiest. Grinding his way through trouble, he allows only a run on four hits and a walk. Lefty reliever Chris Hammond throws three shutout innings behind him. And Crosby, who entered the game with a very rookielike .205 batting average, goes 3-for-4 with a homer and three RBIs to help the A's get out of town on their way to Seattle with a 7–1 victory over Kelvim Escobar, yet another big-ticket free agent signee. Zito's workmanlike outing drops his ERA to 3.32 and raises his record (2–1) and his confidence. "That's a good offense over there, and I'm proud that I was able to bear down when I needed to," he says. "I still need to get my pitch count down so I can get deeper into the game, but this is a step forward for me." Five days later, facing the Angels in Oakland, Zito takes a step back.

In Seattle, Redman and Harden pitch well in the first two games, but the A's offense dries up in consecutive 2–1 losses to open the four-game series. After 6 shutout innings in the third game to extend his streak of scoreless innings to a career-best 21⅓, Hudson gives up a game-tying grand slam in the seventh. But he puts up another zero in the eighth and improves to 3–0 on the year—with a 2.15 ERA—when Oakland gets three runs in the top of the ninth, two of them coming on a double by Dye, and Rhodes gets his sixth save. In the finale on April 22, Chavez's second homer in two days helps Mulder get by with what he calls "crap," and the A's finally win one without late drama, 8–2. "He threw the ball well, but he didn't have his best stuff," Chavez says, as the A's pack up for home. "I can tell when he's really on, and he wasn't. It seemed like he was kind of reaching for it today. He got through six innings with, like, 6 percent of his stuff, if you ask me." Mulder smiles and says, "I don't know if it was even 6 percent. I don't know what I was doing out there today." Mulder's main problem was his sinker. It's what he turns to in particularly dicey situations, and it wasn't there for him against the Mariners. "I just don't have command of it right now," he explains. "I'm not feeling it. I mean, I have enough other pitches to get outs, but when I'm looking for a double play, that's what I need. . . . I got lucky today."

There is no luck for Zito back at home the next night against the Angels. He is hit early, often, and hard. He takes the worst beating of his career in a 12–2 rout that's over by the bottom of the second inning, and that ability to get out of jams that he flashed in Anaheim is nowhere to be found. All of the career-high nine runs he allows come with two out. After getting two quick outs in the first inning, Zito gives up hits to ten of the final twenty-two batters he faces through four rocky innings, and five of the hits are for extra bases. "That," Zito says, "was fucked up." After the game, Hudson stops by Zito's locker. Not as a teammate, but as a friend. Zito is sitting down, staring at the floor, no doubt thinking, thinking, and thinking some more. Hudson puts a hand on Zito's shoulder and says, "Don't worry about it, Z. It's just one of them nights. You'll be all right. Keep your head up, man." The only thing up about Zito at the moment, though, is his ERA. In four innings it nearly doubles, to 6.26, creating a question that, anticipated by Zito himself, will be heard ad nauseam for the next few months but never quite answered to anyone's satisfaction: *What's wrong with Barry?*

6

THE DRILL

The relationship between professional baseball players and the media has undergone dramatic changes over the last few decades, and you'd be hard-pressed to find someone who thinks any of the changes have been for the better. This is why older sportswriters take the cake when it comes to yearning for "the good old days." For them, the good old days were the days when there was a spirit of cooperation between athletes and writers, and that spirit was fostered, in part, by friendship and familiarity.

There was a time, for instance, when reporters traveled with the teams they covered, and some of the expenses incurred were on that team's dime. Players and those who covered their exploits shared planes, trains, and hotels. Close quarters. Some beat reporters even got rings when the teams they covered won championships. This kind of you're-with-us feeling created a certain sense of togetherness. Players and the reporters who covered their teams were, if not friends, at least somewhat friendly.

"It was a totally different world," says Ron Bergman, a semiretired sixty-nine-year-old scribe who covered the "Mustache Gang" A's dynasty of the early 1970s as a beat writer for the *Oakland Tribune*.

To this day, he proudly sports the 1972 World Series ring he was given by the ownership, and he has the '73 and '74 rings, too. "You'd travel with the guys, get to know them. And they'd get to know you. It wasn't uncommon to see a few players and a few writers having drinks in the hotel bar, and that kind of relationship, in my humble opinion, did nothing but help both sides."

The teams were of that opinion as well. Hence the picking up of reporters' tabs here and there. Several teams (but not the A's of notorious tightwad owner Charlie Finley) paid for writers' flights, hotel rooms, and meals. It was a scratch-my-back-and-I'll-scratch-yours kind of thing. Wink wink, nudge nudge. And it was a time when the phrase "conflict of interest" applied to politics and the stock market but not yet to sports journalism. A time before you could get 587 specialty channels on cable television and instantaneous information on the World Wide Web. A time when newspaper reporters were the best vehicle through which the fans could get close to a player. So it only made sense: the closer the reporter was to the player, the better.

Familiarity was a good—no, a *great*—thing. It led to trust, which inevitably led to better stories. "Those days are gone," says Bergman. And so is the trust. Nobody seems to be able to put a finger on exactly when the dynamic started to change, but it's changed to the point that today's beat writers get next to nothing from the teams they cover. They'll get free tickets for friends and family on occasion, and they get the same giveaway bobblehead dolls and trading cards that clubs hand out to fans at assorted promotional games. But they're allowed on the teams' charter flights only in emergency situations, and they all make their own travel and eating arrangements, paying for everything out of their companies' coffers. Not coincidentally, when it comes to behind-the-scenes access or insight, most of them get next to nothing from most players, too. The vibe has shifted from "we're in this together" to "us against them."

"I think most players look at the media as the enemy," Zito says. "I don't know if that's fair, because it might be a case of a few bad reporters spoiling it for all the good ones, but once someone's been burned once by a writer or whatever, it's only natural to be suspicious of the next writer who comes around." Thus, you're more likely to see John Goodman on a treadmill than you are to see an athlete tossing back a few cold ones with a reporter these days. And with the dreaded "conflict of interest" now front and center in the minds of most reporters, the vast majority of them would rather eat glass than be seen chumming around with a player away from the ballpark. A seventeen-year-old high school junior who folds socks and underwear in the clubhouse is more likely to get a World Series ring than an ink-stained scribe is.

"It could definitely be seen as a conflict of interest if you're hanging out with the players now," says Susan Slusser, who has worked the A's beat for the *San Francisco Chronicle* since 1998. "If you get too close and become friends, I think you run the risk of losing—or at least *appearing* to lose—objectivity." This is a fairly new-school way of thinking. Old-school writers hate it, and they blame it on two things: tabloid journalism and the Information Age. Everything is a story, nothing is off-limits, and negativity in modern professional sports is as pervasive as the six-buck beer.

Back in the good old days, a writer might look the other way if a player—say, Mickey Mantle—rolled into the clubhouse reeking of rum, clearly unfit for the rigors of the day. Truth is, that same writer might have been the one plying Mantle with the previous night's libations, and he might have been feeling even worse than Mantle in the morning. But imagine, for instance, Derek Jeter dragging into the clubhouse at Yankee Stadium on game day with an obvious hangover. The city's notoriously rabid reporters would be on the phone with their editors within seconds, and other reporters would be dispatched to every one of Jeter's known nocturnal hangouts in search of incriminating quotes—anonymous, of course—from the bartender who served him. The next day's newspapers would scream banner headlines along the lines of "BRONX BOOZER!" and, in the *New York Post*, there'd probably be a photo illustration of Jeter slumped at a bar, empty shot glasses lined up before his drooping, glazed eyes. Later in the day it would become a national story, with everyone from ESPN to local talk-radio shows across the country chiming in. In fact, there's a chance the story would have been broken even if Jeter had somehow hidden his clubhouse condition from the omnipresent reporters assigned to the team. Because the Internet has spawned an entire generation of amateur watchdogs, and you never know if that bartender who just bought you a shot has a Web site of his own.

It boils down to this, and by no means is it a ground-breaking announcement: for whatever reason, a large segment of the American public has always liked seeing superstars brought down a peg. We dig dirt, so to speak. But with the exception of transcendent athletes such as Joe DiMaggio, Joe Namath, and Wilt Chamberlain, it wasn't until the money in sports started getting silly that players were considered superstars. And now that they are, what they do off the field is considered fair game.

Barry Zito, Mark Mulder, and Tim Hudson are superstars. And, predictably, they have very different theories on—and approaches to—dealing with the press. "For the most part, I like the media," says Zito, and the feeling is mutual. "Dealing with the media is part of the job, so I do the best I can," says Hudson, and the media appreciates the effort. Says Mulder, "I could definitely live without all the media attention." And there have been days when the media could just as easily have done without Mulder. Three different men, three different takes, all understandable when put into context.

From the day he arrived on the big-league scene as a twenty-two-year-old in July 2000, Zito was a hit with the men and the women assigned to cover the A's. He was a reporter's dream, actually. He had every prerequisite for media stardom and then some. He was exceptionally good at his job, for one thing, and if you aren't that, the media doesn't have much use for you. The sports world is filled with guys like Frank Menechino, a 5-foot-8 utility infielder who beat the longest of odds to make it to the big leagues. But Menechino, who was traded from the A's to the Toronto Blue Jays during the 2004 season, is a complementary player, so his story, though inspiring and entertaining, goes largely untold. Barry Zito the rookie, on the other hand, was clearly something special on the diamond, so people lined up to write down whatever story he'd give them. And wow, did he give them stories to tell. "Feeding frenzy," is how Hudson puts it. "Everybody wanted to talk to

Barry." And they still do, says A's public relations director Jim Young. "Mainly because you can go in so many directions with him," Young explains. "Of the three pitchers, we've gotten more requests for Barry's time than anyone."

And why not? In addition to the obvious talent, it was clear from the onset of his big-league career that Zito was just plain different. With the size of contracts climbing out of sight, professional athletes had become corporations unto themselves, but here came Zito, a mom-and-pop corner store to the rest of baseball's Safeway. He was born in Las Vegas to a mom who has been, at various times, an opera singer, a vocal coach, and a new-age minister, and once upon a time his father hung out on the fringes of the Rat Pack. Zito went to four colleges in three years in an effort to improve his skill and draft standing, adding a vagabond quality to his appeal. And when, as part of an A's tradition, he was dressed in a wedding gown for the team's final flight of his rookie season, he played the blushing bride with pride. "Virginal" is how he describes the experience.

All of those eccentricities, however, take a back seat to Zito's sense of style. He forever looks like an extra in a porn flick from 1975. "That's probably my favorite description of the way I dress," Zito says with his Hollywood smile. "My mom likes it, too." But contrary to what some of his teammates felt when Zito was first called up to join Oakland's starting rotation, Zito doesn't dress this way for attention. He does it because he honestly thinks it looks good. Ditto for his naturally brown and perpetually mussed-up hair, which has probably been dyed—blue, blond, jet black—more often than it's been combed.

"I remember when Barry was a boy, maybe eleven or twelve, and he told me he wanted this crazy haircut," recalls his mother, Roberta. "I said, 'Barry, are you sure the other kids are wearing their hair that way?' He looked at me like I was nuts. He says, 'Mom, I don't care how the other kids wear their hair. This is the way I want it.' He's just so comfortable in his own skin, it's remarkable. He's very true to what he thinks is best for him, not what others might think he should do. And that's how he is with his clothes, too. He could care less what I think or what you think or what anyone else thinks. He's going to dress the way he likes to dress."

This is why, when the A's were in Texas during the 2002 season,

Zito showed up for getaway day looking like a rodeo winner. Getaway day in the big leagues is dress-code day; it's the last day in that city, and the team jumps a charter flight out of town right after the game. The sharp dressers go with a suit of some sort. Those with less fashion sense go with a sports coat, a tie, and slacks. On this day in Arlington, after he pitched the A's to a 12–2 win over the Rangers, Zito went with a white ten-gallon Stetson, Wrangler jeans, alligator-skin boots, and a shiny silver belt buckle the size of New Hampshire.

"You like it?" he asked someone who'd stopped by to admire the ensemble. "It'll be even better when I get the belt buckle engraved." But what about the dress code? he was asked. Don't you need a tie? "Got one," he said, pulling a bolo out from the pocket of his baby-blue-and-white striped shirt. "Straight Texas pimp style."

The outfit, noted Mark Saxon, then a beat writer for the *Oakland Tribune*, was detailed the next day in every one of the Bay Area newspapers that sends a reporter out on the road with the A's. "Look at all this ink about what he was wearing," Saxon said as he thumbed through the daily press clippings distributed by the team. "The guy's a marketing genius." Saxon, who covered the A's from 1999 to 2003, likes Zito. Most people do. But he's also among those who think there's something slightly contrived about Zito's public persona. And he's right. Zito has a publicist for a reason. But Saxon's also wrong.

Does Zito cultivate and take advantage of his relationship with the media? Absolutely. He doesn't see the media as the enemy at all. Remember, his father was in show business. Joe Zito knows the importance of publicity and has long encouraged his son to be open and accessible. And when MLB.com or ESPN or *Sports Illustrated*—or even the *Nantucket News*—comes calling, looking for some time, Zito almost always answers in the affirmative. "You're only in this position for so long," Barry said, shortly after winning his Cy Young Award. "I think it'd be wasteful not to take advantage of everything the position has to offer, because if I don't, as soon as baseball is over, I'm right back to being a nobody."

Zito will never be a nobody. Thanks to his high profile, which is the result of his willingness to play ball with the press, he's a crossover star in the making. He does the Hollywood scene in the off-season, and his acting career kicked off in 2002 with a guest spot on HBO's *Arli$$*. Music is a big part of his life, too. He's always been part of his sister's band, the Sally Zito Project, and early in the 2003 season he performed with one of his musical favorites, New York–based singer/songwriter Ari Hest. "Would he be sitting in with me if he wasn't Barry Zito? Probably not," Hest admitted. "But he *is* Barry Zito. And he's a great musician. And people love him."

He is Barry Zito. That's the key, Zito says. He's not Barry Zito trying to be a star. He's just Barry being Barry. Barry being who he wants to be. That's why anyone who thinks he's nothing more than coldly calculating when it comes to enhancing his fame isn't paying very close attention. "I am who I am," he explains. "There's nothing fake about me, and you can't say that about a lot of athletes. A lot of guys spend so much energy trying to be something they're not, or trying to be something they think other people want them to be. And not to toot my own horn, but that's not me at all. I don't do anything I wouldn't do if I was pumping gas for a living, but if something I do draws attention, what can I do? I'm just being me. I think most of the media appreciates that, and so do the fans. I'm the kind of guy who, if a fan comes up to talk to me, I'll talk. I like to think I can relate to anyone."

Unless, that is, you make the flake mistake. It's an easy trap for the national media to fall into, what with Zito's colorful array of outside interests. Plus he's a lefty, and southpaws have always had a reputation for being strange. But calling Zito a flake is the fastest way to get him to shut down. In fact, it happened a mere two minutes into a televised game for which the producers had him wear a microphone in the dugout. The talking head in the booth dropped what Zito calls "the other F word" in his first question to Zito, and Zito all but dropped out of what was supposed to be a game-long conversation. He takes the flake mistake personally. Very.

"I hate that, and I don't throw out the word *hate* very often," he says. "I mean, it's just so tired to call me that, and it tells me right away that the person calling me that hasn't put anywhere near the preparation into our interview as I put into pitching. Because anyone who's bothered to really learn something about me knows I'm anything but a flake. . . . I equate flakiness with irresponsibility, and any implication that I'm irresponsible is kind of a joke to me."

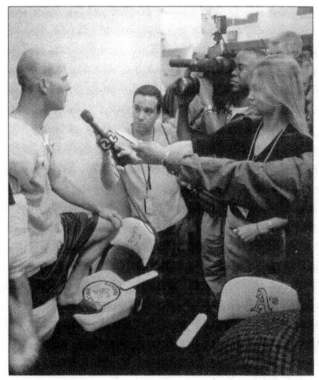

Hudson, who considers dealing with the media one of his responsibilities as a professional athlete, is the most consistent of the Big Three when it comes to handling the drill that follows every start.

A sense of responsibility is what makes Hudson another media and fan favorite among the A's. As far as he's concerned, talking with the press and mingling with the customers is as much a part of his job as is running wind sprints and throwing in the bullpen between starts. So before each game he can often be found standing in front of the A's dugout or down one of the foul lines, fielding cards, balls, and questions from autograph hunters. In that same spirit of cooperation, after each of his starts he patiently waits for the media to swarm his locker. "Think about it," Hudson says. "Without the media, we wouldn't have as many fans. And without the fans, we wouldn't have jobs. So I think you'd be crazy not to take care of both sets of people. It takes a little time and patience sometimes, but in the big picture it's worth it."

Hudson seems to think about the big picture a little bit more than many of his teammates do, and that's probably a function of his age. Though he won't turn thirty until July 2005, he's the oldest member of the A's young core—about two years older than Mulder and three years older than Zito. "Not that Mark and Barry are immature in any way, but Tim is probably more mature," says Beane. "He's a little older, a little wiser, and as a family man he has a little more on his plate." Hudson, whose wife, Kim, gave birth to the couple's first child—daughter Kennedie Rose—two weeks after he turned twenty-six, agrees. "Not that being a family man is a sentence or somethin'; I love it. But there's definitely a little more freedom to being Mulder or Z," he says. "And that freedom gives you a little bit of a sense of . . . I don't know, *invincibility* maybe, like nobody can touch you. But when you've got a wife and kids, you have to think about a lot more than just you. You have more business to take care of. And even when you get to that point where you feel like you've taken care of business, like when you get that first big contract, you start to think about other things you could be doin'."

Other things like charity work. In 2002, Hudson started hosting an annual golf tournament that, through 2004, has raised more than $285,000 to benefit the Greater Bay Area Make-A-Wish Foundation, which assists terminally ill children in fulfilling lifelong dreams, such as meeting sports stars or swimming in the ocean. Children from the foundation are invited to the post-tournament banquet, allowing them to interact with other A's players and staff, and each year Hudson makes an ailing child's wish come true by bringing him or her to a game and playing catch with the child on the field during batting practice. "I've always had a soft spot for kids," he says. "Especially sick ones. I mean, they've done nothin' bad in their lives, and some of them just get a raw deal. If there's anything I can do to help, I'm all for it." Hudson also donates time and/or money to the Special Olympics of Northern California, the Muscular Dystrophy Association, the Juvenile Diabetes Research Foundation, and the A's Community Fund, among others. As a result, he was the A's nominee in 2003 and 2004 for the Roberto Clemente Award, which is presented to a major league baseball player who demonstrates the values Clemente displayed in his commitment to community.

"I didn't come from a lot of money, and all of a sudden I have a bunch of it. I'd be a hypocrite if I didn't try to use it to help some people out," he explains. "I'm not sayin' we were a charity case or anything when I was growing up, but I know what it's like to do without. So if my name or my money or my time can give some people somethin' they wouldn't have had otherwise, I'm all for it. When I was growin' up, my dad worked construction and my mom stayed home with us, and we never did have a lot, but what we had, we were always generous with it, you know? My parents were really giving. I mean, my dad would give a bum the last ten bucks in his pocket, so that's where that comes from." Hudson notes that his wife is an equal partner in the giving. "And truth is," he says, "in a way it's as selfish as it might appear unselfish. It makes us feel good."

Image-wise, it also makes him look good. As does his approachability with reporters. Hudson is not nearly as colorful on the surface as Zito is. He's often decked out in simple jeans and a T-shirt, but he's one of the most colorful quotes in the clubhouse. Whereas Zito sprinkles his answers with flowery phrases such as "positive aura" and "in the moment," Hudson sprinkles his with humor in the form of some priceless one-liners. "Huddy's the guy who will poke fun at himself more than any other guy on the team," says Saxon. "He has great comedic timing."

The drawling delivery doesn't hurt, either. Alabama oozes from his voice, especially when he's animated. One particularly funny moment came after a game in which Hudson surrendered a moonshot of a home run to San Francisco Giants star Barry Bonds. Asked about the encounter, Hudson shook his head in amazement. The pitch Bonds hit was a sinker, right about at shoelace level, and Hudson normally makes his living by getting guys out with that very pitch. "Not the greatest of matchups right there for little Timmy," Hudson said. "I'm a low-ball pitcher, and he's a low-ball smacker."

So widely liked and respected is Hudson that he was the A's recipient of the San Francisco chapter of the Baseball Writers Association of America's 2003 "Good Guy Award," which is given to the player with whom local media members most enjoy dealing. It's an award that once seemed certain to never find its way onto the mantel of Mark Mulder, whose early relationship with the media was characterized alternately by ambivalence and disdain.

"I'm never going to give you guys anything good," Mulder told Saxon, not long after arriving on the big-league scene. Why? Because Mulder is basically of the mind that the media is the keyboard-punching embodiment of the old adage "Give 'em an inch and they'll take a mile." His fear is that if he opens up and lets everyone see his wit and boyish charm, he'll become a go-to guy for reporters and never be left alone. He's seen the amount of attention Zito has gotten, and he insists that he doesn't want it. "It was kind of painful talking to Mark the first couple of years," says the *Chronicle*'s Slusser. "And it was painful for everyone. He was horrible in interviews, to the point where he seemed *really* uncomfortable. And that kind of made everyone else uncomfortable."

So Mulder made a point of being boring, and he was great at it. If he pitched well, you could be sure his postgame comments would fall somewhere along the lines of, "I felt pretty good out there. For the most part, I hit my spots. I don't know what else to say. Things worked out, I guess." On the rare occasions that he pitched poorly, the comments were nearly identical: "I felt pretty good out there. For the most part, I hit my spots. I don't know what else to say. Things just didn't work out." So predictable was he that after one of his starts in Seattle, all of the A's beat writers were in an elevator on the way down to the clubhouse, their deadlines fast approaching, when one of them broke the silence by volunteering to play the role of Mulder for the night in the name of expediency. "I felt pretty good out there," said the scribe. "For the most part, I hit my spots. I don't know what else to say. Things worked out." And when Mulder opened his own postgame assessment by saying, "I felt good out there," several writers had to turn away to keep Mulder from seeing them laughing.

One early theory: dealing with the media is not always easy, and Mulder's life had never been all that hard. He'd always been the All-American boy for whom most days were a cakewalk, so when faced with the option of dealing with something difficult—and make no mistake: interacting with the media is definitely optional and often painstaking—he'd take the easy way out. His thoughts on that theory? "Oh, jeez. I don't know," he says, laughing and rolling his eyes. "That's a question for a psychologist, isn't it?"

Whatever the reason, Mulder played personality possum for most of his first three years in the big leagues. What was interesting, though, was that he was boring only in front of groups. Reporters generally travel in packs after games, and while Mulder insists that he has no fear of public speaking or claustrophobia or anything of that nature, it sure seemed that way when he was facing a scrum. But at some point during the 2002 season, his third in the majors, the people assigned to covering the A's realized that if you managed to get him one-on-one, Mulder was often clever, thoughtful, and expansive.

"Totally different guy when he's alone," says Laurence Miedema, the A's beat writer for the *San Jose Mercury News* in 2002–2003. "It's amazing. Especially if it's in the dugout or somewhere away from the rest of the guys. It's like he finally drops the act and becomes the real Mark Mulder."

And the real Mark Mulder can be every bit as interesting as Zito or Hudson is. He's bright and funny and absolutely loves to talk about the game. He's personable. And in direct contrast to the popular perception that he's arrogant, he's actually a bit self-conscious. It's endearing in a way. Example: Mulder has long had a habit of shrugging his shoulders when he talks to the media. It's almost a defense mechanism, a nonverbal addition to his air of disinterest. Amused by the regularity of the shrugging, a beat reporter decided to keep a "Mulder Shrug-O-Meter" during a five-minute group interview at spring training 2003. When the interview was over, Mulder was told that he'd shrugged thirty-seven times, give or take a few. Two weeks later, after an even longer group session, he pulled the same reporter aside and said with a smile, "Did you count? Zero shrugs, bitch." Then he actually thanked the guy for pointing out the habit—"I had no idea I was doing it that much," he said—and that said everything about the difference between Mulder of 2000–2002 and Mulder of 2003 and beyond.

"It's like a light switch went on for him in the [2002] off-season," says Saxon, who now covers the Anaheim Angels for the *Orange County Register*. "All of a sudden he's a great interview, whether it's in a group or not. I swear, he used to be one of my least-favorite guys to talk to. Now he's one of my favorites." Adds Slusser, who has dealt with Mulder longer than any reporter on the current beat has: "It's like night and day. He is, by far, the most improved guy with the media I've ever covered."

What changed? Beane and Hudson think it's a simple matter of maturity. Zito thinks it's a matter of confidence. Others still think it relates to Zito; Mulder has seen what being open and accessible has done for Zito's off-the-field image, and now he wants a piece of the popularity pie, too. What does Mulder think? Typically, he says it's all much ado about nothing. "It's not like all of a sudden I love giving interviews, or I'm trying to improve my profile," he offers. "Believe me, I'd be happy if I never had to do another interview again. People say I've changed, and that's great if they think I'm better at it now. But I haven't consciously changed anything. Maybe I'm just more used to it." To which Hudson laughs and says, "That's a bunch of bullshit, man. Come on, now. Mulder's just tired of me and Barry gettin' all the love."

7

DON'T MIND THE MAGGOTS

Going into Yankee Stadium is always something of a test for a team, but for the 2004 A's, it's more than a test. It's their version of the SATs, letting them know just how prepared they are for the proverbial next level. If you want to be considered one of the big boys, you have to hang with the big boys, and heading into the 2004 season the Yankees are the biggest boys in school. If big-league ball were a playground, they'd be the hyperactive twelve-year-old with an equally hyperactive pituitary gland—a 6-foot bully knocking down overmatched classmates with dodge balls to the dome.

Once known for a star-studded pitching staff, the Yankees lost starters Roger Clemens, Andy Pettitte, and David Wells in the offseason. So in addition to bringing in top-flight starters Kevin Brown and Javier Vazquez, along with relief reinforcements in the form of setup men Paul Quantrill and Tom Gordon, they decided to put together what might go down as the most decorated offensive lineup in history. They added shortstop Alex Rodriguez, a seven-time All-Star, the reigning AL MVP, and widely regarded as the best player in the game—and moved him to third base to accommodate five-time All-Star and 2000 World Series MVP Derek

Jeter. They brought in outfielder Gary Sheffield, a seven-time All-Star who batted .330 with 39 homers and 132 RBIs in 2003. They brought in outfielder Kenny Lofton, a six-time All-Star who went to the World Series with the Giants in 2002 and to the NLCS with the Cubs in 2003. Already in place was 2000 AL MVP and four-time All-Star first baseman Jason Giambi. And five-time All-Star outfielder Bernie Williams. And four-time All-Star catcher Jorge Posada. And outfielder Hideki Matsui, who made the AL All-Star team as a rookie in 2003 and was the best hitter in Japan before he ventured to the United States. So on any given day, the 2004 Yankees could throw out a lineup that, from hitters one through eight, had thirty-nine All-Star appearances between them. It almost made you feel bad for the poor number nine hitter, be it Enrique Wilson or the equally anonymous Miguel Cairo. Almost. "They've got a lineup of Hall of Famers," Hudson said, near the end of spring training. "Most teams have two, maybe three guys you can look at and think, 'Okay, this isn't so bad.' The Yankees, it's gonna be nonstop. People always say the road to the World Series goes through New York, and this year it's a rocky road, man."

About a month later, Hudson gets his first look at the Yankees, and the A's have hit a few bumps in the road already. On the heels of Zito's Friday-night disaster at home against the Angels, Redman was ripped for ten hits over 5⅓ innings on Saturday. Harden surrendered a three-run homer to Tim Salmon in the sixth inning of a loss Sunday, dropping the A's to 10–9 on the year. But while all of this was going on, the Red Sox were doing in New York what Anaheim was doing in Oakland, so with both teams coming off embarrassing sweeps at home to their chief division rivals, something has to give as the A's and Yankees square off on Tuesday, April 27, in the opener of a three-game series in the Bronx.

And something does give. A lot of things, actually. The A's give Yankees starter Mike Mussina a beating, Hudson gives the Yankees fits . . . and Oakland's relievers give Hudson perhaps the most galling of his twenty-three no-decisions since the start of the 2002 season. This one, more any before it, is a straight choke job. "We had a bit of a meltdown there in the bullpen," Macha concedes when it's over. "We just fell apart."

Hudson has one rough inning among his seven. Cairo's two-run single, Rodriguez's RBI ground out, and an RBI single by Giambi give the Yankees a 4–1 lead in the third, but the offense picks Hudson up, scoring three runs in the fourth, one in the sixth, two in the seventh, and one in the top of the eighth. He has an 8–4 lead and a pitch count of ninety-seven to this point, but Macha decides to entrust the final six outs to someone else. And to the delight of 33,191 screaming fans, the Yankees emerge from a season-long offensive slumber to score six runs against relievers Jim Mecir and Ricardo Rincon before even three of those outs are had. The last three aren't needed, because Yankees closer Mariano Rivera shuts down the A's in the top of the ninth for a 10–8 victory that leaves Oakland's clubhouse pin-drop quiet after the sixth loss in eight games. "I probably could've kept going," Hudson says in hushed tones. "But I didn't really have a problem with coming out. I was confident that we could bring it home. . . . We just didn't make pitches when we needed to."

We just didn't make pitches when we needed to. The "we" very obviously means "the bullpen" here, and that's why the comment stands out. It serves as the first crack in the wall of diplomacy Hudson has been building, brick by brick, blown save by blown save, because he's long been extremely mindful not to break one of the more sacred of big-league ball's many unwritten rules: Thou shalt not throw a teammate under the bus. In other words, if the bullpen or a crucial error or a lack of support from the offense costs you a win, keep your trap shut and wear it. And Hudson always has. That's part of being a leader. But every man, no matter how strong, has a breaking point. This—*We just didn't make pitches when we needed to*—obviously was not that point for Hudson, but it was the first he'd bent even a little bit publicly. And when that's mentioned to him in private the following day, the first thing he does is ask about how the comments were played in the press. Told that they were hardly played at all, he's relieved.

"Hey, man, I've taken a lot of bullets over the past couple years, and if I was the type to go off, I've had plenty of opportunities, you know what I mean?" he says. "But that's not me, and I hope everyone knows that. I mean, the way I see it is, look, man, everybody's gonna fuck up from time to time. I'm gonna fuck up, Mulder's gonna fuck up, Z's gonna fuck up, you're gonna fuck up.

The bullpen's gonna fuck up. Macha's gonna fuck up. Even the genius, Billy Beane, he's gonna fuck up. It's inevitable. We're all gonna fuck up. So you got two choices when someone else's fuckup affects you: you can drive yourself crazy and piss and moan about it, or you can try to be a professional and deal with it. Myself, I try to be a professional. I haven't always been like that, but I think over the last few years I've been able to handle that kind of thing a lot better because it's happened so much to me. There was a time two years ago when, I don't know, gettin' mad was just kind of over for me. Gettin' mad, gettin' frustrated, lettin' it wear on you for three or four days afterwards . . . it's kind of like, I'm just past that now."

Asked, after failing to retire any of the five batters he'd faced in Tuesday night's game, whether Hudson might be cursed in some way, Mecir, at whose locker Hudson had already stopped by with a few words of encouragement, took a while to think about it. "It *feels* like a curse, to tell you the truth," he's said. "But then again, this is Yankee Stadium. This kind of stuff just seems to happen here." And more of it happens the following night. New York starter Jose Contreras enters the game with an ERA that looks like a breakfast tab for two at McDonald's—10.64—but he looks like Don Larsen for six innings. Giambi, who will own a Gold Glove only if someone finds him one on eBay, kills the A's only real rally by robbing Chavez of a likely double with a diving snare with two on and two out in the third inning. And Mulder gives up three runs in an ugly first inning as the A's fall, 5–1, to keep him winless in four regular-season starts at Yankee Stadium. "It has nothing to do with the stadium," Mulder insists. "It's putting the team in a hole early."

Mulder pitches pretty well after the first, but Posada drills his AL-leading eighth home run in the third, and Mulder's line for the night is wholly unremarkable: five runs on seven hits over six innings. The remarkable part of his evening comes after the game, when one of the many Japanese journalists assigned to cover Matsui's every move asks Mulder to go over each of Matsui's at-bats. It's part of the drill when you play New York.

"His first time up, in the first inning, I walked him," Mulder says, before rattling off the type and the location of each of the at-bat's five pitches. Ditto his six-pitch strikeout of Matsui in the second. "In the fourth," he continues, "I started him with a four-seamer away for a ball, got away with a pretty average curveball for a strike, he looked at a sinker in for strike two, and then he missed another sinker." The Japanese reporter eagerly writes this all down and looks up at Mulder, who is towering over him. "So . . . you strike out Matsui two times. How do you do that?" Mulder smiles. "I just told you. Curveball, sinker, sinker." The reporter smiles back and tells Mulder that Matsui doesn't often strike out twice to the same pitcher in the same game. "Well, I guess I got lucky, then," Mulder says. Dressing at his locker five feet away from Mulder, Hudson waits for the reporter to walk away and laughs. "Nothin' more in the world you want to do right now, Mulder, than go over every pitch to Matsui," he says. "Yeah, no shit," Mulder answers. "At least it's not every single batter."

But what if it were? Mulder is asked. Do you remember every pitch of every game? "Pretty much," he says. "Maybe not every single one, but most of 'em, yeah." So Hudson tests him, asking him about an at-bat against Jeter. "Which one?" Mulder responds. "Third one," Hudson says. Mulder thinks for about ten seconds and says, "Okay, fourth inning. Ground out to short," he says, then repeats in recounting the Jeter at-bat as he'd done with each of Matsui's. Only this time he tells not just what pitches he'd thrown, but the location of each pitch, whether he'd hit his spot or missed it, why he'd thrown the pitch, and what Jeter did with it. Listening to the level of detail he offers brings to mind an everyday scene from the PGA Tour, where the top golfers are brought into an interview room and asked to dissect their round, shot by shot. The difference is that if a golfer is called to this interview room, he's had a pretty good round, and a pretty good round consists of no more than seventy shots. Mulder has just thrown 115 pitches, and he says he could probably go over every one of them. It's an amazing display of recall, but Mulder, of course, is unimpressed. It takes a lot to impress Mark Mulder. "I don't think it's that big of a deal," he says. "I mean, this is my job. Who doesn't know what they did at their job each day?" Hudson laughs again. "Hell, I don't even know what I had for breakfast today!" he says. But pressed, Hudson says that he, too, can relive most of his pitches in the immediate after-math of a start. "I don't know if I can do every pitch down to the nitty-gritty like Mulder," he says. "But for big situations, big outs, yeah. I could definitely tell you what I threw and why."

The why part of the equation is what's most interesting. If the first pitch is an inside sinker that Jeter looked at for a called strike, why is the next pitch another sinker, only away? And if the first one had been a ball, would that have changed the second one? Why? Or why not? The answers are in the scouting reports each team compiles on opponents, and while most teams have access to the same information, the reports can vary from club to club. This is why Mulder, before leaving the clubhouse, makes sure all of the whys he's just explained *stay* in the clubhouse. "If you write some-thing about how I'm trying to pitch a guy and why, it's out there for everyone to see," he says. "I'm not saying Jeter's going to read it and think, 'Oh, so *that's* what he's trying to do.' He's such a smart hitter, he already knows what I'm trying to do. But what good would our reports be if we just gave that information to everyone?"

Jeter, by the way, could use a little help right about now. He went 0-for-3 against Mulder and 0-for-4 for the night, extending the worst slump of his career to thirty-two hitless at-bats.

For those not accustomed to the mass of humanity, the noise, and the constant hustle and bustle, New York City can be an agitating kind of place. Hudson is from the laid-back South, so maybe that's why, while sitting at a table in the crowded outdoor patio of an Ital-ian restaurant built into the side of busy Grand Central Station the day after Mulder's loss, he's in a bit of a foul mood. Then again, maybe it's being thousands of miles away from his wife less than a week before the birth of his second daughter. Or maybe it's just the lingering effects of the massive hangover he'd endured the day after watching what should have been a series-opening win turn into an epic loss. "Might have tossed back one too many tryin' to drown my sorrows," he concedes. Whatever it is, Hudson has a little fire in his eyes as he addresses, for the first time at length, the future of the Big Three in Oakland. He's reminded of Beane's contention that the economics of being the A's will probably prevent the team from keeping all of their aces beyond their current contracts, but he doesn't entirely buy the whole economic-realities spiel.

"I think all three of us would like to stay," Hudson says, "but there's also that small-market cry that you hear every year. You know, 'We can't afford everyone.' But, man, I don't get it. The Bay Area's one of the richest areas in the country. How the hell are we a small-market team? And the way I look at it, we've put well over $100-million product on the field for these guys for the last four or five years. Forget about what our actual salaries have been. That they've been so low is a credit to Billy and him being smart enough to sign us to multiyear deals when we were just getting established. But if you look at what each guy's market value would be out there—Chavvy, Mulder, Zito, myself, Jermaine Dye—you're talking big, big dollars. So I think it's time for ownership to ante up. They've been gettin' a bargain, man. We haven't won a World Series or even gotten past the first round, but we've been one of the better teams in all of baseball for the last three or four years and at a fraction of the cost. A big-time fraction. That's my whole thing. We've been doin' it for you for a long time, and now it's time to give us our due. And not just us. Now it's time to go out and start signin' some premier free agents. Go to that Steinbrenner School of Business. Start bringin' some guys in. Make this an offensive club with good pitchin', not just a good-pitchin' club with a hit-and-miss offense."

Hudson is on a roll now, getting more animated with each word. It's clear that watching the annual exodus of free agents from Oakland has bothered him more than he's let on, and here, between bites of lunch, he's shedding that diplomacy he typically uses when discussing the yearly reshuffling of the A's deck. But now he pauses, smiles, and laughs at himself. "I can't believe I just said 'Steinbrenner School of Business,'" he says. "What a dumbass. New York must be gettin' to me, man. . . . Look, I know we're not the Yankees. I know we're not the Red Sox. But it does get frustratin' sometimes, 'cause if you take the team we have today and add to it some of the free agents we've lost the past couple years, you're talking about a serious dynasty."

Hudson and Beane, it should be noted, are fairly close. Beane, who played big-league ball for six years and was part of Oakland's 1989 world championship team, chats often with a lot of his players. But he's careful to separate the personal and the professional aspects of his job, and Hudson insists that the topic of his future with the A's doesn't come up when the two talk. "Not really," he says. "Everybody knows that I'm the next guy to be a free agent. There's a line, and I'm the next issue they have to deal with, so we'll deal with it when it's my time. This was Chavvy's year. Next year, hopefully, is mine."

But how hopeful is he, really? The signing of one free agent does not a dynasty make, and Hudson knows it. "You want to win. That's the main thing," he says. "The financial security is there for most players who become free agents. They've played five or six years. So money's not the issue. It's, are you gonna be playing for a championship? I'd love to stay with Oakland. But even if they paid me Boston or New York money, if I thought the organization wasn't committed to winnin'—you know, start tryin' to build the offense up and go with a more offensive-oriented team, I don't know if I would. That's why the Chavvy deal was so big. As startin' pitchers, we want guys who are established, who know how to play the game. . . . Hey, man, it's not the money. It's about the commitment of the organization to put a product out there that's going to be competitive every year. . . . The guys on our team are solid guys who don't care about fame or fortune or all that stuff. And we're already secure financially. It's all about winning and being happy. It's about going to the park every day wantin' to go to the park. If we don't see that as being part of the deal, they're gonna have a tough time getting any of us to sign."

Several hours after Hudson vents, the future is of no concern. The present, on the other hand, has become quite an issue on several fronts. Prior to this series, the A's had sent Hudson, Mulder, and Zito to the mound in a three-game series nineteen times since Zito became the third of the Big Three to reach the big leagues. In sixteen of those series, the A's had won at least two of the games, including five sweeps. Twice the A's had won just one of the games.

Only once had they been swept, and guess where that happened? Right here at Yankee Stadium, back in April 2001. This is the twentieth such series, and when the most forgettable seven-day stretch of Zito's career ends with a thud, the Yanks have another sweep.

Make that four very loud thuds, off Zito. And six straight duds for the A's. While trying to bounce back from giving up a career-high nine runs the previous Friday against the Angels in Oakland, Zito instead gives up a career-high four home runs in a 7–5 loss. "It's strange," says Zito. "It's nothing that I'm used to." Before the Angels roughed him up, Zito hadn't allowed a home run since August 2003, a string of sixty-three innings and 268 batters faced. After these six innings in New York, he's allowed six homers in his last ten innings. And the trouble today starts right away. That wicked hitless string of Jeter's? It ends when he sends Zito's first pitch of the game over the 399-foot sign in left-center field. The game ends with Zito at 2–3 on the year with a 6.83 ERA. Over the last two starts, the numbers are 0–2 and 13.50.

So again the question surfaces: *What's wrong with Barry?*

One theory is that he's tipping his pitches. After Zito allowed eleven hits in his win over Texas, Rob Dibble, a former big-league pitcher working as an analyst on ESPN's *Baseball Tonight*, noted on the air—with video to back him up—that Zito was moving his glove as he reached in to grip his signature curveball. He wasn't moving his glove as he gripped his fastball and changeup, Dibble said, so teams were simply laying off the curve. "The way they were showing it, you could see it easily," A's outfielder Jermaine Dye told the *San Francisco Chronicle*. "And it showed when Barry was throwing his curveball. [The batters] weren't even moving. They were taking it." But why not bang the pitch if you know it's coming? Well, that's how good Zito's curveball is, says Eric Karros, who hit 270 home runs in eleven full seasons with the Los Angeles Dodgers before playing for the Cubs in 2003 and starting the 2004 season with the A's (he was later released). "If a guy has one devastating pitch and you can avoid it, you avoid it," Karros explains. "And Zito's curveball is his one devastating pitch. You take that away from him and he throws two other pitches, a fastball and a changeup, and both of 'em are straight. And trust me, if a big-league hitter goes up there and can just sit on something straight, it doesn't matter how hard you throw or how good your changeup is. You're gonna get hit."

How, then, did Zito manage to shut the Angels down on one run in the start before they battered him for nine? Before that first game, Dye told Zito of Dibble's report and suggested that he move his glove a little while gripping all of his pitches, and very few curveballs that day were hit hard, much less put in play. Then why did the Angels tee off on Zito five days later? Even Hudson, while commiserating with Zito after that drubbing, expressed some suspicion that the Angels had known what was coming. And maybe they did. But Zito didn't think so then—he said he'd gone over videotape of several starts and hadn't seen any evidence of tipping—and he doesn't think so now, after the drubbing at Yankee Stadium. As far as he's concerned, it's all a matter of location. Jeter's homer in the first? "Fastball up," Zito says. A-Rod's solo homer in the third? "Fastball. Also up." Williams's solo homer in the fifth? "Changeup. Up." Cairo's back-breaking, three-run homer with two out in the sixth? "Fastball. Up," Zito says again. "It's weird. Usually you get away with a couple . . . but they didn't really miss any mistakes tonight."

Damian Miller, Oakland's veteran catcher, says he doesn't see any evidence of Zito tipping his pitches, either. "He's just leaving a few balls up against some pretty good hitters," he says. "He didn't really pitch that bad. He got a lot of strikeouts when he needed them and basically pitched his tail off and competed. He's just gotta find it, and it's a matter of time before he does." A similar sentiment courses through the clubhouse when talk turns to the series as a whole. Losing consecutive games started by Hudson, Mulder, and Zito is a rarity, and everyone agrees that it's highly unexpected. But the optimistic perspective that April allows every team rules the day. "They're human, too," Miller says. "Tuesday night, we had that game won and let it get away, but obviously, you have some confidence when you have Mulder and Zito coming in after that. It just didn't work out."

Nor did the A's plan to shed their reputation as slow starters. The sweep assures them of a losing record for the first month of the year. "Some things never change, I guess," Mulder says. "But we'll be okay. This is no big deal."

8

PEAKS AND VALLEYS

"Here we go," Mulder says, throwing his arms up and rolling his eyes to make clear just how ridiculous he finds the line of questioning. "We all knew this was coming." The question today is not *What's wrong with Barry?* It's bigger than that. It's *What's wrong with the Big Three?* It is May 8, about ninety minutes before Hudson takes the mound against the visiting Minnesota Twins, and the last time Hudson, Mulder, or Zito had won a game was April 22, when Mulder "got lucky" against the Mariners in Seattle.

Mulder has made two starts since then, the first being his loss in New York, the second being a deflating no-decision against the Yankees in Oakland. Handed leads of 7–1 and 8–3, Mulder couldn't close the door. He allowed thirteen hits—the second-most in his career—over 6⅓ innings, including a three-run homer to A-Rod in the seventh inning, and left with a one-run lead that Chad Bradford, a righty groundball specialist who throws virtually underhand in a "submarine" style, quickly coughed up as New York rallied to a 10–8 victory. "To be up 7–1 and not get a win out of it, that's discouraging," Mulder said that night. "When the offense comes through the way they did, you have to make sure to shut the door. When you don't, you've let everyone down, and that's the last thing any pitcher wants to do. So am I frustrated? No. I'm embarrassed."

Hudson's start tonight against the Twins will be his third start since the Big Three's drought began. The first was that awful game in New York, where he watched helplessly from the clubhouse as the bullpen blew his four-run lead. The second was in Tampa Bay, where he gave up nine hits and eight runs over seven innings. Only five of the runs were earned because Hudson and Karros each made a throwing error, but as Hudson says, "When the pitcher makes an error that leads to runs, the runs should be earned. So it was pretty much me sucking all day, in every way." The day after his loss to the Devil Rays is a much better day for Hudson. He gets back in town from Tampa in plenty of time to be there as Kim gives birth to Tess Belle at a Bay Area hospital. A day later, after sneaking in some work at the ballpark while Kim and Tess sleep, Hudson, still wearing the ID band that hospitals issue new fathers, says everything went well—and that Kim is stronger than he thought. Seems she was hanging on pretty tight to her husband's right thumb at one point during delivery. "She was killin' me, man," he says with a laugh. "Once things calmed down a little, I said, 'Honey, you know that's my pitching hand, right?'"

Zito has made three starts during the drought, the first two being the beatings administered by the Angels and the Yankees. The third start was a marked improvement, with Zito scattering six hits over six innings against New York in Oakland, but he'd allowed two more home runs (to Sheffield and Giambi), bringing his three-start total to eight. When he left the game, it was tied, 2–2, and an RBI single by Chavez gave the A's a 3–2 lead heading into the ninth. The lead disappeared when A-Rod launched the first pitch from Rhodes over the wall, and in response to his second blown save of the season, Rhodes gave up a pair of walks and a double by Tony Clark. After New York's 4–3 victory, Ken Macha spends far less time discussing Zito's improvement than he does Rhodes's night, even hinting that the closer's job might be in jeopardy. But Zito was quietly encouraged. "I was spotting my fastball a lot better than I have, and that's big for me," he said. "I'd still like to get deeper into games, but I kept us in the game this time, and that's what's important."

Right now, though, on May 8, what's important to the small semicircle of reporters surrounding Mulder's locker in Oakland is this line of questioning he so detests: *What's wrong with the Big Three?* It's no secret that the A's go as Hudson, Mulder, and Zito go. When they're on a roll, it seems to bleed into every other part of the team. When they're not, this is what happens. During the thirteen-game drought, the A's are 4–9. They're 14–15 overall. They're already 5½ games out of the division lead, which is shared by the favored Angels and the upstart Rangers. Things do not look good, and Mulder knows it. "I'm not saying we're not going through a little lull," he says. "Every year, the three of us have funks here or there. Sometimes, they're all at once, and that's kind of what's going on right now. I mean, we aren't going to go the whole season just dealing. But we'll have a lot more stretches where we are dealing than where we aren't."

Dealing is another inside-ball term. It's used to describe a pitcher's dominance. And not long after Mulder is done talking, Hudson deals for nine innings. He gives up a run in the first and one in the fourth, but for the next five innings, the Twins get nothing. And that's exactly what Hudson gets for the effort: nothing. After nine innings the game is tied, 2–2, and Minnesota scores an unearned run off Mecir when Crosby drops a pop-up in the top of the tenth. The A's strike out three times in the bottom of the inning and lose. It's a familiar story for Hudson by now. No run support, no luck, no win, no loss. Just another no-decision, his third of the year. As well as he's pitched, he could easily be 6–1. Instead he's 3–1, and while he's still working from behind that wall of diplomacy, another tiny crack shows when a TV reporter asks him, "Do you ever think, 'Why me?'" Hudson shakes his head and answers, "Man, I stopped asking that a long time ago." The A's have now played fourteen games since one of the Big Three got a win, and they've lost ten of them. Hudson, Mulder, and Zito are a combined 0–4 with a 7.01 ERA in eight starts over that span, and Oakland's division deficit is up to 6½ games. Asked in private if he's concerned, Hudson smiles.

"Naw, man. This is what we do," he says. "We fall behind, everyone starts writin' us off, and we come stormin' back. Watch, Mulder'll get us back on track tomorrow and we'll win us a bunch of games in a hurry." The drought ends the very next day. Mulder gives up four runs in the first five innings, but after the A's score three in the bottom of the fifth to give him a 6–4 lead, he throws shut-out ball the rest of the way to notch his first complete game of the year.

— — —

Six days into a seven-day, six-game road trip, Barry Zito is at peace with his place in the world, which for the moment is a window booth at a Denny's restaurant in Kansas City, just across the highway from Kauffman Stadium, not long after visiting the Negro Leagues Museum downtown. He's Oakland's "bookend pitcher" on the trip, having started the first game in Detroit, and he's scheduled to pitch the last game here, Sunday, May 16, against the Royals. The start in Detroit was nothing special; he allowed ten hits and four runs. But there were plenty of positives. (1) He didn't allow a home run. "That, actually, hadn't really crossed my mind," Zito says, while picking at an Egg-Beater omelet. "But now that you mention it, yeah, that's a big plus." (2) He went seven innings. "That was my

Zito, who finds it difficult to "go deep" with many of his baseball colleagues, chats up A's reliever Justin Lehr at spring training 2004.

goal, so any time I go seven, it's not a bad day for me." (3) After the A's scored a run in the top of the sixth inning to tie the game at 4–4, Zito held the Tigers scoreless in the bottom of the sixth and the seventh. "Shutdown innings are huge, especially when the offense picks you up like that. There's nothing more discouraging for a team than to fight back to tie or take a lead and have their pitcher go back out there and give runs back. It's a huge mental downer." And finally, the A's won the game. It took Miller's two-out RBI single in the fifteenth inning to get it done, but no-decisions aren't nearly as much of an issue for Zito as they've become for hard-luck Hudson. "That's a no-decision I don't mind," Zito says. "For one thing, I wasn't exactly lights out. Four runs in seven innings on some days is a loss. A lot of days, actually. But the main thing is that we won the game. I kept us in it after we came back, the bullpen was amazing, and we got it done in extras. Wins like that, where every part of the team contributes, are a huge confidence-builder."

Confidence is everything to Zito. And as he hands his empty plate to the waiter, he launches into a five-minute soliloquy on the topic. Sitting at this table, oblivious to the whispering people in the restaurant who have started staring at him in that I-know-you're-somebody-but-I'm-not-sure-who kind of way, he is about to do something he *really* likes to do. "I'm gonna go deep here, bro. You ready?" he says. Assured that whatever wisdom he's about to impart probably won't explode the skull across from him, Zito laughs, clenches his teeth, and shakes both fists triumphantly. "I love it, dude," he says. "You don't know how hard it is to get someone to go deep with you, especially in baseball. I'm not saying everyone else is a rockhead or that I'm some kind of genius philosopher, but the environment of baseball doesn't allow for a lot of really in-depth discussions."

And so starts the soliloquy. "A lot of people don't understand how powerful the mind is, and not just in sports, but in everything we do in life," Zito says. "I honestly believe that if I can commit myself mentally to something, whether it's learning something gnarly on the guitar, throwing a 3–2 fastball right down the middle past someone with the bases loaded, or even dropping my rap on some hottie who's way out of my league, I can get it done if I'm 100 percent into it mentally. If you're 98, 99 percent into it, the door to failure opens. But if you can get to that place where you truly believe that nothing can stop you from doing exactly what you want to do, nothing will. If that guy hits the 3–2 fastball, it's not because he's better than me. It's because, mentally, I basically *let* him hit it. It's because, mentally, I wasn't 100 percent committed. And what is being 100 percent committed mentally? It's confidence. If you're confident, truly confident, you can do anything."

To illustrate his point, Zito offers a snapshot from one of his final regular-season starts in 2002. "You've heard of people having out-of-body experiences? This is what that was like," he says. "I was so locked in, so completely committed to what I was doing, that there was this feeling that I was hovering over the mound. It was like my spiritual self controlling what my physical self was doing. Total puppeteer thing going on with myself, and I was just toying with the hitters. They couldn't do anything. But then, for whatever reason, maybe boredom, I decided to do a little experiment. I made a conscious decision to *not* be committed to a pitch. And bang! Double. But then I was able to lock right back in and just cruise from that point on. It was trippy."

But what if, the devil's advocate across from Zito asks, you're 100 percent committed to a pitch and so is the hitter? "That's when the physical part takes over, I guess," he says. "I don't know. I haven't really thought of it in those terms, because so few people really know how to harness that mental power. Physical ability is important, obviously. I mean, if I could only throw the ball 75 miles an hour instead of 89–90, I'm not gonna be in the big leagues, much less get a 3–2 fastball by someone. That's physical. But everyone in the big leagues has amazing physical ability. The separation between good and great is mental. It's about conviction. It's about commitment. I really believe that." How does Zito get into that state of supreme confidence? "I wish I knew, exactly, because I'd never lose," he says with a laugh. "It's not something where you can just go, 'Okay, I'm locked in.' Sometimes you can't get there, and that's the challenge: how do you get back to that place?"

Anyone subscribing to the theories Zito has laid out while going deep at Denny's would say that on the following night, the moribund Royals don't appear very committed. And none of them go deep on Zito, which, of course, is a good thing in an on-the-field context. His second consecutive start without allowing a home run drops his ERA under 6.00—to 5.62—for the first time in more than a month, and a wind-blown, two-run, opposite-field triple by Joe Randa in the first inning is one of just four hits against him over six innings. The A's win 6–2 to close out a Big Three sweep, as Zito evens his record at 3–3. It begs the question: Any puppeteer action going on out there today, Barry? "No," he says, "but I did a good job of staying in the moment, staying convicted with all my pitches. Total confidence isn't easy to achieve. You just have to find a way to get there, and I can feel it coming."

Confidence is not the elusive butterfly for Hudson and Mulder that it can be for Zito. A hard-hit ball, a bad inning, a bad outing? Hudson and Mulder usually have such ironclad confidence in their stuff, their ability, that they can almost immediately erase from their thoughts anything negative that happens during a start. That's not so easy for Zito, says Ramon Hernandez. The Big Three's primary catcher, from the time each broke into the big leagues through 2003, Hernandez was traded to the San Diego Padres in

Mulder, whose stress level generally sits at zero, sports a late-'70s Pittsburgh Pirates cap while lounging in Oakland's clubhouse before a game.

the off-season, but he has more intimate knowledge of the trio's on-the-mound mind-set than anyone. "He loses confidence quick because he starts worrying about things too much," Hernandez says of Zito. "He might be thinking about his last start when he's pitching that day. He really thinks a lot about everything. It's different with Mulder and Hudson. When they pitch, they forget about the last start, even if it was a shutout. They're totally and completely focused on this one, and they make sure they have everything how they want it to be to go out and pitch this start."

For Mulder, that kind of compartmentalization is a must. "When one of my starts is over, it's over," he says in mid-May. "That's why I don't really buy into the whole idea that momentum can carry over from one good start to the next. And at the same time, I don't think a bad start carries over, either. Every time you go out there, everything's different. Maybe not by much, but it's different. Your cutter might be a little better one day than the next. Maybe your split's not as good today. Maybe your arm feels great, so you have a little extra on your fastball. Nothing is the same from day to day."

And because no two starts are the same, looking back at one—good or bad—doesn't do him much good. When Mulder is watching videotape, it's always *before* a game, and he's only doing it to casually check out the hitters he's facing that day. Postgame self-analysis just doesn't work for him. "Everybody learns in different ways," he says. "I'm not saying my way is the best way, but I know there was one game that Barry pitched and he didn't pitch well, and he went up into the video room and I saw him watching the tape. I will never do that. Unless I feel that my mechanics are off and I wanna find something that's wrong, it's like, I don't want to go out and see again what I just messed up, what I totally screwed up out there. If I give up a grand slam, I don't want to go up and watch it again. Because why do I want it running through my head? Why do I wanna see that again? Why do I wanna make myself watch it and go, 'Oh, I can't believe I threw that'? I threw it. It's over. Because whether I throw a shutout or I give up ten runs in two innings, it's done with. Now let's focus on the next one. There's only one tape I ever watch to see myself—a one-hitter I threw at Arizona in 2001—and I only look at it as a way to check my mechanics, because that's as good as I've ever thrown."

Mulder's faith in himself is something everyone around him seems to feel. "He's got a nice inner confidence about himself, and it isn't arrogant, and he isn't a show-off," says A's pitching coach Curt Young. "It's really a nice professional work ethic that he's developed somewhere that makes him very consistent, very calm, with whatever goes on." *Calm* is not a word you'll often hear used to describe Hudson while he's working. He might look calm out there on the mound at times, but inside burns a competitive fire that, when mixed with his full tank of confidence, can produce the occasional in-game explosion. Art Howe was the manager in Oakland from 1996 to 2002, and Hudson will always be one of his favorite players. "The thing I loved about Tim was, on numerous occasions, he'd come into the dugout, and it's nothing-nothing in the sixth inning, or maybe even the seventh inning, and he'd say, 'Just get me one run guys, that's all I need. Just get me one. That's all it's gonna take.' And he'd back it up. We'd get a run, and that's the ball game. Tim would finish up," Howe says. "I mean there's a lot of guys who talk smack, but he always backed it up. And that lit a fire under his teammates. They'd see that passion from this guy

Whether he's pitching or not, Hudson, whom former manager Art Howe calls a born leader, is always vocal in the dugout during games.

and say, 'Geez, he just wants one run. Let's go, let's scratch it out, let's get it.' And like I said, he could back it up. He'd yell at his teammates, 'Let's go, get me a run, that's all I want, get off the schneid, let's get going.' And most pitchers, to be honest with you, just don't say stuff like that. They just come in and sit down and hope the offense gets it going. But Huddy's not gonna sit there and be quiet, and I love that in a pitcher. That's the ultimate confidence. That's a leader."

It's not easy to be a team leader as a starting pitcher, mainly because starters take the field only once, maybe twice, a week. Hudson, though, pulls it off. "Timmy's a born leader," Howe says. "I mean, he's out there, even on days when he's not pitching, pulling for his teammates. He's there for guys. He's into it. And that's part of why he's so good. He's always out there, and he's learning when he's not pitching. He talks to the other pitchers about how to get certain guys out or how he goes about things. Huddy's just a great guy. What a plus. He's special." Told of Howe's praise, Hudson plays modest at first. "Yeah, I'm pretty special," he says. "Special in that short-yellow-bus kind of way." After a few more seconds, though, he's serious and quick to the point on the topic of leadership. His voice lowers to a whisper as he leans forward, squinting, to make his point. "Every team needs a few guys with big fuckin' stones who ain't afraid to flash 'em," he says. "Everyone in the big leagues has talent, so it's a fine line between winning and losing. You need a little extra somethin' to push you over the top. And if me gettin' all pumped up gets a few other guys all pumped up, that could be that little extra somethin'."

Just as Hudson had predicted, Mulder put the A's back on track with that complete-game win over the Twins. And just as Hudson said they would, the A's go on a roll, winning eleven of thirteen games from May 9 to 23. First comes two of three in Detroit, including a 2–1 win, in which Harden strikes out eight over seven strong innings and Rhodes gets his seventh save. Then there's the sweep at Kansas City, where Hudson, in the opener, survives a flashback to that blown four-run lead in New York. After allowing five hits over eight innings, he leaves with the A's up 6–2, but with two out in the ninth, the Royals get two men aboard with Mecir on the mound. "I'm thinking, 'Error here, bomb, bomb, we're tied up,'" Hudson admits. "But that wasn't the case." Mecir gets the final out without incident, giving Hudson a 4–1 record on the year, and the following day Mulder throws his second consecutive complete game, a four-hitter, and improves to 4–2.

After Zito completes the sweep, the A's go back home for six more games against the Tigers and the Royals (May 18–23), and again they win five of six. The home stand opens with a snoozer in which Harden pitches okay—three runs on six hits over six innings—but is beaten by Detroit's twenty-one-year-old Jeremy Bonderman, a first-round draft pick of the A's in 2001 who roomed with Harden in the minors before being traded away in 2002. "I love facing this team," says Bonderman, who improves to 3–1 against Oakland in his short career. "They got rid of me, and every time I go out there, I want to show them what they got rid of." To which the A's respond with a clutch win. Dye hits his ninth homer the next night, and Bobby Kielty hits two out to get Redman (five innings, two runs) his third victory. In the finale, Hudson appears headed for yet another brutal no-decision when an error by Chavez helps the Tigers tie the score at 2–2 with an unearned run in the top of the eighth. "You've got the best third baseman in the league in Chavvy over there," Hudson says later. "I was just thinking, 'Well, that pretty much sums it up.'" But Detroit makes two errors in the bottom of the eighth and the A's capitalize. Rhodes gets his eighth save with a perfect ninth inning, and Hudson is suddenly a winner, now 5–1 with a 2.90 ERA. "I'm hoping this is the game that turns the tide for Hudson as far as his luck is concerned," says Macha. Says Hudson, "That'd be nice. Normally, these are the games I definitely get a no-decision. . . . Maybe the witch is dead."

The following night, Mulder throws his best game since that one-hitter against the Diamondbacks. He takes a no-hitter into the seventh inning, settles for a three-hitter, and a mere two hours and nine minutes after he's thrown the first pitch, his third consecutive complete game is over. So ruthlessly efficient is Mulder that the crew in charge of Fireworks Night in Oakland has to wait about forty minutes for darkness to fall before starting the show. And with typical detachment, Mulder shrugs—yes, the habit has returned—off the place in history he lost when Mike Sweeney singled just beyond the reach of Crosby and into left field to open the seventh inning. "It was a 1–1 splitter, and I didn't want to fall behind 2–1, so I kind of babied it instead of just letting it go," Mulder explains. "I just wanted to throw it for a strike instead of really making a pitch. . . . But that happens. Of course, I'd like to throw a no-hitter. Who wouldn't? But if a guy gets a hit, he gets a hit. What can you do? Give him some credit." He's every bit as blasé when asked if there's any particular reason for his 8–0 career record against the Royals. "I don't know and I don't want to know," he says. "I don't want to put too much thought into it. There's no reason to overthink it."

The A's close out the sweep and the home stand with two extra-inning victories over the weekend. Zito gives up four runs over seven innings, including a solo homer to Sweeney, but Chavez takes him off the hook for a loss with a game-tying homer in the ninth, and Crosby wins it with a single in the eleventh. "It didn't feel like a game where I gave up four runs," Zito says. "But we won, so I'm not gonna worry about it." Harden throws well the next day (six innings, two runs), but it takes Eric Byrnes's tenth-inning single to send the A's, now 25–18 on the year and 3½ games behind the Angels in the AL West, off to Boston and Cleveland for 6 games on a winning note. "Any way we can get it done, we'll try and find a way," Byrnes says. "The most important thing is our pitching staff is just keeping us in ball games. They're doing great for us."

What's wrong with the Big Three? Right now, not much.

9

THE SCENE OF THE CRIME

Bill's Bar is a dark and unassuming little place on Lansdowne Street in Boston, sitting in the shadows of the Green Monster across the street from fabled Fenway Park. Only now there are no shadows. It's past 10 P.M., and having scrambled here from the team hotel after scrambling from the A's charter flight, which was diverted and thus delayed en route from Oakland, Zito is a little frazzled. "Nice casual outfit for a low-key gig, huh?" he says, while making his way to the stage after hurriedly hopping out of a cab. "I didn't even have time to change. Just dropped off my bags and bailed." The A's are about as casual a team as you'll find in big-league ball, as evidenced by the shorts and the flip-flops favored as everyday attire for Billy Beane, but they do have a dress code for charters, so Zito is doing his best to look musician-cool while weaving his way through a crowd of sixty or so people. The jacket is open, the first few buttons of the white-collared shirt underneath are undone, and his hair, as always, is controlled chaos. "Dude, massive chafe," he says of his late arrival. "Sally's been freaking out." Sally, one of Zito's two older sisters, is already on stage, chatting with one of the photographers onhand to capture the scene. Sally is the lead singer/songwriter/keyboard

player for the Sally Zito Project, a six-piece band that's working on
its debut album, but tonight she's performing at Bill's with only
Barry and his guitar at her side.

Two things are immediately obvious here: someone has been
hyping the appearance of Zito and his sister locally, and those who
have come to watch could care less that Zito is in town with the
enemy A's. A good half of the crowd are wearing some sort of Red
Sox gear, but Zito is clearly welcome at Bill's. "I just think he's a
really cool guy, whether he plays for Oakland or not," says Jenna
Davies, a striking twenty-one-year-old who says she drove two
hours for a chance to see the show. "It's not about baseball tonight,
anyway. It's about music. I've heard some of Sally's stuff and really
like it, so when I heard she was playing and bringing Barry, I said,
'There's no way I'm missing this.'" As Zito breezes past Davies and
flashes a shy smile, something else becomes obvious: it's not *all*
about the music tonight for this young woman, who's showing
enough cleavage to prop up a flagpole. She practically melts in his
wake, grabbing a friend's arm in a nonverbal "Oh . . . my . . . god!
Barry Zito just looked at me!" Might she be planning to approach

Music runs in Zito's family, and he takes his guitar with him just about
wherever he goes.

him at some point tonight? "Actually, I'm hoping he approaches me, but if he doesn't, yeah. I'll definitely have to say hi."

Once on stage, Zito's expression changes as dramatically as it does not long after he walks through the clubhouse doors on the day of a start. This is business, the expression says, and that's the air about him as he kneels to take his acoustic guitar out of its case, plugs in, and sits on the stool next to Sally's keyboard for what, from the look of Zito's now-furrowed brow, appears to be a very frustrating sound check. Anything less than perfection when it comes to preparation is unsettling for Zito, and the only member of the A's who ventured out to Bill's to watch him play has seen this look plenty of times. "Every little detail is so important to Z," says bullpen catcher Brandon Buckley. "He has his routine, it works for him, and when something throws him off that routine, he hates it." Zito's game day routine, from the time he gets to the park, is timed by a big black watch he wears. After carb-loading with peanut butter or snack bars, he jumps into a hot whirlpool exactly ninety minutes before the game is to start. Then he showers and stretches in the trainers' room for forty minutes. Ten minutes on an exercise bike follows, before he heads out to the field for some more loosening up. Then he plays catch and long toss and throws forty pitches in the bullpen before finally heading to the dugout right before game time. "You can tell when he's been thrown off because he's looking down at his watch all pissed off," says Buckley.

There isn't a single mention of Buckley in the A's media guide. The clubhouse manager at Phoenix Municipal Stadium is in there. The guys in charge of the scoreboard dot races in Oakland are in there, too. So is the charming woman who handles the switchboard at the team's offices. But Buckley, a former minor league catcher who over the course of the season spends as much time with the A's pitchers as anyone, gets no love. And that's okay with Buckley, which partly explains why he's one of Zito's best friends on the team. "Buck is so real, dude, he's amazing," Zito says, after ending the hour-long set with his sister by singing a cover of "She Don't Use Jelly" by the Flaming Lips. "You can talk to him about anything. Pitching, life, whatever. He's one of the few guys I can go deep with. He's not interested in attention, he doesn't try to 'live the life' with the guys on the road or anything like that. He's just a regular dude. I love Buck, man. He's awesome." Buckley doesn't hear the praise being heaped upon him now, though, because he was gone almost as soon as the show came to a close, leaving Zito to live the life solo while Sally cozies up to the bar.

The fans come in small waves. A pudgy young man in a dirty Red Sox hat asks for an autograph, and Zito, now without his jacket, happily obliges. A good-looking woman who appears to be in her late thirties asks Zito to pose for a photo. He does, and after the woman disappears into the crowd, he smiles and assigns her the label he gives attractive older women: "Cougar, right there." Jenna Davies, having figured out that Zito is not here fishing for females, gets her time, too, though it lasts for all of two minutes. This procession goes on for twenty minutes or so, after which the requests for a piece of Zito fade, and, eventually, he's just one of the many patrons. Just hanging out, talking, and laughing. About an hour later he hops into a cab with Sally—she's his roomie at the team hotel while she's here—and declares the night a success. "That was cool," he says. "Everyone was just chill. No yahoos, no Super Fans. Just a bunch of people having a good time."

The last time Zito had hopped into a cab after leaving a Beantown bar, with Hudson on the eve of game three of the American League Division Series, the scene wasn't nearly as nice.

After tearing through the first inning of game four of the 2003 ALDS at Fenway Park on nine pitches, Hudson took a couple of warm-up pitches before the second inning and walked off the mound, holding his side in obvious pain. And the very next day, a story broke back home that hounds Hudson to this day. The headline in the *San Francisco Chronicle* was straightforward: "Muscle Strain Sidelines Hudson." Fair enough. The subhead, though, reeked of the speculative sensationalism that's contributed so mightily to the adversarial relationship between athletes and the media: "Bar Incident Might Be Culprit." Not so fair, says Hudson. The story, written by Susan Slusser, opened a can of controversy that still gets his goat. "I thought it was super irresponsible," Hudson says. "I just thought the whole thing was unnecessary."

The first five paragraphs of the story provided the details of the injury: exactly what area of his body was hurting, what the next step in treatment was, and how Hudson's absence might affect the rest of the series. There was even a quote from Hudson, explaining at what point during the game he knew he'd have to shut it down. The last seven paragraphs got into Hudson's history with the injury (a similar strain bothered him late in the 2002 season) and how the injury can hamper an athlete. Hudson doesn't have a problem with these twelve paragraphs. It's the six paragraphs in the middle—and the unwanted attention they brought—that earn his ire:

Three sources suggested Sunday that Hudson's injury might have stemmed from an alleged altercation on Friday night at Q, a Boston nightspot.

According to a security guard and a member of the bar staff, Hudson got into a skirmish with a Red Sox fan and threw several punches, including one that clipped a bartender.

"It was a big melee. He was throwing haymakers," said the security guard, who spoke on the condition his name not be used.

"Honest to God, he's 160 pounds and it took eight big guys to hold him back," the staff member said of Hudson. "It was five minutes of mayhem."

Hudson was unavailable for comment about the alleged incident on Sunday night, and the manager of Q, Noel Gentelles, strongly denied that any clash had taken place.

"Tim and Barry (Zito) were both here, and they couldn't have been nicer," Gentelles said. "Barry even played with the band. There was no altercation."

To be fair to Slusser, she made several failed attempts to reach Hudson about the bar incident, and she didn't write the headline. Newspaper writers never write their own headlines, and rare is the athlete who knows that. As a result, it's not uncommon for an athlete to see a not-so-flattering headline attached to a fairly harmless story and angrily confront the story's author without reading anything *but* the headline. Hudson did not angrily confront Slusser, but he did read the rest of the story. "She just wrote whatever was going to be the most interesting article without gettin' the true facts," he says. "She just listened to, number one, Boston fans, who wanted to do whatever they could to cause some turmoil for our team. . . . I'm the most nonconfrontational guy you'd ever meet, and she's paintin' me with a broad brush right there. It bothered me a lot. My wife was really mad at the whole article, too. We had a talk, and obviously she didn't agree with the fact of me being out or gettin' mixed up in something like that, but she was really bothered by that article, too. She obviously knows me better than anybody, and she knows that's not me."

Slusser and fellow *Chronicle* writer Ron Kroichick were the first reporters to explore the alleged brawl. As Slusser wrapped up her coverage duties for game four, Kroichick went to Club Q and interviewed several employees. Slusser did the same when she was done at Fenway, and she stands firmly behind what she wrote, while stressing that she investigated the incident based on a tip from a source she considered far too reliable to discount. "I would not change a thing," she says. "I had a source I know and trust and who knows Hudson and was a witness. And let me add, the source only said, 'Check to see if Hudson was in a bar fight in Boston in the past few days. I think that's why he's hurt.' The rest was all from interviews with bar employees, all of whom said the same things to both me and Ron. . . . I couldn't possibly sit on that information, given the circumstances and the magnitude of the game. Star pitcher possibly hurt in a fight two days before a big start? That's not a story I can avoid following up on. And I feel absolutely confident about the sourcing. . . . I think it's important to note that I was given the information about the incident because the source believed it was the reason Hudson left the game. I would never write about something that happened away from the field unless it either affected performance or was against the law. I have no interest in their personal lives whatsoever, unless it's a performance issue or a legal issue. In this case, it was potentially both."

It's also important to note that the bartender to whom Slusser and Kroichick spoke was fired shortly after the story broke. "He had no reason to lie about it, knowing his job might be at stake," Slusser says. And that firing, she contends, counters Hudson's complaint that the anonymous quotes detailing the incident were played higher in the story than the quote from the manager deny-ing everything. "I had at least five people all saying the same thing—that it had happened—including one who later got fired for saying it," she explains. "I frankly felt more comfortable with their version than [that of] the lone management type who, by that time, had ordered his whole staff not to talk to me. If there was nothing to talk to me about, why order them not to? That to me was fairly telling. . . . And Kroichick, who went to the bar first, heard the same things. We also heard some other things that I didn't write about, because they weren't relevant to Tim's performance."

When such a story breaks, other scribes scurry to follow up on it. And a couple of days later, Gayle Fee and Laura Raposa, who tag-team a glorified gossip column on BostonHerald.com called "Inside Track," provided a loosely written account that featured interviews with several people who said they were witnesses, including Marc Cerone, the bartender who was fired. "Hudson seemed pretty intox-icated," Cerone told Fee and Raposa, who also tracked down the man most witnesses say started the fight. Identified only as "Lee, 24, a former Army M.P.," he accused Hudson of being the instigator, contending that the ace was "throwing out bad lines" to the girl-friend of one of his friends. "My friend comes in and tells me that Zito's cool, but Hudson's drunk and being an idiot," Lee is quoted as saying. "So I went in and said, 'This is a Boston bar. Get the hell outta here. We don't want you in here.' He's got his middle finger inches away from my face. So I grabbed his finger, threw some beer on him, and after that, I was being hit from every angle." But the column noted that Paul Daley, who described himself as a Red Sox fan and said that he was standing next to Hudson, "contends it was Lee who gave Hudson the finger and that the pitcher tried to avoid an altercation until he was covered in beer." Said Daley, "[Hudson] tried to laugh it off and back away, and then this idiot sprayed him with beer. That's when Hudson hit him—with his pitching hand. . . . Hudson was basically defending himself." Witnesses added that all hell broke loose thereafter, and Cerone reiterated his suggestion to Slusser that Hudson was out of control. "Hudson threw his drink; it hit me in the chest, bounced off me," he said. "Then he started throwing punches over and over again."

Hudson's version of the night's events, offered during the same lunch in New York at which he addressed the future of the team, corroborates several details. "We were just hangin' out. Me, Zito, my brothers, some other buddies. You know, a night at the bar," he says. "It was real cool, actually. A lot of Boston fans were there, and they recognized us, but they were being cool. You know, sayin' things like, 'Hey. You guys are great, but we're gonna kick y'all's asses.' Things like that, just supportin' their team, and that's cool. . . . And that pretty much goes on all night. Everybody was bein' pretty cool. But there was this one guy, off to the side, wearin' his Boston hat, and you could tell he was pretty wasted. He just goes, 'Hey, the A's fuckin' suck,' this and that. He was the only one that ever cursed or was, like, being a dick about it. So I kinda looked at this guy and gave him, you know, the you're-a-dumb-ass kind of look. I just kind of looked at him and smirked like, 'Why you wanna be a jerk?' So then he comes toward me, pointing at me, and then he touched my face with his finger. He said, 'You fuckin' suck.' So at that point I'm doin' what any man would do in that situation, so I knocked his hand out of my face, and when I did that, his drink went flyin'. I kind of hit him and pushed him off me at the same time. Hey, whether you're a baseball star or some Joe Schmoe off the street, you have to protect yourself in that situation." Adds Zito, who was in another area of the club at the time, "I only got second-hand what happened that night, which was that someone came up to Huddy and put his fingers in his face and was like, 'You suck,' which is as violating as you can be to another man, basically."

Hudson disputes that he was drunk: "I had probably three or four drinks, which isn't too bad." He disputes that he was hitting on anyone: "Maybe some guy got pissed that his girlfriend asked for my autograph or a picture or somethin'." He disputes that he was machine-gunning punches all over the club: "After I pushed him off me, the bouncers came over real quick, and my brothers came over and were kind of pushing this idiot off me. And that was it. The lights came on. The bouncers came over and kicked him out. It might have looked like this big to-do, but it wasn't." And most vehemently, he disputes that his injury had anything to do with his early exit from game four two days later: "It was really frustratin'. To be honest with you, what happened that night never crossed my mind. But then after the game, next thing I know, that's the rumor flying around. That's frustratin' for me because I know that's not why I came out of the game. It's the same injury I had the year before. That's what I don't think a lot of people understand. It was a recurring injury that happened the same time the year before."

What Hudson does not dispute is that he learned a valuable lesson about judgment in the wake of the incident. His wife was right. He had no business being in a Boston hotspot that night. Not with a 2–0 series lead. Not in a town where desperate fans were one loss from another crushing end to a season. "Obviously, hindsight is twenty-twenty," he says. "You have to think about it. Places like Boston and New York are places where their fans are way more passionate about their teams than in most places. A lot of people, that's what they live for. So that's one thing that I don't think we really understood. You look back, it wasn't a smart thing to do. I mean, we weren't in the wrong one bit as far as what happened, but looking back, I shouldn't have gone down to the local bar to have a drink. I should have stayed at the hotel. . . . It just takes one guy in a bar, one wise guy that gets liquored up and sees an opportunity to cause trouble for somebody that's playing his team, and all of a sudden you're in the paper. I can guarantee that won't happen to me again."

As for Hudson's relationship with Slusser today? It's fine. Good, even. Both have moved on. "I didn't like the story, but I know Susan's not out to get me," Hudson says. "I respect her. She's just doin' her job." Says Slusser, "He's been great to me ever since. He always has been and has never changed one bit."

The night after Zito's gig with his sister at Bill's Bar, Boston is no kinder to Hudson than it had been to him eight months earlier. But this time all of the damage is done on the field. The worst start of Hudson's season and the best night of former A's infielder Mark Bellhorn's career give the Red Sox an easy 12–2 victory in the first game of a three-game series. In what many expected to be a classic pitchers' duel with Red Sox righty Curt Schilling, Hudson allows five runs on nine hits, four walks, and two hit batters over four innings in his shortest outing since lasting just three innings on

September 3, 2003, in Baltimore. The fifteen base runners allowed are a season-high for Hudson, who is now 2–2 with a 4.18 ERA in his last six starts since opening the season by going 3–0 with a 2.15 ERA in his first four outings. "It was a rather unusual performance for Huddy," Macha says. "I don't think he hit his spots too well." Hudson and his catcher, Adam Melhuse, concur. "They just caught me on a bad night. There's not much else to say," Hudson offers from behind a pained smile. "My command was as bad as it's been in a long time." Adds Melhuse, "It's hard to put your finger on any one thing. He wasn't putting it where he wanted it a lot of the time, but more than anything, they just came out hacking and put a lot of balls in play hard."

Hudson has often said that when he's especially excited for a game, he tends to overthrow. That, in turn, takes some of the sink out of his sinker. "The harder I throw, the flatter it gets," he says. But he insists that he was on an even emotional keel this night: "They just got me. That team can rake." The Red Sox bang out a season-high nineteen hits on the night, including a career high–tying four by designated hitter David Ortiz, but it is Bellhorn who does the heaviest lifting, setting one career high by scoring four runs and matching another with five RBIs while going 3-for-5. "Fuckin' Horny," Hudson says of Bellhorn, who played at Auburn before Hudson and batted .198 in 323 at-bats over parts of four seasons with the A's. "Where was that when he was with us? He was all over the place tonight." So was Hudson. The four walks are a season high, as are the five doubles he surrenders. "It happens," says another former teammate of Hudson's, Boston center fielder Johnny Damon. "We'll take it. You never want to see him on his game; that's definitely not fun." It was a far cry from what had transpired the previous August in Oakland, where Hudson shut the Sox out on two hits in a ninety-three-pitch masterpiece to beat another Red Sox stud, Pedro Martinez. "They've seen the best and the worst of me," Hudson offered. "And a little bit in-between."

Fenway has become a haunted house for the A's. They lost Mulder for the season in a game here last August. They lost games three and four of the 2003 American League Division Series here, both in agonizing fashion, and they lost Hudson to the aforementioned injury in the process. And a day after losing the series opener, they lose their streak of five consecutive winning series by losing 9–6 after Redman gives up a game-breaking three-run homer to Jason Varitek. "I can only speak for myself because I've only played here two games," says Crosby, whose three-run throwing error was the other key play of the game. "But even in college and in the minors, there's always that place you go to where strange things seem to happen to you." Oakland bounces back the next night with a 15–2 win, though, and the only thing strange about it is that the offense is so effective that Mulder's fourth consecutive win isn't much to talk about. His quest for a fourth consecutive complete game essentially dies when he throws thirty-one pitches in the first inning, and he finishes with a career-high seven walks. But he starts the game with five shutout innings and allows only four hits before being lifted with a pitch count of 117, with two out and two runs across in the sixth. "I couldn't throw a strike," Mulder says. "I was a mess." A mess with a 6–1 record and a 3.00 ERA.

You want messy? Take Oakland's visit to Cleveland (May 28–30) after the Red Sox series. In the Friday-night opener of a three-game series, Zito's claim that his confidence has returned is backed by his eight shutout innings of three-hit work. He gets "Hudsoned," though, when Mecir gives up a walk-off home run to Casey Blake. "We scored fifteen yesterday and came out tonight and were shut out," Zito says. "But that's just the nature of the game. I feel like I've thrown the ball more or less the way I've wanted to the last month, and it came to a head tonight." Things come to a negative head for the bullpen—the *first* negative head, actually—two days later.

Harden is spotty Saturday (five innings, six walks), but the A's have a 6–5 lead going into the bottom of the eighth when rookie reliever Justin Duchscherer gives up a leadoff triple to Alex Escobar. Macha turns to Rhodes, who gets Matt Lawton to hit a chopper to short, and Crosby throws wildly to the plate. Tie game. Omar Vizquel singles. Jody Gerut singles. Travis Hafner singles. The A's lose, 8–6, with Rhodes getting his second loss and third blown save. On Sunday he gets his third loss and fourth blown save when the Tribe erases a 3–2 deficit with two runs off Rhodes in the bottom of the ninth, and the game-winning run scores in torturous fashion. Rhodes and catcher Melhuse get their signals crossed, resulting in a wild pitch that ends the game. Quietly fuming over the three losses, two blown saves, and 8.78 ERA put together by the bullpen on the six-game trip, Macha grimaces and says, "You've got to get three outs the last inning."

Oh, and guess who got Hudsoned this time? That would be Hudson, whose eight strong innings went for nothing more than another no-decision. "'Hudsoned,' huh?" he muses. "So I'm a verb now? Stay hot, Huddy. Stay hot."

10

HELPING HAND?

Remember when Mulder was so put off by the early-May questions about the Big Three's struggles? There's more to it than his contention that it was too early in the year to hit the panic button about a collective rough patch. A lot more. What *really* bugged him was that several of the questions did something Mulder has long been loath to do. They assigned what he feels is an inordinate amount of credit for the Big Three's prior success to Rick Peterson. That's what he meant when he said, "Here we go. We all knew this was coming." A few days after the off-season announcement that the A's were allowing Rick Peterson to end his six-year term as Oakland's pitching coach to take the same job with the New York Mets, Mulder made the following prediction: "I guarantee that the first time one of us struggles, everyone's going to say it's because of Rick. 'Oh, they miss Rick.' I guarantee it. I'd bet my life on it." He was right, too, but that doesn't mean the media were necessarily wrong in posing the Peterson questions. In fact, they were perfectly justified. *Of course*, people were wondering about just what sort of impact Peterson's departure would have on his three star pupils. Peterson was the only pitching coach they'd had as big leaguers. He's all they'd known. And that all three of them appeared to be struggling at the same time so early in the season made the questions fair and legitimate. Mulder reluctantly concedes as much, but he's even more reluctant to heap the kind of praise upon Peterson that so many others have done over the years.

"I'm not going to sit here and say that Rick didn't help me. He did," Mulder says. "But do I think he gets too much credit? Yeah. I mean, look at what he was working with. I was a first-round draft pick. Zito was a first-round draft pick. Huddy wasn't, but he should have been. He's got as much talent as any of us, maybe more. So, obviously, we were all pretty good pitchers when we got drafted, and Rick didn't have anything to do with that. It didn't take any of us very long to get to the big leagues, either. Was that all Rick's doing? No. He wasn't with us in the minor leagues. He worked with all of us some, and he helped with my delivery when I was in triple-A, but it's not like he was there the whole time."

Understand that Mulder holds no malice toward Peterson. In every walk of life, there are certain employees who will never be into holiday-card swapping with their bosses, and a pitching coach is essentially the boss of a pitching staff. But there is a specific point in time to which Mulder points where the relationship took a turn for the worse. It came during his second season in the majors, while he was on the way to a 21–8 record, a 3.45 ERA, and a runner-up finish in the 2001 AL Cy Young Award voting. It was a dramatic turnaround from the previous season, when he'd gone 9–10 with a 5.44 ERA as a rookie, and Mulder took exception when it was relayed to him via reporters that Peterson had suggested that the turnaround was the result of Mulder more closely following the game plans Peterson had so meticulously mapped out. "That was pretty much when it went a little sour for me," Mulder recalls. "It was like, 'Mark's so much better now because he's finally listening.' And that wasn't it. It was almost like, 'When he was going bad, I had nothing to do with it.' So, yeah, that bugged me. Look, I didn't go from 9–10 to 21–8 because of Rick Peterson. Did he help? Yeah. I'm not saying he didn't. But for the most part, the improvements I made was just from pitching. From being out there. From seeing what works, what doesn't, and just kind of learning from it. I just felt like Rick always wanted to be in the spotlight. That's why he's always talking to the media. He just wants to make sure everyone knows that he's good at what he does, and I'm just not like that, I guess."

That Mulder isn't the biggest Peterson fan in the world comes as no shock to Peterson. He was a constant target of Mulder's practical joking when they were together in Oakland—"My only goal on the days I wasn't pitching was to fuck with Rick," Mulder says— and Peterson is a smart and perceptive man. It was apparent to anyone close to the A's that Mulder didn't buy into all things Peterson, so Peterson himself had to be well aware of the subtle frost that

Mulder never quite meshed with the hands-on style of former A's pitching coach Rick Peterson (right), suggesting that Peterson was too quick to take credit for his pupils' success.

developed on the relationship over time. But despite having never seen a notebook he couldn't fill, with either quotes or elaborate, multicolored charts, Peterson bristles a bit at the suggestion that he sought credit for any of his pitchers' success. "I've always said I get way too *much* credit, if anything," he says. And while he admits that he's been a little hurt by having heard about what he calls Mulder's "animosity" toward him since his leaving the A's, Peterson has nothing but good things to say about Mulder. The way he sees it, their differences were all about personality. "Exactly," he says. "It's because Mark is a very independent guy who has so much pride in who he is and what he does and his abilities. I respect that." Peterson does, however, want to set the record straight about 2001. This is when *his* pride comes out.

Peterson's motto as a pitching coach is simple: "In God we trust. All others must have data." And Peterson is the baseball equivalent of IBM when it comes to data. On cue, he can tell you that Ray Durham is 34-for-199 when he swings at an offspeed pitch or that Juan Gonzalez hits .230 when the count is two balls and a strike. He uses that information to formulate a plan of attack on each hitter, and Mulder's supreme confidence in his own stuff occasionally clashed with Peterson's reliance on statistics. "Well, that was a huge part of our system," Peterson says. "But here's Mark, in his first year, and he's got [runners at] first and third with one out and he's throwing a cutter with the first pitch. So I say, 'Mark, we need a grounder. You've got heavy sink. Your ground ball–flyball ratio, you were second in the league. You've got a ground ball–flyball ratio off the charts, and you're throwing a cutter on the first pitch? That's not preparation, that's a bad decision.'. . . Look, Mark is one of the most talented guys I've ever seen. I mean, he does everything well. I remember seeing some day-in-the-life thing they did with him on ESPN, and he had a T-shirt on and long jeans, and he gets pushed into the pool and he gets out of the pool and he gets on the diving board and he sticks a one-and-a-half gainer. I said to Mark, 'Are you kidding me? You can just get up there and stick one with wet jeans on, soaking-wet jeans on?' I mean, that's a tribute to Mark. And it's the same thing with golf. He doesn't need to practice. He's just gifted. But talent does not equate to performance at this level. And he equated, when was 9–10 with a 5.44 ERA, he equated talent with performance. 'Not here,' I said. 'Yeah, before you got here, in college or the minors, yeah, it does, it'll equate there. But when you get on *this* field, talent doesn't equate to performance. You have to prepare better, and I can help.' But to have to tell him all that, that didn't go over real good with Mark."

Zito was—is—the anti-Mulder when it comes to Peterson. No shock there, either. Zito is the anti-Mulder in a million ways. Zito surfs and practices yoga. Mulder golfs. Zito is into photography and philosophy. Mulder is into video games. Zito studies tape of his performances. Mulder avoids tape study like it's the plague. Zito admits to sometimes thinking too much on the mound. Mulder says his goal on the mound is to think as little as possible. It's fascinating, really, because Zito and Mulder get a kick out of each other. They're friends. Not the let's-hook-up-in-the-off-season type, but friends nonetheless. You'd have a hard time, however, finding two people on such opposite ends of the spectrum in virtually everything they do, and their relationships with Peterson—Zito calls him "Pete"—could not be more different.

Former pitching coach Rick Peterson (left) is a huge proponent of video study, and Zito followed Peterson's lead at every turn. The two started working together in 1996, when Zito was still in college.

"I think it's a personality thing, more than anything," Zito says. "I was probably more open to everything Pete had to say, and that's not a knock on Mark at all. I'm not saying that everyone else is closed-minded, but when you stop being open to new suggestions and new learning, you stop learning. And then, at that point, you're getting worse. So you know, I'm always learning. My dad's motto was, 'Leave no stone unturned.' We would try everything. If we had to read a whole book to get one little mechanic different, one little mental concept, it was worth it." Mulder is slightly wrong about one thing, too. Peterson did have a considerable impact on Zito's development before he got to the big leagues. They've known each other for years, and the story about their initial contact is priceless.

"In 1996, I was a [pitching] coordinator for Toronto," Peterson says, "and it's about six o'clock on a spring training night, about a week to go in spring training, and the facility is basically empty. I've got a stack of tapes, going through all this stuff, and the clubhouse guy comes in and goes, 'Rick, there's a long-distance phone call.' And I say, 'Is it real important?' and he says no, so I say, 'Get me his number and tell him I'll call him back in about ten minutes. I've gotta finish this.' So the guy comes back thirty seconds later

Oakland's cramped video room isn't just for studying. Here Mulder makes a phone call while Zito catches up on his e-mail.

and says, 'The guy says it's urgent.' And so I go, 'Who is it?' 'Joe Zito.' Joe Zito? Who the fuck is Joe Zito? So I take the phone and I say, 'Hi, this is Rick Peterson,' and he goes, 'Hi, Rick, this is Joe Zito. I'm Barry Zito's dad and he's a freshman in college, and we've hired everybody to work with Barry Zito, from Randy Jones to this guy and that, and we've done a background check on you, and we've selected you to finish off my son as a big-league pitcher.' I'm thinking, 'This guy did a background check on me? Are you fucking kidding me?' So I said, 'Joe, I'm totally flattered, but with all due respect, there's a lot of dads who think their kid's gonna be the next, you know, whatever. Call me back in ten days, after the end of spring training. Let me find out if I'm even allowed to do this.'. . . Well, he's pitching up in the Cape Cod League with Mark, and I'm down in New Jersey for a few days, so he drives with his sister so we can finally meet face-to-face. So, I'll never forget, it was a soft summer rain in New Jersey, and we go to a local high school, and we're in the parking lot shadowboxing his delivery and showing him all these drills. And we're playing in a fucking parking lot by a high school, so that's where it started. I spent two years with Barry prior to the draft. You know, looking at his system or his program and adding or subtracting from it."

Zito remembers that time very well, too. In fact, he remembers one little detail about Peterson's availability for such duty that Peterson left out. "At that point, Rick was the pitching coach with Toronto and, you know, he got fired, so he kind of was a freelance guy," he says. But that didn't matter to the Zitos. *Leave no stone unturned.* Peterson had something Barry needed, and he got it in that rain-soaked parking lot. "He wrote me out this whole program that I'm sure I have somewhere," Zito says. "It was like, uphill throwing behind the mound, sixty-feet long toss, and you come down and do this and that, and you wanna throw up this way. We went into the school library and he was writing down all this stuff and talking about it, and that was it. We met for about an hour and a half, and I went back to the Cape with my sister. And cut to, basically, two years later, in '99, when I'm just getting drafted by the A's, and I ended up being back with him." Peterson, Zito says, has the two most important elements of pitching—the mental and the mechanical—down cold. "Pete's so good mechanically, he could, like, see something wrong with someone and just go, 'No, your hands are here,' or your foot, or your timing, this, that," Zito says. "And half the time he wouldn't say anything; he was just sitting there watching me and he wouldn't say a word. But the whole time he was watching with a frickin' careful eye, man, because the instant an arm slot would change or a hand movement would change, he was on it."

It wasn't just Peterson's mastery of mechanics that appealed to Zito, of course. In Peterson, he had someone with whom he could go deep. "Definitely," Zito says. "He wasn't just a pitching coach for me. He's a friend. You know, Pete and I are both guys who are a little different. I think we're similar in our spiritual beliefs and our beliefs that everything in life is really a lot more about the mind than people believe. And I think that kind of was the initial background that we really vibed on together."

If Zito is the anti-Mulder regarding Peterson, Cory Lidle was Mulder on a 'roid rage. He and Peterson did not vibe on anything. Lidle, who through the 2004 season had played with six big-league teams in seven years, was with Oakland for two of those years, 2001–2002, and his beef with Peterson is a forty-eight-ounce porterhouse to Mulder's carpaccio. Peterson's game plans, the product of countless hours of studying video and charting tendencies, were always an issue with Lidle. "He watches a lot of tape, and I do, too," Lidle says, "but if I didn't agree with his plan, he got insulted. And it's not that I never agreed with his plan, but if you're out there on the mound and you're supposed to get somebody out with your curveball and he takes a good swing at it or hits a home run just barely foul, now I might not want to throw him another curveball. On tape, maybe he doesn't look like he's a good curveball hitter. But what if he puts a good swing on my curveball? Maybe he's a good curveball hitter that night. So, for me, to go into a game with a plan, I think I should be able to change my plan if I see hitters acting differently than what I thought it was. Rick didn't believe in that. He thought, if you watch it on tape and he doesn't hit a curveball, you just keep on throwing the curveball. And that's where it was hard for me."

Lidle also resents what he perceives to have been a star system employed by Peterson. "Mulder, Hudson, Zito? They had the freedom to do what they wanted to do," he says. "Me? Even when I was going good, he would still put me in a different category. My first year [with Oakland], I had a good season. I mean, I won thirteen games and there was nine blown saves, and that equals a lot of wins if everything goes my way. But then the following year, one of the first things Rick said to me was that I don't have the freedom to pitch the way that I really want to pitch, and that *really* chafed me. . . . Rick is the ultimate totem-pole guy. If he is higher on the totem pole, he will treat you like a dog. He was not higher than Hudson, Mulder, Zito. But for a number four guy who just signed there, yeah, he thought he was higher. He would talk down to me, and you should see the way he talked to our video guy. If he was higher on the totem pole, then he would treat you like shit, and that just shows you what kind of person he is."

Without denying that they existed, Peterson takes the high road when talking about his battles with Lidle. But he does suggest that a look at Lidle's career numbers might prove interesting. And sure enough, there are dramatic differences in the ERAs that Lidle has posted with and without Peterson's guidance. The year before he joined the A's, Lidle's ERA was 5.03 with Tampa Bay. In his two years with the A's, it was 3.59 and 3.89, and in 2002 Lidle flirted with the Oakland record for consecutive scoreless innings with a thirty-two-bagel run that earned him AL Pitcher of the Month honors for August. The year after he left the A's as a free agent, Lidle's ERA ballooned to 5.75 with Toronto.

"I'll give Rick credit," he says. "He helped me out, there's no doubt about it, 100 percent. When I came over here, I came over here from the Devil Rays, and we didn't have pitchers' meetings over there to go over hitters like Rick has. We had a video room in Tampa Bay, but it wasn't even about watching tape. I went into every game just saying, 'Okay, I'm gonna throw my fastball inside and my changeup away and throw my backdoor curveball,' not really knowing. I think I became a much better pitcher once I started watching film, so that's what helped me a lot. Rick taught me how to prepare. I'll give credit to Rick where it's due. But I'm not giving him as much credit as he gives himself for what I did. He's very much a self-promoter. I commend him for doing the amount of work that he does, but he got this job when Mulder, Hudson, and Zito were coming up, and how do you go wrong there? Honestly, how do you go wrong? He stepped into a great situation."

Lidle and Mulder weren't the only pitchers to go at it occasionally with Peterson. Ted Lilly, who played for the A's in 2002 and 2003, is another high-profile example, and some of Oakland's relievers over the years have made their displeasure known. But nobody got after it with Peterson like Lidle did. "I saw Mark have some words with him, but with Mark it's always been a nonchalant, joking way to get his point across," Lidle says. "I tried to stay pretty calm, but sometimes I got pretty aggressive. There was one time I had a talk with Rick, and he basically told me that with my stuff, if he'd have called every pitch, I'd have been a twenty-game winner. And it was basically a slap in the face that I didn't know what I was doing. I almost got in a fight right then. Another time he was out on the mound and talking about that same type of stuff, and the whole team's out there, and they saw me get in his face. Mark yelled over, 'I've got my money on Lidle, I've got my money on Lidle.' And Rick said, 'Don't bet on it.' Like he could kick my ass or something." The third instance came in Lidle's second year with the A's, after he'd signed a two-year contract worth $7.6 million as a reward for his strong 2001 season. "We were in a pitchers' meeting in Boston, and we had a disagreement. And he, in front of everyone, said, 'I didn't see you complaining when you got that contract you got.' Like he got it for me. I got up to fucking grab Rick by the neck. . . . Rick knows a lot about pitching, but there's one thing that he never did. He never competed at this level."

And there it is, ladies and gentlemen. Lidle has played the you've-never-been-in-the-big-leagues card. In his own nonconfrontational way, Mulder played it on Peterson, too. But Peterson had the perfect response. It was 2001, and Mulder had taken the page from Oakland's media guide on which Peterson's less-than-stellar minor league stats appeared and enlarged it on a photocopy and posted it for all to see. Peterson says that Jason Giambi, then the team's leader, asked Peterson if he should take it down. Peterson said no. Instead, he says, he walked over to Mulder and appealed to the golf fan in him. "I said, 'Hey, Mark, who's Tiger Woods's coach?'" Peterson recalls. "He says, 'Butch Harmon.' I say, 'Tell me, how many PGA Tour wins, how many majors, did Butch Harmon have?' He says, 'None.' I just kind of stood there and smiled for a second. Then I said, 'Keep up the good work, Tiger,' and walked away."

—   —   —

Whatever is said about Rick Peterson, Hudson insists, it also must be said that he gets the job done. In 1998, Peterson took over an Oakland staff that had the worst ERA in the majors the previous season. In 1999, Hudson's rookie year, the A's finished in the top three in AL ERA for the first of five consecutive years. In 2002 and 2003, Oakland led the league. And in his first year with the Mets, Peterson was good enough—New York's ERA was the seventh-best in the NL—to have been the sole survivor of a purge that saw Howe and the rest of his staff fired at the end of the season. "When I got drafted, he was the minor league roving pitching guy," Hudson says, "and from day one he was hands-on with everybody. I mean, he's really passionate about teachin' pitchin' and teachin' mechanics and teachin' whatever it is that he knows about pitchin', which is great for young pitchers. I learned probably more with Rick than I ever have pitchin'. Most everything that he worked on with me helped me get here as quick as I did and have as much success as I did. And I think for any young pitcher, Rick is unbelievable. His methods might rub a few guys the wrong way, but he means well and he knows his shit. I also kinda like that he's a battler, man. It took him a while to get where he is now, but he never gave up."

The son of former Pittsburgh Pirates general manager Pete Peterson, Rick Peterson is a baseball lifer, having kicked around the minor leagues as a player and a coach for nearly twenty years before Beane, who has never been afraid of anything unconventional, gave him a shot in Oakland. Peterson has a degree in psychology from Jacksonville University, and in addition to putting that degree to use on his pitchers, he's been heavily involved in famed orthopedic surgeon Dr. James Andrews's American Sports Medicine Institute (ASMI) since meeting Andrews while coaching with the Chicago White Sox's double-A club in Birmingham, Alabama, from 1989 to 1991. Peterson says ASMI has studied more than nine hundred baseball injuries, and that data is the foundation for a throwing program—closely monitored pitch counts are a part of it—designed to reduce injuries. He calls it "prehab."

He also takes many of his pitchers for off-season visits to ASMI, where they're put through a battery of computerized tests, in which thirty-five segments of each pitcher's delivery are recorded by video cameras at 240 frames per second. But as scientific as he is, Peterson has an air of mystery about him. He does not, for instance, share the results of these tests with his pitchers, as Zito found out during the off-season after winning the Cy Young Award in 2002. "Two years ago we went back to Birmingham—we took Harden and a bunch of guys—so I called Z to get the dates," Peterson says. "And he goes, 'Rick, why am I even going back to this? You didn't even show me any of the analysis.' I said, 'Exactly, but remember we did this instead of that, we did that instead of this.' And I went through six specific things and I said, 'You had a pretty good year last year. You won a Cy Young. That analysis is for me to understand. You need to drive the car. I'll make sure the car is running the right way.'" Another Peterson oddity: his pitchers are occasionally asked to throw in the bullpen with their eyes closed as a visualization method. "Timmy laughs about it now," he says of Hudson, "but we were doing some throwing with our eyes closed in the Instructional League one day, and he goes, 'Look what the fuck we are doing! Throwing with our eyes closed!' And it's like, 'This is so far off the wall.' This is why I have the reputation I have. But you wanna go to the highest level? This is what you do."

Consider Hudson, who tends to take a broad view on everything, sold. "I had a great relationship with Rick, because he was so passionate about us," he says. "He's not just a pitching coach. He truly cares about you, not only as a coach but as a person. And he's good at what he does, so you gotta show him some respect. Obviously, a lot of guys gave him a hard time. A lot of the older guys didn't really see eye to eye with him, and Mark didn't really see eye to eye with him, but that's just personality stuff. Mark's personality, he was a guy who was always good in anything and probably didn't ever need to listen to any coaches. He was just that guy, he didn't need to be coached, that kind of thing. Barry's on the other end of the spectrum. He needs his head massaged more than anything, and I think Rick was really good for him in that respect. I mean, if you're willing to open up to Rick, and give him your honest attention, he'll be good for anybody, whether you're young or old. Most old guys, old pitchers, they're kind of set in their ways and can kind of understand what makes themselves tick, and maybe they don't need some pitching coach to tell them to do balance drills with their eyes closed and that kind of thing. Young guys, they're very easily influenced by people, especially kids who wanna get better, and Rick's that kind of guy. . . . I don't think any of us would be as good as we are without him."

As for Curt Young, the man who replaced Peterson? Like Mulder and Zito, Hudson came quickly to Young's defense when the early-May struggles brought Young's ability to handle the staff into question. "We're still doing the exact same stuff with Curt that we did with Rick because it's our system, and just because Rick is gone doesn't mean the system has changed," Hudson says. "Curt, he's one of the best coaches I've ever been around. He's easy to get along with, he's always got a smile, he's always there to try to help you, but it's not like he's pressing the issues all the time. I mean, if there was one thing that I probably didn't see eye to eye with Rick on, it was that. He'd wear you the fuck out about what you need to do. But I think that with me and Zito and Mulder and some of the better pitchers in the game, the hitters have to adjust to us, you know what I'm saying? It's like, this guy may be great at this pitch, but he hasn't been great at hitting that pitch off *me*."

So was it a good time for a change? Hudson thinks about it for a good thirty seconds. "To be honest with you, I think whether Rick was here or was gone, I think me and Mark and Zito are at the points of our careers where it really don't matter who's our pitching coach," he says. "You know, I think we're developed enough and we understand our game enough to the point where our success and failure is gonna be determined from us, what we do and how we prepare. I think Curt's the perfect fit as far as that goes."

11

BREAKING DOWN

Baseball is a game filled with unmistakable sounds. The crack of the bat. The gentle thump of a ball enveloped by leather. The persistent shouting of vendors hawking peanuts. All very *ball*. All very welcome. There is one most unwelcome sound of the game, though, and the A's have to hear it the night of their first game back after the miserable trip through Boston and Cleveland.

In the first game of a season-high twelve-game home stand, on June 1, Redman is solid on a perfectly mild Tuesday evening, holding the visiting White Sox to one run over six innings. Dye's tenth homer of the year gives Oakland a 4–1 lead going into the seventh. But then the bullpen takes over. Bradford gives up a two-run homer to Frank Thomas in the eighth, Jose Valentin ties it up with a solo shot off Mecir in the ninth, and there goes blown save number ten of the year. This, as it turns out, would be the least of the A's worries. Facing hard-throwing southpaw Damaso Marte in the bottom of the eleventh inning with nobody out and a runner on first, Chavez tries to spin away from an inside fastball but fails. The result is the sickening sound of ball against bone that can be heard throughout the stadium, and as Chavez hops around in obvious pain, a sense of doom descends on the paltry crowd of 14,000-plus.

"I thought I was going to be fine," Chavez says later that night. "Obviously, I was wrong." Very wrong. Chavez, who leads the American League with thirteen home runs and leads the A's with thirty-four RBIs, says he has a broken right hand and will miss at least three weeks. He'll be going on the disabled list for the second time in his six-year career, and it's awfully tough to be a badass from the disabled list. "It didn't swell up too bad because after I came out of the game, we got some ice on it," he says by cell phone, after leaving a nearby hospital. "So I wasn't too worried about it. I mean, I knew I wasn't going to be able to play tomorrow because there's no way I could grip a bat, but I thought maybe I'd be out a couple of days at the most." After gloomily explaining that doctors had told him they might have to place a pin in the hand to stabilize it, Chavez says he didn't ask for, nor did he get, a best-case scenario regarding his return to action. "I've never broken anything in my life," he says, "so I have no idea how long this is going to take. It all just depends on how I heal. It's gonna be at least three weeks, they said, but it could be more."

Six weeks is typical with such breaks, and the injury is a huge blow to Oakland's offense, which entered the night's game tied with Toronto for the lowest batting average with runners in scoring position in the AL (.247) and ranked eleventh among the league's fourteen teams in overall batting (.263) and runs scored (227). "Yeah," Chavez says. "It's not good." Macha, who had left the stadium after the game unaware of Chavez's prognosis, had already gotten the bad news when he, too, spoke by phone later in the night. And he, too, knows that Chavez being down for *any* amount of time is a potentially crushing blow. "Obviously, Eric's an important part of our team, offensively and defensively," Macha says. "You've just gotta play on and do the best you can." Looking for something positive, Macha points to his team's response to the season-ending injury suffered the previous August by Mulder, who was having a Cy Young–caliber year. The A's played the last month and a half—about six weeks—without Mulder and still managed to win the AL West. "Guys stepped it up when Mark was hurt, and now we've got Chavvy hurt," Macha says. "Injuries are part of the game." But Mulder works once every five days. Chavez will be missed every day—every time a ground ball is hit to third base, and every time the number three spot in the batting order comes up.

In the short term, Macha says, it's likely that veteran utilityman Mark McLemore, a thirty-nine-year-old in his nineteenth season of big-league ball who underwent knee surgery in the spring, will take over at third base. Marco Scutaro, who started the season at second base but has recently been sharing time there with McLemore, will again be the everyday starter. Other possibilities include a trade, which could prove a challenge, or the promotion of one of Oakland's prospects. Another option is Esteban German, who played third for the first time this spring and has been up with the big-league club in each of the last three seasons. "I don't know what they're gonna do," Chavez says. "This is pretty brutal."

The next day, Beane is holding court in the hallway that takes players from the clubhouse door to the big room of lockers, and he looks like someone just put his collie, Taggart, through a wood chipper. "I don't think I need to state the obvious in terms of his overall importance to this team. Chavvy arguably has a chance to go to the Hall of Fame," he says. He had known the extent of Chavez's injury by late Tuesday night as well and says, "That's the first time in two years that I didn't sleep very well." And just in case dealing with the Chavez crisis isn't enough of a drain, Beane is hit with another question about the bullpen. Clearly, he's not in the mood. "My guess," he says with the trademark trace of condescension that creeps into his voice when he's not pleased with a question, "is that we'll continue to try to find the guy who gets the most outs." As Beane speaks, players file in past him, getting ready for the afternoon game and Day 1 of Life After Chavvy. Most of them have already heard the news, including Mulder, who had gotten a call from Chavez the night before.

"Shitty," he calls the situation. So does Hudson, who, like Mulder, is a ground-ball pitcher and relies heavily on Chavez's brilliant defense. "Chavvy's our number three hitter, but we've got eight other hitters in the lineup every night," Hudson says. "But we don't have any other three-time Gold Glove third basemen in here. This deal here? It ain't gonna be easy."

— — —

What happens in the immediate aftermath of Chavez's injury is nothing new. It happens all the time in sports. A superstar goes down, and the team somehow raises its level of play to compensate for the loss. The night Chavez is hit by a pitch, Bobby Kielty, whose playing time has been cut dramatically by the solid play of Byrnes, wins the game with a walk-off homer in the twelfth inning. The next day, after Scott Hatteberg sends the game into extra innings with a pinch-hit single in the bottom of the ninth inning, Mark Kotsay hits his first homer of the year in the tenth, marking the first time since Dwayne Murphy and Mike Heath did it to the Angels in August 1981 that the A's had won consecutive games with walk-offs. "That's awesome," says Mulder, who'd allowed two runs on eight hits through seven innings but left the game trailing 2–1. "If we're gonna get through this stretch without Chavvy, that's the kind of thing we need. That's two huge wins, right there." It wasn't a bad couple of days for Beane, either. Hatteberg was a relative unknown when Beane rescued him off the scrap heap in December 2001. Kielty and Kotsay were two of Beane's key acquisitions in this last off-season. And the three Chicago pitchers who gave up Oakland's three biggest hits in the two-game sweep—Neal Cotts on Tuesday, Billy Koch and Jon Adkins on Wednesday—are former members of the A's organization, traded away by Beane. "That hadn't even crossed my mind," Beane says. "But we'll take it." The very next day, more extra innings and a 2–1 victory over Toronto. Byrnes bloops a two-strike leadoff double into right field in the bottom of the eleventh, Hatteberg moves him to third by grounding out to second, and Dye sends the smallest crowd of the season—10,879—home to the victorious strains of KISS. That the song the A's celebrate with is "Rock and Roll All Night" is making more sense by the day. Oakland's last five games at home have gone 11, 10, 12, 10, and 11 innings. "The most important thing is winning games," says Zito, who nursed the 1–0 lead he was handed in the first inning until the Jays scratched out the tying run in the eighth, ending his streak of scoreless innings at sixteen. "And the fact is that we're winning." Zito, of course, doesn't get credit for the win, but he doesn't seem to care. Since that vicious beating at

Yankee Stadium, he's lowered his ERA by nearly two and a half runs, from 6.83 to 4.44. "I'm trying to focus more on the process," he says, "and less on the results."

With most teams who lose a star, sustaining that elevated level of play for more than a few days is very difficult. The crushing reality of the loss—*Oh, shit! Chavvy's out six weeks!*—eventually hits home, and the struggle commences. There's a glimpse of that when, with the exception of Dye's twelfth homer of the year, the offense goes quiet, and the bullpen, which had been nails in extra innings the three previous games, again stumbles in the late going. After Harden leaves with the game tied at 1–1 after seven strong innings of four-hit work, Bradford and Hammond give up five runs over the final two innings and the A's lose, 6–1. But a day later enters irony, and a remarkable run follows. With the A's on the verge of setting a major league record for most consecutive no-decisions by a starting staff, Hudson, the Mayor of No-Decision Land, steps up and throws an eight-hit shutout. "I was glad to put an end to that streak," Hudson says, after improving to 6–2 with a 2.93 ERA. "The starters have gone out and pitched their hearts out pretty much all year, and it's nice to go out and get a decision in a tough game." During the game, Hudson debuts a mechanical adjustment in which, in the middle of his delivery from the windup, he hesitates and taps his toe before going to the plate. It's something A's pitchers do during drills, and Hudson hopes it will stop him from rushing his delivery, which he says he'd done during his latest debacle in Boston. It's odd to see an established pitcher make such a dramatic change, but it speaks to Hudson's willingness to try anything that might help. "I'm sure it looks pretty funky," he says, "but it helps with my balance a little, and who cares if it looks funky if it works?" It works in part because one of only four hits for Oakland on the day is Hatteberg's three-run homer in the third inning. "We only had four hits, and that's nothing to brag about, but a win breeds confidence," Hatteberg says. "With Chavvy out, we've had to move some people around in the [batting] order, but I think we'll bounce back. I don't think we're this poor offensively." And the A's spend the next seven games proving Hatteberg's point, makeshift batting order and all.

Oakland scores eight runs to help Redman beat Toronto in

the series finale, which signals the start of interleague play, and the drubbings the A's drop on the visiting National League teams— Cincinnati and Pittsburgh, June 7–13—are nothing short of astounding for a team missing their biggest offensive weapon. It all begins with a welcome-back beating of Lidle, who gives up nine runs in 3⅔ innings. "I can hear it now," Lidle says. "'*See? He misses Peterson too!*'" Mulder gives up two runs over seven innings, and the A's win 13–2. Zito's roller coaster continues when he gives up five runs in five innings the next day, but he's the winning pitcher because the A's pound out ten runs. Harden then gives up five runs over seven innings, but that's hardly a problem. A's win, 17–8, to close out the sweep, set a franchise record with forty runs over a three-game series, and take a one-game lead over Anaheim in the AL West.

And still they keep hitting. *Eric who?* After a day with no game, Hudson opens the Pirates series by allowing one run over seven innings and wins 6–1 when the A's explode for five runs in the seventh and the eighth. Redman gets beat up for seven runs over 5 innings the next day, and the A's trail 10–6 through 7½ innings, but they score five in the bottom of the eighth and win 12–11 on a single by Dye in the bottom of the ninth. "It's the most impressive thing I've ever seen in the big leagues," Byrnes says of the team's offensive surge. "It's fun to be a part of. It's fun to watch."

The home stand ends with the offense getting Mulder thirteen runs for the second straight start, while extending Oakland's winning streak to 8 games—the A's are 37–24 on the year now—and its division lead to 2½. After whipping through the first three innings without allowing a runner, Mulder allows three runs on two homers over the next two innings as the Pirates tie the game, 3–3. The A's score six in the bottom of the fifth, three in the sixth, and one in the seventh to give Mulder his sixth consecutive win. "With our offense clicking the way it has been, I can get away with a mistake or two," Mulder says. "Let's just say the confidence in the dugout is pretty high right now." Mulder is averaging eleven runs of support over his past four starts, and as he talks, Hudson can be heard chirping something over and over. It's hard to make out above the din of Tupac's "How Do U Want It?" which is among the songs on a mixed CD that plays in the clubhouse after every victory, but outside the clubhouse doors a few minutes later, Hudson laughs as he explains. "I was yellin' 'Run whore!'" he says. "This clinches it, man. Mulder's a fuckin' run whore."

Busch Stadium in St. Louis and Wrigley Field in Chicago are two of the National League's legendary yards, for two totally different reasons. Built in 1966 along the same boring, cement, multi-use lines as Cincinnati's Riverfront and Pittsburgh's Three Rivers Stadiums, Busch was remodeled not long ago, but it remains nothing spectacular from a venue standpoint. The attraction in St. Louis has always been the fans, considered among the best in baseball. Clad in hometown red, they pack the place whether their beloved Cards are ten games up or ten games out, and they lend a joyful innocence to the game, win or lose. Wrigley, built in 1916, is special for other reasons. History oozes from every crumbling corner, the ivy-covered walls bring an unexplainable freshness to the proceedings, and the surrounding neighborhood turns into a massive extended block party before, during, and after every game. So as Oakland pulls into St. Louis for the start of a ten-game road trip (June 15–24) that features three against the Cards, three against the Cubs, and four against the rival Angels, there's a palpable sense of excitement among the players. Everything about them seems to suggest the same mindset: *This is going to be fun.*

And then the games start.

Zito, whose name has started popping up in the trade rumors that often surround a struggling star, has another uneven outing in the opener of the St. Louis series. He gives up two runs in the first inning and one in the second, and despite leaving with a 4–3 lead after the fifth, he's pissed about needing 115 pitches to get that far. "I didn't have anything today," he says. "The outs weren't coming quick at all. They were working the count, they hit a lot of foul balls, and it was just a rough night as far as my stuff was concerned." Another rough night for the bullpen, too. Three Oakland relievers give up five runs in the seventh inning, and the A's winning streak ends with an 8–4 loss. The one positive, if only for the sake of humor, is Zito, in his first plate appearance in a year, taxing Cardinals starter Matt Morris in an eleven-pitch, second-inning at-bat. After working the count full, Zito fouls off five pitches before flying out to left. "I tried to get the pitch count up. You know, give 'em some of their own medicine," Zito says, tongue firmly planted in cheek. "I was in full-on hack mode."

Harden takes the loss in the second game of the series, but again the bullpen is the center of attention. Rhodes, asked to make his earliest entrance of the season, helps keep the A's within a run of the lead, at 3–2, by getting the final two outs in the bottom of the seventh, but after glaring long and hard at home plate umpire Bruce Dreckman after a 2–2 pitch is called a ball, Rhodes gives up a three-run homer to Reggie Sanders in the eighth that kills any comeback hopes. Rhodes doesn't even wait for Sanders to cross the plate before yelling at Dreckman, who responds by throwing Rhodes out of the game. "[Sanders] should have been out on the 2–2 pitch, and we should have been out of the inning," Rhodes fumes later. "I can't tell you what I said. It wasn't good, I can tell you that." Later in the night the team announces that Rhodes, who leads the AL with five blown saves and has a 5.00 ERA, has left the team for a couple of days to attend a family funeral in Texas. They say he'll rejoin the team in Chicago on Saturday. So maybe his mind was elsewhere. But this isn't the first time Rhodes has had words with an umpire, and he suggests that he's been squeezed—pitcher-ese for "screwed"—on several occasions. "I'm fed up with it," he says. "You get frustrated, and I got frustrated tonight." Mulder, asked if he's ever been frustrated by an umpire's tight strike zone, quietly laughs. "Only every start," he says. "The thing is, you can't show that out there, or it might get worse. You just have to wear it and focus on the next pitch. You can't show that frustration at all."

Ah, frustration. The backbone of baseball. A 70 percent failure rate makes you a great hitter, and losing two of every five games gives you a decent shot at the playoffs. Frustration is part of the fabric of the game. For Hudson, though, the fabric is starting to fray. On opening night he left after five innings with a 3–2 lead and got stuck with a no-decision. On April 27 he left with an 8–4 lead after seven and got stuck with a no-decision. On May 8 he went nine but left with the score tied 2–2. Another no-decision. On May 30 he left after eight with a 3–2 lead. Another no-decision. And here at Busch, in the series finale, he hands off a 4–2 lead after

7⅓ innings and has to watch the bullpen implode. Again. Specifically, Mecir faces five batters in the bottom of the ninth and
doesn't record a single out. Scutaro's two-run error with the bases
loaded that allows the Cards to tie it certainly doesn't help, but it
was Mecir who loaded the bases, allowing two hits and hitting a
batter to start the inning. Sanders's game-winning, two-run single
up the middle sends Mecir walking off the field a 5–4 loser. "Huddy
pitched a great game, we had a two-run lead, and I couldn't get an
out," Mecir, now 0–5 on the year with a 6.17 ERA, says in the
funeral home that is the A's clubhouse. "It's just an embarrassing
situation. That's all I have to say."

Hudson is still 7–2 with the second-best ERA in the AL (2.78)
and a virtual lock to make the All-Star team, but he could very well
be 12–2, and his twenty-sixth no-decision over the last two-plus
seasons makes displaying the diplomacy of a team leader a tough
task. In front of reporters, he shows some restraint at first: "It's hard

The most openly competitive member of the Big Three,
Hudson insists that hitters can smell fear, so he brings
an intensity to the mound that everyone can see.

to say why it happens, but it has been. It's just something we have to overcome." Then comes yet another little crack in the wall: "I think we just need to start getting the job done. I know they're out there trying, but sometimes trying isn't good enough." And finally, an unmistakable flash of the frustration he's been suppressing for quite some time. He says it with a smile, but it's gallows humor at best: "Every bullpen's gonna have their ups and downs, but it seems like when they have their downs, it's usually in my games." Sadly for the A's, that's not quite true. Mecir's blown save is Oakland's thirteenth of the season—in just twenty-five chances.

The A's are 37–27 on the year, with a 1½-game lead in the AL West. Throw in those thirteen blown saves, and it doesn't take a math whiz to see that the bullpen is killing the A's. This, more than anything, is why, ten minutes after he's done talking to the media, Hudson is still hot. White-hot. And it's not about the wins he's not getting. It's a team thing. "I swear, man, if I leave [as a free agent], this is gonna be why. This kind of shit right here," he says with that angry whisper dads use to scold their kids in a crowded grocery store. "I mean, you know I do the best I can not to throw anyone under the bus, but fuckin'-a, man. And it ain't just the bullpen. I mean, can I get a four-run lead just one time? We should be runnin' away with the division right now."

Mark Redman seems to have a knack for throwing a big game just as he's reaching a point of irrelevance, and his performance in the Friday-afternoon opener at Wrigley fits the bill. He'd gotten through the sixth inning just once in his previous five starts and his ERA was up to 4.52, but with eight innings of four-hit ball against the Cubs, he spins his best start as an Athletic when the team needs it most. But they still need those final three outs to secure a 2-1 victory, and when Bradford gets the last of them— Rhodes is due back tomorrow, so Bradford is the closer du jour—by striking out Sammy Sosa to cap a 1-2-3 ninth, the bullpen finally warrants a little positive attention. Bradford, though, isn't much of a talker. He's cheerful, funny, and observant, but put him in front of a pack of notebooks and microphones and he clams up in a hurry. "Don't make it a bigger deal than it is," he says, but when the A's nail down a save these days, it is a big deal. And Macha, who has tiptoed around the festering problem all year, admits as much.

"Like Huddy said yesterday, we know the relievers are trying their best. It's a matter of getting it done," he says. "Today Bradford got it done. We've got to stay behind those guys." The A's have been trying, but Saturday's game proves that it's easier said than done.

Mulder allows ten hits over eight innings, and the Cubs put at least one runner aboard in each of his final seven innings of work, but a couple of double-play balls and some gutsy work under pressure limit the damage. He leaves with a 3–2 lead. It's the exact situation for which Rhodes was signed, but Rhodes isn't there when Macha calls for his closer in the ninth. He's AWOL, still in Texas. The problems in Oakland's bullpen don't just *seem* to get worse by the day. It's really happening. Rhodes was supposed to be back in time for the matinee, but his absence is conspicuous, as Bradford gives up two runs before getting two outs, and the A's lose another heartbreaker, 4–3, robbing Mulder of his seventh consecutive win. "Rhodes didn't make it back," Macha explains angrily after the game. "I spoke to him the other day and he said he would be here for Saturday, but he wasn't here." Mickey Morabito, the A's traveling secretary, later says he'd spoken to Rhodes in the morning, at which time Rhodes said he'd changed his morning flight plans for a late-afternoon arrival. "I would have liked to have his services, yes," Macha says. "I don't know what the circumstances [are] of him not being here today, but we'll find out."

When a member of a player's immediate family passes away, the team can place the player on the "Bereavement List" for up to seven days and bring in another player to take his spot on the roster. The funeral Rhodes attended, though, was for an uncle, so the A's couldn't replace him. Macha says he and assistant GM David Forst, who is on the trip, spoke with Rhodes before he left and made it clear that his absence would be excused for only two days: "We told him that we didn't have the luxury of the bereavement thing, so we'd like him back as soon as possible." The more Macha talks, the more his composure erodes. "We're beating this . . . this is a dead horse," he says. "This bullpen . . . I don't know how many blown saves it's been. It's been a whole bunch. But I can't blame these guys. Sometimes they get put in a position where they will not be successful due to other circumstances. Rhodes wasn't here. I can't blame Bradford for that. It's a shame. Mulder went out there and gave us his heart and soul." Had Mulder not already thrown a season-high 123 pitches, Macha suggests, he'd have been allowed to at least start the ninth. "I felt fine," Mulder says, "but I'm not saying I'd have gone out there and done well in the ninth. I could have gone out there and done the same thing [as Bradford]. . . . I'm not going to sit here and talk shit about anybody. The bullpen's just struggling. Everybody knows that. . . . Somebody needs to step up and make good pitches."

Zito throws fifty-three pitches in the first two innings of the series finale, and even the good ones turn into trouble. Struggling with command, particularly of his curveball, he needs thirty-nine pitches to get through Chicago's three-run first, which features a home run by Moises Alou, a swinging-bunt single by Aramis Ramirez, a bad-hop single by Derrek Lee, and a two-run double by Corey Patterson. When Dye loses a ball in the sun in the fifth inning, it helps the Cubs take a 4–1 lead. Zito leaves after the fifth with a pitch count of 110 and falls to 4–4 with a 4.81 ERA. "Some crazy things happened out there," Zito says. "Some strange things happened in the first inning, and that sun ball was strange as well." Strange is a pretty good description for Rhodes's return. Forst won't go into much detail, other than to say that Rhodes finally called Beane on Saturday night to explain his absence, and that the club was satisfied with the explanation. Forst won't say whether Rhodes was fined, either, and while that usually means he was fined—if he wasn't, why not just say it?—Rhodes insists that he wasn't.

The family man in Hudson is empathetic toward Rhodes, who says the uncle who passed away was like a father to him. "That kind of thing takes precedence over anything else," Hudson says. "Yeah, we needed him, but his family needed him more, and that's hard to not be okay with." What isn't okay with some of the veteran A's is that Rhodes apologized to Beane but didn't feel the need to apologize to his teammates. On a club that prides itself on cohesion, particularly when the chips are down, this is unacceptable. And while the A's still hold a slim lead in the division as they head for Anaheim, the chips are definitely down.

12

HEAD GAMES

hat's wrong with Barry? The theories are running wild now, with everyone and their uncle weighing in on the great mystery of Zito. One popular theory is that he very much misses Peterson. "Yeah, I'm sure Barry misses him," says Hudson. "I mean, who knows? But I do think Rick can massage him mentally more than Curt, because that's an area that Curt just doesn't deal with. That's not his job. He's not a psychiatrist. He's a pitching coach. But I think Barry and Rick, they see so eye to eye that it's obvious that Zito wishes every now and then that he was still around." Mulder obviously thinks Zito misses Peterson, too. While the A's were in St. Louis, an article about Peterson that appeared in the *New York Times* came to the attention of Mulder and Hudson, who spent a little time laughing about it in the clubhouse. At the time, the Mets pitching staff was on fire, and even a staid publication like the *Times* isn't above a little bandwagoning. Peterson's background and philosophies were detailed in the article, and several Mets pitchers were interviewed. Based on the quotes they'd seen, Mulder and Hudson decided that veteran lefty Al Leiter was the Mets' version of Zito and made a pact as they walked through a tunnel leading from the clubhouse to the dugout. "We can't let Zito see that article," Mulder told Hudson with a laugh. "He'll get jealous of Leiter and want to go play for the Mets."

Zito doesn't wholly disagree that he misses Peterson, but he doesn't wholly agree, either. "I would say that personally, I do miss him. I miss just having a guy that I got along with, a guy that, you know, took a different approach than everyone else in this game, someone who kind of sees things the way I might be seeing them." In other words, someone else who likes to go deep. "But on a professional level, I mean, the game is the game. Coaches move on. They go here and there. That's not why I've struggled."

Another theory: Zito needs a new pitch. By major league standards, Zito does not throw particularly hard. He tops out at about 90, whereas Hudson and Mulder can run it up there in the mid-90s on a good day. But Mulder says velocity is overrated. "If a guy's looking fastball and gets it, he's got a pretty good shot at hitting it hard, even if you throw absolute gas," he says. "The only chance the pitcher has in that case is if he's got good movement on his fastball." That's a problem for Zito. His fastball is ramrod straight most of the time. Former All-Star catcher and current A's broadcaster Ray Fosse calls Zito "the only left-hander I've ever seen with no natural movement."

Most pitchers, including Hudson and Mulder, throw two types of fastball. One is a four-seamer, gripped with the first two fingers of the pitching hand draped, perpendicular, across the "C" created by the seams on a baseball. It cuts the wind and doesn't move much at all. The other is a two-seamer, generally gripped with the fingers more or less parallel to and on top of the seams where they come closest together, where they frame the commissioner's signature on a ball. The two-seamer, depending on the wrist action with which it's thrown, runs in on, or away from, a hitter. Zito throws only the four-seamer, and while Hudson and Mulder get a little bit of action on their four-seamers because they throw from a three-quarters arm slot, Zito has to throw his fastball from straight over the top. "He's like that pitching machine, Iron Mike," Hudson says.

Why doesn't Zito just drop down a little and throw from a three-quarter arm slot? Because throwing from straight over the top is what makes his curveball so devastating. The same pitch thrown from a three-quarters slot is what's known as a "slurve," and rather than breaking straight down, from 12 to 6 on a clock, it breaks from, say, 10 to 4. That gives the hitter a better shot at identifying the pitch, and Zito can't afford that. His curveball is too good to change. And because he throws it from straight over the top, he has to throw his other pitches from the exact same arm slot. If he doesn't, hitters will be able to distinguish what pitch is coming before it even leaves his hand, which would turn everyone into Barry Bonds, who is said to be able to identify what's coming even if a guy is throwing from the same slot every time. Bonds's hawk-like vision, it is said, allows him to pick up a pitcher's wrist just prior to the release of the ball. If he sees the flat underside of the wrist, he knows it's something straight. If he sees the wrist slightly turned, he's looking for a slider. If he sees the side of the wrist, he's thinking curveball, because a curve is thrown with a wrist motion akin to turning a doorknob while standing with your chest squared up to the thin side of the open door. "All the hitters I know can't pick up the ball until it's been out of a guy's hand for a few feet," explains Dye. "But if the arm slot is different on one pitch, you can pick that up pretty easy." So Zito's arm slot can't change. But what about adding a two-seamer from the same slot? "It's something I've thought about," he admits. "Part of me wants to say, well, I won a Cy Young with these three pitches I've been throwing all this time, but that's probably a little closed-minded. We'll see."

The theory that's gaining more and more steam by the day, though, is that Zito is getting in his own way, mentally. That place in his mind that he described at the Kansas City Denny's? It's not an easy place to find, and a major league mound is no place to be searching for something. It's either there or it's not. Does Zito simply think too much during a game? In a six-page essay by Michael Silver, "Inside the Head of Barry Zito," that appeared in a June issue of *Sports Illustrated*, Hudson and Scott Hatteberg, Oakland's first base-man and a very cerebral man himself, seem to answer in the affirmative. "He's constantly bombarding himself with the mental part of the game," Hatteberg says. "Everybody's trying to get a mental edge, but he takes it to another level." Hudson adds that Zito is "too ana-lytical when it comes to baseball. It's a sport that'll drive you crazy, and he puts too much thought into things that sometimes have no rhyme or reason." What does Mulder, who isn't quoted in the article, think? "I definitely think Barry has a tendency to get in his own head," he says, while admitting that he hadn't read the article. Then he laughs and offers, "That's why I very rarely talk about pitching with him. I'm afraid he might get into *my* head! Like I've said, I try not to think at all out there. That's the catcher's job. My job is to make pitches."

Zito hears this and laughs, too. "That's perfect Mark Mulder, right there, and that's cool. That's what works for him. And maybe I *do* think too much. But what am I going to do? Just decide one day to stop thinking? I can't do that. This is who I am. I can't just change who I am."

Sitting in the A's dugout a couple of hours before one of the games in Chicago, Hudson watches his teammates stretching before batting practice and tries to explain why too much thinking can get a pitcher in trouble. "There was a time a couple years ago when I was really struggling. Like six starts in a row," he says. "And at first it didn't really affect my confidence, but then, after four or five in a row I was just, like, 'Jesus. What's goin' on?' Because usually I'd struggle for two, maybe three starts at the most, and then I'd get back on track and be nails for seven or eight starts. Those six starts, though, I didn't know what the hell was goin' on. I think it was in 2002, and it started with a couple bad starts in Chicago and Boston, and they were bad, but those were two pretty good teams at the time. So we came home, I had Cleveland, Toronto, and Tampa coming up, and I'm thinking, 'Okay, these three starts, I'm gonna get it back together.' And I got my ass handed to me in all three of those starts. It kind of hit the fan. And I was just like, 'What the fuck, man?' I was freaked out. The last one was against Tampa, and the team spotted me a six-run lead and I couldn't hold it. I went like, four innings, gave up six or seven runs, and I came out of the game and I was almost in tears." The problem? "I didn't think it was mechanical," he says. "It was just mental and overthrowing, and whenever I would overthrow, I'd try to make everything so nasty that they couldn't hit it, but instead it would just flatten out. And for me, to get out of it, it wasn't about trying harder. It was trying less. I needed to back off. Rick and I talked about it, and he's the one who said, 'Just back off a little bit.' And my next start, it was against Tampa again, at their place, and I went six innings and gave up thirteen hits, but I only gave up one run. One run. And that was a solo homer to Ben Grieve. The other twelve hits were nothing, all ground balls, ten-hoppers through the hole, which is fine. For once it wasn't dick-high balls over the plate getting hit in the gap for doubles. Instead of throwing 94, 95 miles an hour and getting hit into the gaps, it was 89, 90, 91 with sink, locatin' it. I just backed off. And that game got me right back on track. I just got back to concentrating on making pitches. And after that, I just stayed with it, and as I was honin' my location and my pitches after that, I could gradually get after it a little bit more. Once I started pitchin' more, I could start letting that hard fastball, that 94, fly a little bit more often. Instead of just throwin' the piss out of it and not worryin' where it's goin', you've gotta locate first, and *then* get after it. Worry about your location first, and *then* try to make your pitches nasty as hell."

It's suggested to Hudson that the mistake he might have made was in taking the lesser teams for granted. No, he says. His mistake was in taking the game of baseball itself for granted. "Every team's got talent, man, and beyond that, even the guy with the most talent doesn't win every time," he says. "You boil it all down, and on the physical side, it's about making good pitches. But unless you just have one of those days where you're unstoppable, you're gonna get hit around a little bit. And then there's a time when you're not making pitches at all and you're *really* getting your ass handed to you—that's when you're going three or four innings and giving up seven or eight runs. But it's weird, man, because there's a lot of times when you'll go out there and make great pitches all day, and there's times you'll go out there and you're not throwin' shit on the corners, you're throwin' down the middle, but you're still getting' guys out. That's why you just can't fucking read into this game too much. It's so different. And it's all upstairs."

Curt Young, who has known Hudson since the year he was drafted, says Hudson's greatest strength as a pitcher is upstairs. "From the moment he came to the big leagues, he felt like he belonged," Young says. "And I think he's kept that same belief from day one. It's just that total belief in himself." Asked about Hudson's weaknesses, Young can come up with only one, and it's one that few people would consider a drawback. "Maybe trying to be too perfect," he says. "The people you're competing with up here believe that they're on the same level as you. And sometimes, if you try to be too perfect, you can get frustrated in what results or things that happen in the game. So there's times when Tim will throw a shutout inning, and he'll come in on the bench and he'll be angry at himself, mainly because of missed location or the quality of pitch he was looking for. That's how competitive he is. But I guess sometimes if you are looking for perfection, which I think Tim does, it happens quite a bit. And I never see that his fire takes him away from concentration in what he's trying to accomplish."

As Hudson outlines his approach to pitching, it becomes evident that it's a pretty simple outline. His motto: act like you belong. To his way of thinking, the way you carry yourself on the mound has everything to do with what happens out there. "If you think that you're a bad motherfucker out there, and you think you're gonna make pitches and you really think you're gonna get this guy out, you're gonna get him out," he says. "Because that confidence that you're showing out there on the mound, they see that. They set up in that fuckin' box and they see you out on the mound and they see that you're thinking and you're walking around like you're a bad motherfucker—they're not too comfortable."

It works the other way, too, he adds. Big-league hitters are like dogs. They can smell fear. "When I was strugglin', they knew I was strugglin', and I wasn't feelin' real good about myself out there on the mound," he says. "So that can give them a little more confidence comin' in. If you show them that lack of confidence out there on the mound, you're halfway beat. You've gotta show confidence up there. You've gotta give off that energy that you're a bad motherfucker and you dare 'em to fuckin' get in the box. And most of the time when people are strugglin', like Barry has at times, I think you just lose that energy, that confidence out there. I believe it's 80 percent of the success for a pitcher. It's not the tools. It's not the pitches, because the pitches are gonna be the same. Maybe 10 percent is gonna be tools and 10 percent is actually just making pitches. The other 80 percent of the game is being out there knowin' you're about to kick some ass."

It's interesting. Take Hudson's simple philosophy and put it through a refinery. What do you have? Basically, you have what Zito explained at the Kansas City Denny's, only with a lot more f-bombs and without the out-of-body imagery. Put *Zito's* philosophy through a refinery and it becomes one of the oldest adages around: mind over matter. "It's not going to work every single time," Hudson admits. "I mean, you might feel locked in, but maybe the guy in the box feels locked in, too. You see superstars who get locked in, and it's like you can't get them out. They just have that zone, you know? That's gonna happen. They're gonna hit you. But it's not easy to fuckin' hit, man. It's not easy. So maybe the superstar's locked in. Okay. But that motherfucker behind him probably ain't locked in. So give that guy who's locked in his double, his single, whatever, and get the next bunch of fuckers out."

Hudson and Zito have a look about them when their confidence is off the charts. Hudson has something of a scowl going on; he really *does* look like he's daring hitters to get into the box. Zito's is more subtle. It's a serious look, but if you catch the cameras zooming in on his face during a game that he's taken by the throat, you can see the slightest trace of a smile. It's in his eyes more than his mouth, actually. It's a twinkle. It's almost as if he's amused by the control he's exerting over everything around him. "You can see it in his walk, too," Hudson says of Zito. "When he's dealin', he's struttin' a little bit. That's part of the look." Mulder, though, doesn't really have a look. He has an *air*.

"Yeah, he stands out there, he's 6 foot 6 with the perfect build, a left-hander, and he's got no wasted motion and no fear," says Young. "If you have the diagram of a perfect pitcher, that's it, right there. He's the most gifted guy I've ever seen. When he first got drafted, I kind of compared him to Steve Carlton. Just a powerful presence standing out there. 'I'm coming at you, I don't care what you have, I'm just gonna keep coming at you time and time again.' And that's why Mark is so good. He takes that same stuff and knows it's gonna work game in and game out."

"The perfect pitcher?" Mulder says. "I don't know about that. If

Part of Mulder's "air" on the mound comes from how he holds himself. He always appears calm, relaxed, and in complete control.

I was the perfect pitcher, I wouldn't have sucked so bad when I was a rookie." But nine wins isn't all that bad for a rookie, and Mulder is indeed a powerful presence. Above-average height is a big plus on the mound. The taller a pitcher is, the closer to the plate he seems when releasing the ball. The closer to the plate he seems, the quicker the ball seems to get there. And if that tall pitcher happens to throw in the low- to mid-90s, well, it's getting there plenty quick. "Being tall is definitely an advantage," Mulder says. "That's why what Huddy's been able to do is so impressive." But Mulder's presence—his air—is about more than being tall, and it's not discernible in his expression. It's in his *lack* of expression.

"There's always been something about Mark that's really hard to describe," says Chavez, one of his closest friends on the team. "Of all the guys I've played with, he's the one guy that you can honestly say you don't know if he's throwing a no-hitter or getting lit up. It's almost like he doesn't even care sometimes, even though I know that's not true. Obviously, he cares. But if you didn't know him and you were out there, you'd probably think he didn't. I think it's just that he kind of knows how good he is, and he knows that if he does things the right way, there's no need to get excited about anything out there. Just go out there, do your thing, and come back." Chavez is one of the few A's insiders who has an informed take on Mulder's mind-set. Most everyone else is just guessing, because Mulder doesn't let many people get close to him. He's as outgoing as anyone on the team when it comes to the standard collegial clubhouse interaction, but he's just as content keeping to himself, so it's possible to mistake his air for insolence.

"It's so easy to look at somebody who doesn't say much, someone you can't get a read on, and say that they're arrogant," says Frank Menechino, who shared a house with Chavez and Mulder. "But I would have to agree that if I didn't know Mulder, I would think, 'Oh, he's an asshole.' But people don't get to know him, so they draw their own conclusions. But he's not like that at all. People would be really surprised that he does a lot for his friends and family. When his friends come into town and people that he knows, there's no expense spared, and he'll go all out to make his friends comfortable and do things for his family. Assholes don't do that. . . . And out on the mound, that's just an extension of what he's like off the field. Nothing demonstrative, nothing flashy. He's just quietly going about his business, and you can take it any way you want to."

Ask Mulder about all of this, and he nods in agreement. He seems to understand that some people might think he's full of himself. He seems to understand why. And that's another thing to which he gives little thought. "Why would I care about what someone who doesn't know me thinks?" he says. "And if someone wants to judge me based on whether I stop and say hi to every single person on the way to my locker, whatever."

There it is. *Whatever.* That's the air about Mulder on the mound. He's working on a three-hit shutout? *Whatever.* A journeyman middle infielder takes him deep? *Whatever.* Live goats are being sacrificed in a black magic ceremony behind home plate? *Whatever.* And to this point in the season, the combination of Mulder's air and his arsenal make him an early Cy Young favorite. After the no-decision in Chicago, he's 8–2 with a 2.91 ERA. "I'm just not that guy who's ever going to let you know how I'm feeling, one way or another," he says. "Everyone has a different style that works for them, and I guess that's mine. Or maybe it's not a style at all. It doesn't mean I'm not intense out there. It doesn't mean I don't get pissed when I fuck up. It doesn't mean I'm not pumped when I get a big strike-out. It just means I'm a little different in the way I show it or don't show it. My philosophy is that if you stay calm out there, chances are that'll help things stay calm around you."

There's nothing calm about the A's as they pull into Anaheim for four games. Chavez's absence is finally a factor. They'd averaged three runs a game in St. Louis and Chicago. The bullpen had gone 0–3 with three blown saves and a 13.97 ERA in the six games. The road trip thus far is a smoldering wreck. So what does Arthur Rhodes do? He pours kerosene onto the pile and drops a match.

Harden takes a 10–3 loss in the Monday opener, dropping the A's into a tie for first place. Hudson loses 6–1 on Tuesday, dropping the A's to 38–31 and a game behind the Rangers, who are still the surprise team of baseball. And on Wednesday, Macha has to call a team meeting because Rhodes, upset by what Hudson and Mulder had said about the bullpen the week before, has ripped into them in a national column. "We had two starters on this team say the bullpen needs to step it up," Rhodes told CBS.SportsLine.com's Scott Miller. "You shouldn't say that. If we lose as a team, we all lose. If we win as a team, we all win. . . . If you're not man enough to come to somebody on the field and tell them to do a better job, don't say in the paper that we're doing a bad job."

The timing is astoundingly poor. Hudson and Mulder's public comments had been fairly tame, for one thing. The team is strug-gling, too. And Rhodes is the *last* guy who should be popping off. He's been a massive flop as a closer, he'd given up a run in one inning of work the night of Hudson's loss to jack his ERA to 5.28, and his little AWOL incident in Chicago certainly hadn't earned him any esteem in the clubhouse. So after meeting briefly with his team, Macha leaves the players to hash it out among themselves. "I told them they need to take care of this on their own," Macha says in the visitors' dugout at Angel Stadium. "Everybody's frustrated, but we don't need this. We need to get everybody back on track." Mulder and Hudson are caught off-guard by Rhodes's rant. "We didn't say anything all that bad," Mulder says, and two days later he issues a nonverbal response. Among other things, Rhodes had suggested during his tirade that if the starters were so unhappy with the bullpen, "Let 'em go nine." So a day after Redman again comes up big to end Oakland's four-game losing steak, Mulder does just that, throwing his fourth complete game of the year to end the ugly trip with a 2–1 victory.

Mulder's gem, however, is nothing compared to the good news that comes an hour or so after the game. Beane, a Southern California native who had joined the team just in time to watch it hit rock bottom with more than a little help from Rhodes, officially removes Rhodes from the closer's role by acquiring Octavio Dotel from the Houston Astros. It's classic Beane—a three-team deal that sends Carlos Beltran, the biggest name on the trade market, from Kansas City to Houston, while the A's part with only two prospects in addressing their most glaring need. There's a reason Beane has a reputation as one of the most creative front-office minds in the game, and this is just the latest example of his ability to pull off midseason moves that prime his club for one of its patented second-half surges.

In 2001, he stole Dye from the Royals on July 25, and Dye led the A's with fifty-nine RBIs in sixty-one games down the stretch. Beane picked up infielder Ray Durham, the leadoff man they'd been lacking all year, on the same date a year later. And on July 30, 2003, he added outfielder Jose Guillen, who was Oakland's best hitter in the playoff loss to Boston. All of those moves, though, were made with the July 31 trading deadline fast approaching. At that point in the season, teams that are out of the race are eager to deal. The Dotel deal comes more than a month before the deadline, with more than half of the teams in baseball still harboring some kind of hope about playing meaningful games in October. "I don't think you ever envision getting a player of Dotel's quality this time of year," Beane says, and few can disagree. Dotel, a thirty-year-old righty in *his* first year as a closer, throws in the mid to high-90s and has fourteen saves in seventeen opportunities, including a 7-for-8 rate for the month. "Octavio Dotel," Beane says, "is one of the most talented relievers in the game." Asked what made Dotel so attractive to the A's, he blurts, "He throws twelve thousand miles an hour."

Rhodes has one save for the month, and he's blown three of his last four chances. But Beane is the man who raised so many eyebrows when he signed Rhodes to a three-year deal to close, and he's not the kind of man who admits many mistakes. Thus, he chooses not to view Rhodes as a failed experiment. "Arthur has been one of the premier left-handed setup men in the game," he says. "I view that as a positive." He does vaguely concede, however, that he knew making Rhodes the closer was risky: "We knew we'd probably have to address the bullpen—even as far back as spring training."

The acquisition of Dotel is huge on two fronts. On the field, it's expected to provide some stability to the beleaguered Oakland bullpen. Rhodes had been so inconsistent that Macha had already started giving other relievers the occasional audition, and when relievers' roles are constantly changing, success rarely follows. "You like to have some kind of an idea, when you get to the ballpark, exactly how you're going to be used," Bradford had said in Chicago. "We don't have that right now. We're not even close." Beane and Macha had even stopped using the word *closer*. And on several occasions, Macha used the phrase "bullpen by committee," and anyone who followed the 2003 Red Sox during the regular season knows what a disaster that approach can be. So the question is posed to Beane: Will the A's start using the word *closer* again now that Dotel is in the mix? "Uh . . . yeah," he says with a laugh. "We now have a better committee."

And a better overall frame of mind. Hudson calls the trade "another miracle by Billy." Mulder calls it "awesome." Zito calls it "amazing." Beane calls it an absolute necessity, a way of massaging the whole team's head. "This move was made as much for our collective psyche as it was for on-the-field improvements," he says. "I think the guys needed some sort of acknowledgment of what they've been going through, and this is certainly that." Later in the evening, Beane is asked about the trade rumors involving Zito and squashes them. "There's been absolutely no impetus to trade Barry," he says. "Do I get calls? Sure. Do I listen? Sure. Am I actively considering trading my twenty-five-year-old Cy Young winner? No."

13

ANOTHER BIG BLOW

Dotel's debut with the A's, on Saturday, June 26, is a mixed bag. The San Francisco Giants are in Oakland, and a night after Zito falls to 4–5 on the year by losing the opener of a three-game series, the whole Bay Area is watching as Dotel enters the game. The Giants, down 6–3, have the bases loaded with one out in the top of the eighth, so it's a save situation for Dotel, and he gets out of the jam with a pop-up and a strikeout. The A's portion of a sellout crowd of more than 55,000 goes nuts, and the cheers get louder as Oakland pads the lead with a run in the bottom of the eighth. The cheers turn to a little nervous chatter, though, in the top of the ninth. Dotel issues a leadoff walk to Barry Bonds. Pedro Feliz singles. The chatter turns to hand-wringing when A. J. Pierzynski pumps a three-run homer to cut the lead to one, and the hand-wringing turns to forehead-slapping when the Giants string together a double, a hit-by-pitch, a sacrifice bunt, an intentional walk, and a sacrifice fly to tie the game. The look on every face in the A's dugout says the same thing: *This cannot be happening*. And although Dotel stays on and gets credited with the win when Scutaro ends the game with a two-out RBI single in the bottom of the tenth, the next day's *San*

Francisco Chronicle runs a mocking reference to Oakland's season-long bullpen problems as its headline: "Dotel fits right in." It's definitely a bummer, but it pales by comparison to the really big news of the day: Hudson's side strain is back, and he's been placed on the fifteen-day disabled list. Again, *This cannot be happening.*

The technical term for what's ailing Hudson is a strained left internal oblique muscle, which involves a small tear in the muscle near his left hip. His term for it is "pain in the fuckin' ass," and this is the third time it's put him on the shelf. The injury first popped up during Hudson's last start of the 2002 regular season, and he pitched with it in the playoffs that year, going 0–1 with a 6.23 ERA. When it resurfaced the following October in Boston, he says, there was no way on earth he could have pitched through it. And to hear him tell it, the Red Sox caught a big-time break that day.

"I went into that game knowin' that we were going to win," he insists. "I was about to shut them down, bro. I was gonna fuckin' carve that day. I felt that good. Some days you're out there and you're just on, and you know it. You're thinkin', these guys are going to be doin' good to get a hit off you. And that's how I felt." He says he was fine in the bullpen, but with his ninth pitch of the game, on which Boston's Todd Walker popped out to end the first

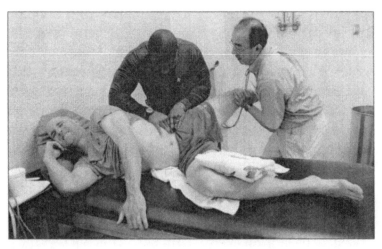

Hudson's problematic hip, which has bothered him at some point in every season since 2002, has gotten plenty of attention from Oakland's medical staff.

inning, he felt something familiar. "I went into the dugout and Chavvy and Frankie [Menechino] were there and I said, 'Man, I think I pulled somethin' in my side.' But I thought maybe I just tweaked somethin'. So I went back out there and threw a couple real slow, and there was a little pain there, but I thought, 'If that's it, I can deal with it.' But then, as soon as I tried to get after one, it felt like a knife went through my side. It was really frustratin', man. Like I said, I thought I was gonna give us a chance to win. Especially after what had happened the last three years in the playoffs. I thought this was going to be it. And that happened. It's tough. You feel helpless. I felt like I let the team down. I felt like they were really on my back and needin' me to have a good game to finally get us to the next round. And I thought I was gonna do it, until then."

That frustration lingered into the off-season, which Hudson dedicated to fixing the problem once and for all. "I changed up my ab workouts big-time," he says. "I was doing a lot more stretching, different stretches. Medicine balls, lot of twists, lot of oblique stuff, lot of side workouts. I was working out at Auburn, and they've got a machine you sit in that totally concentrates on your side muscles. I used that as much as I could. It's like everything I did was to keep this from happening again, and I went to camp pretty confident that it wouldn't. Nobody's invincible, but I did everything anyone could think of to avoid it." Yet here it is again. He felt a tweak when he was warming up in Anaheim, but he pitched through it. He says he could pitch through it now, too, but the team is being understandably cautious. So imagine the frustration now, and forget about the wins that have been pulled out from under him. The A's are in a dogfight, and their biggest bulldog has to sit on the sideline. It's all out of his control, but Hudson feels like he's letting his team down again.

"The fact that I focused on it in the off-season and it shows up three months earlier than it ever has really burns my ass," he says. "I mean, I'm prob'ly only gonna miss a couple starts, but we're already missin' Chavvy. We've got a lot of talent on this team, but you can only get by without the big boys for so long. I feel like I've been throwin' the ball this year as well as I ever have, for the most part, and me being out, Chavvy being out, that puts a lot of pressure on the other guys. There's enough pressure already built into this game, man. This is just pilin' on."

Just then a thought hits Hudson. A silver lining. A wicked smile crosses his face. "You wanna know the one good thing about this deal?" he says. "All those fuckers who said I got hurt in a bar last year can kiss my ass now. It's a *recurring* injury, dammit. Now leave my bony ass alone."

— — —

Redman can't get through the fifth inning of the Giants series finale, which the A's lose 5–2, and when the Rangers win on Monday while the A's are idle, they push their lead in the division over Oakland to 2½ games. It's still early, but the schedule immediately in front of the A's looks daunting. Nine of the final twelve games before the All-Star break will be against legitimate playoff contenders in the Angels, the Giants, and the Red Sox, and nine of the twelve will be on the road. Cleveland, which hosts Oakland in the final three games before the break, hasn't exactly been a pushover, either. "It doesn't look great right now," Mulder says after Redman's loss to the Giants. "Chavvy's out, Huddy's out, Barry hasn't pitched as well as we know he can. But you can't feel sorry for yourselves. It makes things tougher, but everyone has got to pick it up. We're not the only team that's been hit with injuries. Look at the Angels."

Anaheim leads the world in injuries as they come into Oakland for a three-game series. Third baseman Troy Glaus, reliever Brendan Donnelly, and center fielder Garret Anderson, all 2003 All-Stars, have missed huge chunks of time. Veteran Tim Salmon, first baseman Darin Erstad, closer Troy Percival, and starting pitcher Aaron Sele each missed a month. Catcher Bengie Molina has missed a few weeks. These are not bit players, either. Every one of them was a big part of Anaheim's plan to storm the division. And former All-Star Raul Mondesi, picked up to help out in Anderson's absence, didn't last nine days before tearing a quadriceps muscle. Aside from Hudson and Chavez (and don't forget Mark Ellis), the A's have been without only Hammond and little-used backup outfielder Billy McMillon for extended periods of time. Anaheim's injury issues are a severed limb to Oakland's paper cuts. "It got a little ridiculous for a while," Donnelly says. "It was a 'What's next?' type of thing." Adds Percival, "I always have sympathy for individual players because

I know what they're going through. It's tough to be out of the lineup. But as an organization, you never feel for another team, especially when you have to battle them. They weren't feeling for us." And in a bit of preseries boldness, Donnelly says he'd rather the A's were healthy right now. "For me, pitching against Chavez is a big challenge. It's better for me when he's in there. You beat a team, you want to beat them at their best."

Mulder is definitely not at his best in the opener, allowing four runs on nine hits over seven innings. But Crosby strokes a two-run single in the bottom of the seventh off, ahem, Donnelly, to give the A's a 5–4 lead, and that bullpen stability that was promised with the Dotel deal kicks in. Rookie Justin Lehr throws a perfect eighth and Dotel throws a perfect ninth. Mulder is 10–2. "This was one of those nights you battle as long as you can, try to make some pitches," he says. "I never really got into a groove. I'd get the first out on a couple of pitches and then I'd throw the ball down the middle or up or whatever and they'd double. I didn't make great pitches at times when I should have, but the offense picked me up." Of Dotel, he smiles and says, "I could definitely get used to that."

The Good Zito/Bad Zito pinwheel stops on Good Zito the next night; he gives up four hits over seven solid innings. But one of the hits is a two-run homer by Adam Kennedy, and he leaves with the score tied at 2–2. The A's don't score in the bottom of the seventh, so when the A's rally for a 4–2 win and Dotel gets another save after some solid work by Rincon and Bradford, Zito gets a no-decision. He has just one win over his past eight starts, in fact, but this night of dramatic improvement—he'd been tagged for eighteen runs and twenty-nine hits over twenty-two innings in his previous four outings—gives him hope. And a chance to go deep. "Maybe over those last starts, I was too *aware* of pitching," he says. "When that happens, I'm usually no good. I just had to believe in myself and pitch. I seemed more calm tonight. That helped."

And why so calm? "I felt like I had a little bit of a breakthrough against the Giants," he says of his previous start. Crosby had made a huge mental error in the first inning of that one, failing to cover second on what would have been an inning-ending double play, and Zito didn't respond very well. He walked Bonds—so would you—to load the bases, and after a sacrifice fly, he gave up back-to-back homers to put the A's in a 5–0 hole. "After that I kind of said, 'Fuck it,'" Zito says. Okay. Not the deepest thought in the world, though, is it? "No, but that's the point," he says. "I went back out and got through the seventh inning that night. I didn't worry about what happened in the past. I just believed in me, right now, not them."

On July 1, five home runs from the offense and five shutout innings from Kirk Saarloos, brought up from triple-A to take Hudson's turn in the rotation, help complete a sweep of the Angels, and the A's move on to take two of three in San Francisco. Mulder, a. k. a. "Run Whore," wins the Sunday finale, 9–6, and later in the same day it's announced that he and Hudson have been named to the AL All-Star team. At 11–2 with a 2.95 ERA, Mulder has a good shot at being named the starting pitcher in the game, which will be held at Houston's Minute Maid Park. At 7–3 with a 2.98 ERA, Hudson is no lock to even make it to the game.

Oh, and Rhodes is on the disabled list now, with a bad back. Nobody seems to notice.

The road trip that ends the first half for the A's is the same trip that ended their May. Three in Boston, three in Cleveland. The results—one win, five losses—are the same, too, only this time the lone win comes against the Indians. But the trip is notable in several ways. Some good, some not so much.

(1) Chavez is back. He returns in time for the Cleveland series and looks pretty badass, going 6-for-12. The A's have somehow weathered the storm, and they've done it with encouraging contributions from up and down the lineup. Kotsay hit .340 in June. Hatteberg hit .333 with five homers and a team-high twenty-seven RBIs. Crosby hit .337 to win AL Rookie of the Month honors. Dye hit .330 with a team-high six homers and seventeen RBIs. Miller drove in twenty runs in nineteen games. Designated hitter Erubiel Durazo hit .343. "I wouldn't be being honest if I said I expected all that," Chavez says. "I think it says a lot about our team, and it's exciting to think what we could do in the second half if I get in there and start pulling my weight."

(2) Boston is still a bad place for Hudson. He's already missed the two starts the team originally said he'd miss, and after the A's fall 11–0 in the opener of the series at Fenway, Hudson mopes out of

the clubhouse and into the night. The A's had been hoping that he'd be able to return to the rotation over the weekend in Cleveland, but that's not going to happen. "I'm shuttin' it down," he says of his rehab. "This thing ain't gettin' any better, so I'm shuttin' it down." The pain in his side is less now, but it's still there. And as long as it's there, throwing is a bad idea. "So now we're gonna see if rest works," he says. The bright side is that Hudson is now assured of going to Houston to take part in the All-Star festivities. Macha and team trainer Larry Davis had hinted that they'd like to see Hudson go back to Oakland for treatment over the break, but Hudson has already booked flights for his parents, his family, and a babysitter. "There's nothin' I can do in Oakland that I can't do in Houston," he says. "Man, let me have *some* fun this year."

(3) Mulder seems to have mastered the art of what Hudson so eloquently calls "pitchin' with a rabbit's foot up his ass." He blows a 3–0 lead at Cleveland by giving up five runs in the fourth inning, but the A's roar back to score seven times in the top of the sixth on the way to a 16–7 victory. Oakland has scored 102 runs in Mulder's twelve victories, and overall his support is 7.45 runs per game. "I must be living right," he says after his tenth consecutive win pulls him into a tie for the major league lead. Yankees manager Joe Torre, who will manage the AL All-Stars, won't announce his starting pitcher until the day before the game, but even Mulder's competitors for the honor—Rangers lefty Kenny Rogers and Red Sox righty Curt Schilling each have eleven wins—have conceded. "He's fantastic," Rogers says in the *San Francisco Chronicle*. "I'm not in his league. I'd pitch that guy, too, he's awesome." Says Schilling, "You look at everything across the board, and Mulder's been the best. He's been very, very consistent."

(4) Zito is as much of a mystery now as ever. The fuck-it approach doesn't work so well against the Red Sox in the first game of the road trip. He gives up seven runs (six earned) in four innings, and his somewhat cavalier comments leave a lot of people scratching their heads. "I was making my pitches," he says. "A lot of balls they hit were good pitches, changeups down and fastballs inside. It's not like they were hitting stuff over the middle." He trots out an old favorite, too, noting that "the results weren't good, but I'm more concerned about the process, and I thought the process, the

preparation, was good tonight." The problem with saying something like that, though, is that it opens the door for Sammy Smartass to say, "Well, guess what, Barry? I opened the newspaper this morning, and I couldn't find any 'process' statistics. All I saw were those pesky 'results' numbers. And guess what? Yours suck." Because let's face it: as much as a very free thinker like Zito would want otherwise, numbers—results—are all that matters in pro sports. And at this particular point in time, Zito's numbers, relative to the standard he set for himself by winning the Cy Young Award at age twenty-three, absolutely do suck. He's 4–6 with a 4.76 ERA, and the day after he's roughed up in Boston, *Oakland Tribune* columnist Carl Steward takes on the literary role of Sammy Smartass and takes Zito to task:

> What's wrong with Zito? Wish I could tell you. Better yet, I wish Barry could tell us all. But his standard response throughout his 1½-year slide from 2002 Cy Young Award winner to 2004 sub-.500 pitcher is that he's perfectly fine and that he's making all of his pitches.
>
> Sure enough, after being fleeced at Fenway Tuesday, Zito took up the familiar stump.
>
> "A lot of pitches they hit were good pitches," he said. "I had great stuff. The preparation was great."
>
> And . . .
>
> "I threw mostly changeups down in the zone and fastballs in," he said. "So I think it was a matter of guys sitting on certain pitches."
>
> And . . .
>
> "Baseball is a crazy game," he said. "You can make lousy pitches and get outs and make really good pitches and have this happen."
>
> And . . .
>
> Well, there's a lot more in the same vexing vein, but enough. At some point, it all starts to sound as if the dog ate Zito's homework, or at least his scouting report. In this latest shellacking, Zito even tried to float his own hazy conspiracy theory that maybe Red Sox hitters were somehow getting advance word of what was coming. Just throw that one on the

lame theory pile, along with the one about Zito having adjustment issues with new pitching coach Curt Young or new
catcher Damian Miller or that most basic of baseball hypothe-
ses, that AL hitters simply have "figured him out." Amazing
how none of these things seem to be affecting Mark Mulder.

Zito makes one more start before the break, in the last game of
the second half. He gives up six hits and two runs in seven innings
but loses, 4–1. He's made eighteen starts and won four of them. The
Big Three, people are saying, is now the Big One and a Half—an
injured Hudson being the Half. Yet here are the A's at the All-Star
break: they'd lost their best hitter for six weeks. Their bullpen—
Dotel blew his second save in four chances in the opener at Cleveland—has been mostly awful. The heart and soul of their pitching
staff is hurt. And they're 47–39 on the year, just two games behind
the Rangers. "Right where we want to be," Hudson says. "Time for
that second-half run."

The last time Hudson was an American League All-Star, he'd been
married less than a year and didn't have any children. He was a
twenty-four-year-old phenom, fresh off an 11–2 debut season. And
because the 2000 All-Star Game was played in Atlanta, not far from
Hudson's birthplace of Columbus, Georgia, he was busy as all get-
out. "It was crazy," Hudson says on Monday, July 12, while taking
part in All-Star Monday's media session at a downtown Houston
hotel. "I had thirteen people to take care of, it was my first time as
an All-Star, I was younger. . . . It was a pretty big deal, and it was just
crazy, man." Now he's the father of two, a six-year veteran, and on
the disabled list for the first time in his career. He'll be allowed to
suit up for the game, but because he's not on the active roster, he's
of very little interest to the hundreds of journalists on hand,
despite having the best ERA in the league. Virtually alone, Hudson
now admits that he probably won't be back on the mound until
late July but tries to put a positive spin on a bad situation. "It's a lot
different," he says of this All-Star experience. "But I think it'll be a
little more fun this time, even though I'm hurt. Not having to

worry about pitching, I'll be able to just sit back and enjoy it a little more. I mean, this is what every ballplayer strives for, to be an
All-Star. So when you get a chance to take part in something like
this, and share it with your family, you gotta do it." Even if part of
the family doesn't quite get it. Kennedie Rose Hudson is a preco-
cious little one, nearly three years old now, but as far as she's concerned, this is just another road trip for Daddy, with one big
difference. "I don't think she understands the whole All-Star thing,
so she's not that impressed," Hudson says. "But I think she knows
the hotel we're staying in is different." The Hudsons, along with
the rest of the All-Stars and their families, are staying at the swank
Four Seasons downtown. "We walked into the room," Hudson
says, "and Kennedie said, 'Oooooh, Daddy, I *like* this hotel.'"

The last time Mulder was an All-Star, it was 2003, in Chicago,
not far from where he grew up. He would have loved to start that
game, but he settled for two innings of relief work and allowed a
run on five hits. Now, with a 12–2 record and a 3.21 ERA that's
third-best in the league, he's been named the AL's All-Star starter for
2004, but it's just not that big of a deal. At the press conference
announcing the news, he's an afterthought. All of the attention is
on hometown hero Roger Clemens, who will start for the NL.
"That's cool," Mulder says the next day, while sitting at his All-Star
locker. "This is Roger's show. I'm just the guy pitching against
him." At the locker next to Mulder is Hudson, who has been giving
him a hard time for weeks about the incredible run support he's
been getting from the A's. A few hours later, Hudson is at it again.
Ichiro Suzuki opens the game with a double off Clemens, Pudge
Rodriguez follows with a triple, Clemens's Astros teammate, Jeff
Kent, makes a costly error at second base, and Manny Ramirez and
Alfonso Soriano each homer to give Mulder a 6–0 lead before he
even steps foot on the mound. Mulder works two innings, allows a
run on two hits, and gets the win.

He doesn't stick around to discuss his night with the media,
though. He's out of the clubhouse before the press is allowed inside.
"I've got family here," he says, while walking through one of the
stadium tunnels with Hudson, who is wearing him out over the
easy win. "Oh, Huddy's been all over me," Mulder says. "When we
got the six runs, he was like, 'That's odd—shocker that you'd get a

bunch of runs.' But hey, I'll take it." Says Hudson, "Some things never change, even in the All-Star Game. I need to get me some of whatever magic he's got working." Rodriguez, the AL's starting catcher, says Mulder had a little magic working on the mound, too. "I like catching him," Pudge says. "Everything is so smooth, so easy. He kept the ball down and threw strikes, just like he always does."

Along the way, Mulder retires Bonds on a routine fly ball to center field, and that pleases him as much as getting the win. When AL reliever Esteban Loaiza walked Bonds later in the game, the sellout crowd showered him with boos. "There's no way I was gonna walk Bonds," Mulder says. "I didn't care if I had to throw him a cockshot right down the middle and he hits it eight hundred feet. My whole thing was not to walk Bonds, and I didn't, so everything was good tonight."

The last time Zito was an All-Star was also in 2003, and it was a strange experience. While taking part in the mass media session in Chicago, he was taken by surprise when a reporter pulled him aside and whispered that he'd been removed from the active roster to make room for Clemens, who was then with the Yankees and was said to be retiring at the end of the year. Like Hudson, Zito got to suit up but didn't play. Unlike Hudson, he was perfectly healthy and looking forward to playing.

Zito's 2004 All-Star experience is a little strange, too. Part of it, at least. A good portion of his three-day break from baseball is spent on a surfboard in the Pacific Ocean off San Diego, thinking about life the way only Zito can. "Just being out there is so peaceful," he says. "It's so different from everything we're programmed to want to do. Sometimes it's good to just let something else be in total control, and that's what the ocean is." Zito on a surfboard is not unusual, though. How he spends another portion of his break is very unusual: Barry Zito, a Cy Young Award winner less than two years ago, takes a pitching lesson. In a very rare concession to the physical side of the game, he goes back to his roots and asks his childhood pitching coach, fellow former Cy Young–winner Randy Jones, to teach him a two-seam fastball.

14

THE NEW GUYS

Rich Harden, Damian Miller, Curt Young. Three different men, three different jobs, three different kinds of pressure. Harden is the baby. The twenty-two-year-old pitching prodigy. Miller is the wise man. The thirty-four-year-old grizzled veteran of a catcher who's been there, done that, and probably invented some stuff along the way. Young is, in a sense, the boss of both. In fact, as Oakland's first-year, forty-three-year-old pitching coach, he's in charge of Harden's moundmates and Miller's backup, Adam Melhuse, too. Yet he entered the 2004 season knowing that he'd probably never get an ounce of credit for the success of any of them. "My job," Young said, early in spring training, "is to not screw this up." Halfway through the season, he hasn't. He hasn't done a lot of things, and that's why he's been so well received. The man he replaced, Rick Peterson, was a micromanager with his finger in every pie. Young is more middle than micro.

"Curt's not really a hands-on kind of guy," says Hudson. "I think he understands that we're all big-league pitchers, you know, and I think he lets us . . . he trusts our judgment. He trusts that we know what we need to do to get ready and that we're as professional as we should be. And I think guys appreciate that, because some people might come into a situation like this and think, 'I've gotta put my stamp on this.' Curt's never done that. He trusts the system and he trusts us."

"I'd say *trusting* is a good word for Curt," adds Zito. "If you want to try something new, he'll say, 'Okay, let's check it out.' Rick would say, 'Something new? Why? What you've been doing works. Why fuck around?'"

Young trusts the system because he knows it. His coaching career began in 2000 as the pitching coach for Oakland's double-A club in Midland, Texas, and in 2003, he was moved up to triple-A Sacramento. By the time he got the big-league job, everything was rote. "We had a thing organization-wide that we did throughout," he says.

And what, exactly, is that thing? Oakland's director of player development, Keith Lieppman, laid it out in an interview with athleticsnation.com, which might be the most comprehensive baseball "blog" on the Web. Even Beane has submitted to a sit-down with the site. "From day one in the organization, pitchers are instructed on the use and command of the fastball to both sides of the plate," Lieppman told Tyler "Blez" Bleszinski, who runs the site. "We want over 60 percent usage during a ball game. Ideally with our starters, we would use 15 percent changeups and the rest with the breaking ball. Early outs—find contact within the first three pitches—are stressed, using pitches to the lower part of the zone. After pitchers learn these aspects, we go to elevating the fastball, using the changeup in fastball counts, and finally using put-away pitches, properly called 'sequencing.' Since pitching is so individualistic, the organization cannot lump any pitcher into groups or a mold. Pitch development, mental training, and other aspects are geared toward each individual since they are so varied and different. There are other programs that involve side work, pregame, weight work, and care and maintenance of the arm that are very regimented and geared toward the group." Keeping track of pitch counts, Lieppman adds, is an important part of it all. "We keep starters below seventy-five pitches at the rookie league level," he says. "We keep starters at the other levels below a hundred pitches. Early in the season, we operate around seventy-five to eighty pitches. Side work is strictly monitored by pitch counts, and pregames are also counted. Long-toss programs, daily warm-ups, and all volumes are kept and recorded by the pitching coach. Unnecessary throws are all eliminated. Relievers cannot throw three days in a row in a game. They are limited to getting up in the bullpen three times, and if they are not in the game by then, they are done for the day. Their warm-up pitches are numbered. If they exceed a certain number, they are unable to pitch for two, three, or four days, depending on the volume during the game."

Young isn't just familiar with this system. He was one of the architects. "We did the same thing from rookie ball to the big leagues, with Rick and [A's minor league roving pitching instructor] Ron Romanick and all of us coaches involved," he says. "So I felt comfortable with the physical part of it, what guys do on a daily basis, relievers, starters. That was the easy part."

Acceptance was fairly easy for Young, too, mainly because he has a big-league pedigree. Young pitched for eleven years in the majors. Ten of them were spent with the A's, and he was part of the starting rotation for the "Bash Brothers" teams—Canseco, McGwire, et al.—who went to three World Series from 1988 to 1990. "I definitely think it helps to know you've got a guy who's been through all the same shit you're going through," Mulder says, and Hudson agrees. "Having pitched for this organization and knowing what it's like to get guys out at this level, he understands that it's not easy," Hudson explains. "You may have the right pitch and the right location, and you can still give up a hit or something, because this is the big leagues and that's what big-league hitters do. For the most part, if you do make the pitch, you're gonna get them out, but that's not gonna happen all the time. Sometimes you've just gotta tip your hat to them, and he understands that."

The real challenge for Young was the same challenge anyone faces in a new work environment. Getting to know people. Building relationships. Establishing rapport. That was particularly important with the Big Three, because if you can't get along with the leaders, the followers will never follow. "All of that needs to be done on a one-on-one basis," Young says, "so I went to them early and found out their needs and what they like from a coach. Whether it's hands-on, whether you want some advice throughout the game, whether you want to talk after the game. I've taken that approach with basically every guy on the staff, including those three, where, with communication, you've gotta pick your times and make sure you go to them at the right times talking about improving or doing something with their game. With Mark, you've kind of got to let him come to you. He keeps to himself, so you just leave him alone until he asks you about something. Barry's more of a guy who wants to know what you think. He wants to know what the catcher thinks. And Tim, he's somewhere in the middle there."

The middle seems like a comfortable place for Young. He'll tell you the truth, but he'll be damn sure the truth doesn't rub anyone the wrong way. Ask him about how his style differs from Peterson's, and he beats around the bush a bit. "Well, see, I was never around Rick the entire season. I was around him in spring training. I know he was always in a mode of helping guys improve. We all are. And that's the art of coaching, how you communicate to each individual how you think you can make their game better. And that's how I'm gonna say the style was different. How he talked to people

Emerging ace Rich Harden (foreground) and Hudson are the most openly intense of Oakland's starting pitchers, and their intensity carries over into their clubhouse video game battles.

was definitely different than how I communicate." As for how his personality differs from Peterson's, Young is a little more giving. Peterson's willingness to talk is legendary, and Young didn't have to spend a full season with him to know that.

"He may be a little more outgoing with the press," Young says coyly. "He may be more involved with the press, I'm not quite sure. I think [reporters] know, you've gotta come to me to find stuff, I don't come to you. Telling you what guys should be doing, that's not me. It's all about making the guys on the field better, and I try to do it with a style and the way I learned throughout past coaching experiences. I knew Rick during spring training, and he was very organized, very technical with all the things that went on, and that may differ from me, too. I may be a little simpler."

But when posed a simple question, Young again reaches for that middle ground. Say you somehow had Hudson, Mulder, and Zito all fully rested and heading into the biggest game of the season. Who gets the ball? "Wow," he says, getting up to end the interview before another sticky question comes his way. "Well, I think I'd go three innings with each guy. That's it, right there. That's nine innings. And I'd make Hudson the closer." Says Hudson: "I think closing would be fun, but I'm a starter, and I want the ball in my hands as much as possible. Maybe I'll be a closer when I'm forty and all broken down, pitching for the Devil Rays."

Get Rich Harden talking about the differences between Young and Peterson. Get him talking about the Big Three. Get him talking about just about anything. The kid's eyes light up. And make no mistake, this is a kid. A kid living a dream. Whereas Hudson, Mulder, and Zito were major-college studs ticketed for stardom from the get-go, Harden kind of snuck up on everyone. A native Canadian, he grew up playing hockey but excelled at baseball, and the Seattle Mariners took the first crack at turning him into a pro when they picked him in the thirty-eighth round—in a typical year there are fifty rounds—of the 1999 draft. Harden turned them down and found his way down from Victoria, British Columbia, to Central Arizona Junior College, where he caught Oakland's eye by leading all Division I Junior College pitchers with 127 strikeouts in 2001. The A's used a seventeenth-round pick on him that year, and two years later he was in the big leagues to stay.

So no wonder he's always smiling in the clubhouse. The only time he's not smiling is when he's on the mound. "You know, Rich is a little different," Hudson says. "He's a Canadian hockey player, so he has that hockey player mentality; he's pretty intense. He's gonna fuckin' bite your head off, which is good, I think. You definitely wanna be aggressive. You wanna feel like a badass out there. It's something that you need, but it's just something you have or you don't, and he has it. He has that fire lit up under his ass, you know, that a lot of people don't have. A lot of people want it, but it's just not part of their makeup."

That part of Harden's makeup, though, is what needs to be tamed to a degree before the youngster reaches his full potential. "He's getting there," Young says. "I think he's really starting to enjoy the game more than fight with it. When you've come through the way he did, going through the minors so fast and being compared to the guys already here, he expects so much of himself. And I think he does fight himself on results in the game, and it makes it tougher on him for the next start. So I think he's learning that you're not gonna be that dominant every time you go out and pitch. There may be an outing where things don't go his way, and he used to get angry out there when one of those outings would come. But he's been able to adjust and kind of get right back on it the next time out. If I had a knock on him, it's that maybe he doesn't put enough fun into it. I tell him, 'Enjoy what you're doing out there. If things don't go well, you don't want to beat your head against the wall.'"

That's not always easy for Harden, who says he watches Hudson and Mulder intently when they pitch and wants to find a way to emulate both. "I'd say it's a fine line between being too intense or just kind of too laid-back out there," Harden says. "Finding that balance is different for everybody. For somebody like Huddy out there, he really gets into it, gets fired up, and that's kind of what works for him. But somebody like Mark, he's the complete opposite. I've gone through both. I've gone through being more intense out there and I've gotten maybe a little bit too relaxed trying to back off, so I'm trying to get to that point where I can just stay level." But he is still a hockey player at heart, which means aggression—and probably that temper—will always be a part of his game. "Well, I just get frustrated with myself. I make a bad pitch or something like that, yeah, I'm gonna be frustrated. I'm very competitive in everything I do, and I guess I just need to back off of that a little bit, but it's hard just because that's what I grew up with."

"I talked to him about that," Mulder says. "He said guys would get on base and it happened so fast that he gets pissed, so when guys get on base, he tries to make nasty pitches. And I said, 'Okay, but you've gotta stick with what got you there.' And I think he's really done a good job lately of, when he gets in trouble, not trying to make the nasty pitches he used to try to make. Don't try to throw your fastball through a wall. Try to paint the corner. It's like, 'What got you those previous five shutout innings? Okay, so why change now just because there's guys on base?' When he needs the strikeout, he'll go 92, 94, 98, I'm gonna throw this one by you. And it's silly that he can do that, but he's gifted enough to do that and you're gonna be tempted to do that all the time. But you've gotta pick your spots, and he's starting to do that."

Harden is 3–5 with a 4.52 ERA at the All-Star break, but Mulder, his mentor and housemate, is expecting a big second half from Harden. And Mulder is not one to throw out compliments for the sake of it. "He's got better stuff than all three of us," Mulder says. "I mean, that's the bottom line. That's just the way it is. It's not that he hasn't figured it out, but once he matures and gets more big-league starts, he's gonna become better, and I wouldn't put it past him to be better than all three of us at some point. It wouldn't surprise me, if one of these days it all clicks. I'm not trying to say that he's not doing well, but in a couple years, if it just clicks, it could be unbelievable, some of the stuff he could do. I mean, he could be that guy who honestly could pitch two hundred innings and give up a hundred hits. It's that kind of silly stat that you could see out of this guy. Maybe. I hope."

Better than the Big Three? Now *that's* pressure. And it's pressure to which Hudson can't relate. "When I came up, the pitching staff was struggling, and I was kind of the first one to get things going," he says. "With Rich, he's coming into arguably the best rotation in baseball. So he stepped right in and was expected to be one of the boys, which is a lot of shit to throw on a twenty-one-year-old. And he came in and he done great, he done what everybody expected him to do when he first came in. But, once you play this game at this level, you know there's gonna be a time when it ain't so damn easy. I've gone through it, Mulder's gone through it, Z's gone through it. It's just one of those things, the nature of the game, and everybody goes through it. And that's what he dealt with the second part of his first year."

There's another school of thought that says the presence of Hudson, Mulder, and Zito alleviates the pressure on Harden. Does Mulder attend that school? "Yes and no," he says. "People expected him to come out and just blow everybody away. And he did at first, and he was just outstanding, but in all honesty, I think it was also easier on him because he didn't have to come out there and be the savior of the team. And it's not that I had that. I didn't have that, Huddy didn't have that, Zito didn't have that. But it could've been that way if we weren't there or whatever, as hyped as he was. I think having us there was probably a good thing for him as far as pressure goes. But it's good and bad, because with us here, obviously he's gonna put a lot of pressure on himself. He wants to be just as good. He wants to do just as well."

Young suggests that Harden forget about trying to keep up with the Big Three for now. "At his age, it's gonna be hard to put up the numbers that those guys do," he says. "But the more he's around them, the stronger the friendship he builds with these guys gets, the better his chances are going to be. At this point I think he's kind of still finding his way, but I think he feels like he can be at their level." When Harden hears what Mulder has said about his potential to be better than each of the Big Three, he shakes his head in amazement. "You never know what's going to happen," he says. "I mean, that's really nice to hear, and obviously these guys give me a great goal to shoot for, but it's really not something I worry about. I've still got a long ways to go, and I need to work on a lot of stuff and get a lot of experience. When I first came in, it was a little more pressure. You always hear so much about the Big Three and this and that, so you know that you really need to do well to fit in. But once you've kind of been here a little bit, I'd say there's less pressure. Those guys are so consistent out there, going out and getting wins, that they always get the attention, so I just pitch and kind of worry about pitching and doing nothing else, so it kinda helps me."

Hudson is wary of the expectations placed on Harden, and he was particularly dismayed by the "Fab Four" talk that surrounded Harden's impressive 2003 arrival. He'd like to see everyone back off a little and let the kid grow into things. "That 'Big Four' stuff or whatever, that's putting way too much on a guy like that too early in his career," Hudson says. "It's great to boost somebody's confidence and tell 'em they're great, but it doesn't take a genius to know that a young guy's gonna struggle in the big leagues when he comes up. I mean, for me, my first year was pretty good, but I tricked a lot of people my first year. I didn't really learn to pitch until the next year. You know, when people got the scoutin' reports on me, knowin' what I throw and where I throw things, and guys wasn't swinging at a lot of pitches that they normally swung at. And I was just like, 'Shit,' you know? Now you have to kind of start all over and figure out a way to trick 'em differently. It's not as easy as it looks."

At the same time, Hudson's eyes are working just fine. He sees Harden's power and sees exactly where the expectations come from. "I think he probably has the best arm out of all of us," he says. "Shoot, he throws almost 100 miles per hour. Where we differ is, he's more of a power pitcher, and we're just more polished as far as knowing how to pitch and using our game. I think we probably understand our game more so than he does, but that's gonna come with time with him. When you've got pitches like Rich, you don't need to be as polished." What you really need in a situation such as Harden's is patience, Zito says. "The way our culture—the culture of pro sports—works is, everyone wants you to just crush people *right now*," he explains. "And when you're young and you know you have a lot of talent, it's so easy to get caught in that trap. And then, if you don't achieve the way other people expect you to achieve, you're going to get caught up in the negativity. That's something Rich has to watch out for, definitely."

In the meantime, Harden has plenty of people looking out for him, and Young is the one he's known the longest. "I worked with

Curt in double-A and triple-A, and we knew each other well when he got the job here, so that helped a lot," Harden says. "And even in A-ball, they always try to work the same program in. The minor league guys really prepare us. Everyone's on the same page in this organization, and I think that's why we're successful."

~ ~ ~

When Zito first heard that Ramon Hernandez had been traded, he sounded very concerned. "I don't quite understand it yet," he said. "Guys could totally rely on him; he operates the staff. . . . I hope we can bring in somebody that knows the league, knows the hitters." Well, the A's did not bring in someone who knows the American League and its hitters. They brought in Miller, whose AL experience prior to 2004 was the twenty-five games he played with the Minnesota Twins in 1997. He was picked up by the Arizona Diamondbacks in the expansion draft that year, and seven years later, including one with the Cubs, he probably knows more about catching top-flight pitchers than anyone in his generation. And if he's good enough for Randy Johnson, Curt Schilling, Kerry Wood, and Mark Prior, he's good enough for Tim Hudson, Mark Mulder, and Barry Zito. "His credentials are ridiculous," Zito says. "When we picked him up, I was like, 'Okay. Works for me.'"

It works for Miller, too, and part of the reason it works is that he's careful not to play favorites with the pitchers. He tries to give the middle reliever with a 5.67 ERA the same attention to game detail that he'd give Cy Young himself. "I don't like to treat those pitchers any different than any other pitchers," he says. "Randy Johnson is a Hall of Famer, but to me, he was just a teammate. You try to treat a guy like that the same as everybody. On good teams, there's no favoritism." Along those lines of equality, Miller doesn't like to compare one batterymate with another. "They're all great pitchers with their own strengths and ways of doing things," he says. "And the fact that they're great, I think, definitely it makes my job a little easier, but at the same time it's a challenge to keep them performing at that level." That doesn't mean there aren't differences, though. "That's the fun part of the job," Miller says. "The physical part is always going to be the same. One finger for a fastball, two for breaking ball, block the ball in the dirt, whatever. The mental side of it is the challenge, and it starts the first day of training camp. You have to sit down and get to know each guy, find out what makes him tick. Any great pitcher you find is going to have something in common with other great pitchers, and that's that he's going to be a very competitive guy. If he's not, he's not going to be great. The trick is to find out what buttons to push to bring that extra bit of competitiveness out. That's what I find interesting."

Also interesting is that Miller quickly discovered that he doesn't need to push many buttons at all with the Big Three. "They're all actually very similar as far as their pitching personalities go," he says. "They're not the kind of guys that you need to get in their face. You don't have to go yell at 'em or fire 'em up or anything like that, because the fire's already there. They have a track record to prove that they know how to win ball games. They're very low-maintenance. It's actually zero maintenance whatsoever with these guys. . . . There's been guys I've caught that do need a little kick in the ass, but that's not really bad. Sometimes you just have to remind guys of how good they are. They forget that sometimes, so you just remind them. . . . You know, 'Let's fucking go!' Stuff like that. A lot of f-bombs. But these guys, I never once had to say that to these guys." Not even Zito, who makes no bones about losing confidence occasionally? "No," says Miller, "because when you're really struggling, the last thing you need is someone yelling at you. You've already got enough shit in your head as it is. Sometimes if you try to tell a guy this or that, it can make it worse. So with guys like Zito, with Mark, with Tim, when they're struggling, you just have to let them work it out on their own, because like I said, they know how to win. It's in there somewhere. They just have to find it." Besides, Miller says with a smile, "Zito, man, there's enough wood-burning in there to heat a pretty big house as it is."

Just how much does a catcher really influence a game? That depends on whose game he's catching. "Oh, it's huge," Harden says. "I really trust the catcher a lot. They really know the hitters. They're really studying them, and we talk about it before the game, so I really have an idea of where they want to pitch them. And Damian's been around a long time, and he's really good at judging hitters' swings. That's something that I'm just learning." For a cock-sure hurler like Mulder, the impact isn't quite as dramatic. "When I was first coming up, the older catchers I had—Sal Fasano, for example—were a big help," he says. "Now that I have a better idea of what I'm doing, I think I could work with anybody. My whole thing is just know my stuff and what I like to throw. Don't make me think. If you know my stuff, we'll be fine. That doesn't mean I don't think Damian's awesome. He is. I mean, look at what he's done. People always point to the big names he's caught, but don't forget that he won a World Series, too. That's more impressive to me, to tell you the truth, because that means he really handled a whole staff. Catching Schilling and Randy Johnson and Prior and Wood is great, but those guys are so good that they'll make *any* catcher look great."

Miller agrees. "It's not me," he says. "I've definitely been lucky. Fortunately, when I was in Arizona we had a good pitching staff and won a World Series, so you sort of get this reputation. I don't even know if I merit that, really. I just happened to be in the right place at the right time. With Randy and Curt specifically, they said a lot of good things about me in the media, and that spreads out, and then maybe other teams look at that and think, 'Well, he's had some success there. He might work here, too.' It's worked out well for me. I've just been very fortunate."

According to Mulder, "It's the catchers that work well with the nonstars on a staff that deserve the attention," and Hernandez got that kind of attention in Oakland. He was seen as a key to the pitching staff's success. He provided what former A's manager Art Howe says is essential in baseball: comfort. "That's important, and Ramon had a feel for what Timmy and Mark and Barry, and every-one else, liked to do," he explains. "Any time a player's comfort-able, he's confident with what he's doing, with his surroundings. And after all those years, Ramon had almost an innate sense of what our guys wanted to throw in situations, and the guys had the confidence that he was gonna put down the right fingers. A lot of their success was due to Ramon knowing what to do, and that takes the pressure off you. If you have to call your own game as a pitcher, I think that's gonna be pretty taxing."

Fortunately for the A's, the transition from Hernandez to Miller was seamless. "It's been fine with me," Hudson says. "I haven't seen much of a difference, to be honest with you. It hasn't been that big of a transition at all. Damian's come over and he's handled us well, he's called good games. I think, with every game that they catch, him and Melhuse, they understand the game more, they understand the teams better. It's a totally new league for Miller, so he's learning all the hitters, and he's learning us, how we pitch. But by the end of spring training, the transition was pretty much over." Miller says the better the pitcher, the easier the transition. "These guys know what they're doing out there, all three of them. That helps a lot. Catching in the big leagues is hard enough without having to babysit."

15

"ROADIE FROM HELL"

he A's are feeling pretty spunky as the second half of the season begins. For one thing, they're only two games out in the division—closer than they've been at this point in the season since 1992. They're also home for twelve of their first fourteen games after the All-Star break, and they went 27–12 at home in the first half. And then there's the understandable excitement about the return to health of Chavez, who, a few hours before the second-half opener against the visiting White Sox on July 15, is pretty excited himself when talking about Oakland's history of dramatic postbreak runs. Each of the A's previous playoff appearances was made possible by a huge summer surge, and their 198–97 record in the second half since 2000 is 11½ games better than anyone else's in baseball over that span. The A's pitching staff, still sans Hudson, has been completely underwhelming—5.18 ERA—over the last thirty games, but Chavez is certain that something special is on the horizon. "Our pitching staff is going to make or break us," Chavez says. "That's probably a little unfair, but this team, since I've been here, has been built around starting pitching. And we have the best starters in baseball, top to bottom, so to me it's just a matter of time before they start going off. If we get Huddy back healthy pretty soon, get Zito back to being Zito, keep Mark on track, and get Harden going a little bit, we're capable of doing a lot of damage in a hurry. Like we've always done." This, of course, is all assuming that Oakland's bullpen reverses its own trend of doing damage. In 2003, the A's had twelve blown saves. Thus far in 2004, the number already sits at seventeen, to go with sixteen losses. Yet even those failures represent hope of some sort. "There's no way the bullpen's not going to come around," Mulder says. "Personally, I think we've got a great bullpen. I know the numbers don't show that right now, but I'll bet you that before it's all said and done, they end up coming up huge for us."

The game that night provides even more hope. Chavez hits his first homer since returning from the disabled list, Harden allows four hits and a walk over eight dominant innings, and while Dotel makes it interesting by walking Willie Harris to open the ninth inning, he quickly dispatches the next three White Sox to wrap up a tidy 4–2 victory. "Nobody likes to walk the first guy," Dotel says with a smile. "But it's what you do with the last guy that matters the most." Asked if he's starting to feel comfortable as Oakland's new closer, Dotel smiles again. "I'm always comfortable, *papi*. If they hit me, they hit me."

The next night, more promise. Dye hands Zito a 3–0 lead in the bottom of the first inning with his seventeenth homer of the year, and the debut of the two-seamer is a huge success. Zito scatters four hits and a walk over seven innings and snaps his personal losing streak at four games. The overall numbers remain messy—5–7, 4.42 ERA—but Zito's ERA over his last five starts is an acelike 3.38. "More than anything," Zito says, "over the last five games I've just felt I've had a pretty good rhythm. The outcome sometimes makes people think things are different, but the process is the only thing you can control." Obviously, the criticism Zito has been enduring locally hasn't changed his global outlook. "You start to feel as though your performance defines you as a person because there's so much scrutiny on a daily basis," he says. "But when you give in to that, you lose sight as a human that you're still a valuable person. I think every guy goes through that, and you need to get away from that." When Mulder hears these comments, he rolls his eyes and laughs. "I think it's great that Barry's feeling better about himself, but I don't get that whole you're-still-a-valuable-person stuff," he says. "That kind of thing never enters my mind. Baseball-wise, I don't give a shit what people think of me. . . . But hey, whatever works for him. It's just awesome to see him pitch that kind of game." Macha agrees. "It's important to us as a team, but it's also important to Barry as a pitcher to feel like he's got something positive going now. . . . He can be a little fragile sometimes, so every bit of confidence he gets is great."

Earlier in the day, Hudson had gained some confidence from a simple game of long toss. Having played catch the day before, he wasn't scheduled to throw at all, but he reported to work rarin' to go, and after playing catch in the outfield, he'd thrown to Buckley from in front of the mound for about ten minutes. It's Friday, July 16, and while Hudson says he'd like to return to action the following Saturday at home against Texas, A's trainer Larry Davis doesn't sound so sure. "I'm not gonna put a projection on it," Davis says. "That just sets the player up for a sense of failure if he doesn't meet the projection." Hudson concedes that he's still "aware" of the injury when he throws and agrees that a few extra days of caution might prove prudent. "We're still going to have to be pretty careful with it," he says, while playing cards in the clubhouse. "I'd rather miss a couple more starts to make sure it doesn't come back and bite us in the ass later than rush back and have it linger all year." The massive wrap of ice surrounding his side as he speaks suggests caution, too. "Hey, man, everyone knows I'm a gamer, and I want to be out there battlin' with everyone," he says. "But really, if I can just make it back soon and stay healthy and strong through the playoffs, whatever time I miss until then is gonna be worth the wait. If we can tread water or make up some ground until then, we're gonna be in good shape, 'cause we got the roadie from hell comin' up."

The Roadie from Hell, a three-city, eleven-game trip through Texas, New York, and Minnesota, starts in thirteen days. Hudson has already missed five starts, and while the A's won't announce it for several days, Hudson privately concedes that he'll miss a few more. "They don't want to let this out right now, probably because everyone in the media's gonna panic, but I ain't comin' back until the trip," he says. "It sucks, but I need more time."

The twelve-game stretch before the trip gets off to an unpleasant start. With a runner on first base and one out in the seventh inning on July 17, Redman gets White Sox catcher Ben Davis to hit a ground ball to second base that has inning-ending double play written all over it. But after taking the feed from second baseman Scutaro, Crosby struggles to get a good grip on the ball. Davis, understand, is to fast what Tony Soprano is to subtle, but Crosby makes one of the hundreds of split-second decisions that must be made over the course of a game and opts to hang onto the ball rather than risk air-mailing it into the stands behind first base. Shit happens. Redman, though, can't let it go. In clear violation of baseball's rule against showing up a teammate, he throws his arms up in apparent disgust and glares in the direction of Crosby, letting every one of the 26,285 people in attendance know that he's upset with the rookie. Three pitches later, Aaron Rowand hits a three-run homer that helps turn a one-run game into a 5–3 Chicago victory. Speaking to reporters about the play after the game, Crosby, unsolicited, unloads. "You never do that on the field," he says of Redman's gesture. "I know the play should've been made. Everyone in the stadium knew the play should've been made. It doesn't mean you throw up your arms and look at me. It doesn't matter if you're a rookie or in the league ten years. You don't do that. . . . I wasn't too pleased by it, to say the least." Redman had left the clubhouse by the time Crosby's comments were made, but before he left he'd said, among other things, "That's a play that should be made and usually is." The local press ran with it as the central angle of Oakland's loss, which extended Redman's personal losing streak to a season-high four games, and upon arriving at the park the following day, Redman, who's about as cuddly as a porcupine on a good day, is particularly prickly when the topic is revisited.

"I didn't even know about it until I read the paper," he says. "I think you guys blew it out of proportion." He also says he doesn't plan to speak with Crosby about the incident. But several hours later, after Mulder improves to 13–2 by running his winning streak to a career-high eleven games with 8⅓ innings of three-hit work, Redman says he and Crosby—who homered in support of Mulder, by the way—did indeed speak during the day. "I didn't think we really had to resolve much other than the fact that the media fucked up, the way we looked at it," Redman says. "We came to that conclusion right off the bat. . . . I said, 'Are you all right?' He said, 'Yeah.' I said, 'Did the media blow it out?' He goes, 'Oh yeah.' I said, 'I agree.'" This is pretty standard stuff, a player blaming the media for something, but it has to be mentioned that not once did Crosby publicly suggest that the media blew anything out of proportion. "That's because Bobby's a pro," says infield coach Ron Washington. "He's a man. He ain't gonna blame nobody. He don't make no excuses. He just goes out and works his ass off." Washington stops short of accusing Redman of lacking Crosby's professionalism, but he makes it very clear that he's on the rookie's side on this one. "In my opinion, Bobby did the right thing by not throwing it away," Washington says. "But when you're in the heat of the battle, things happen. . . . It's unfortunate Red did it out there in front of the fans. He just lost it for a minute."

Careful not to alienate one of his starting pitchers, Ken Macha tries to straddle the fence on the issue. He's the kind of man who takes eight to ten seconds before responding to any question that isn't a softball, and you can almost see the editor in his head feverishly working to concoct a politically correct (read: boring) answer. "All I know," he says, "is that I picked up the stats this morning, and no team in the American League has turned more double plays than we have." It's a subtle backing of the kid, followed by a not-so-subtle poke at Redman, who has already annoyed the manager on occasion by complaining about his starts being pushed back a day or two after breaks in the schedule to keep the Big Three on regular rest. For example, if Mulder pitches on a Thursday, he wants to pitch again Tuesday, with his regular four days of rest instead of five. It's the difference between being an ace and a journeyman, but Redman obviously doesn't see himself as a journeyman. Says Macha, "Everybody's just gotta concentrate on their area."

It's a phrase Macha has applied to a number of situations over the course of the season, including Rhodes's blowup over Hudson's and Mulder's benign bullpen comments. It also applies to how a pitcher should handle himself when all about him is falling apart.

Says Hudson, "If you show a guy up over an error, what's to stop that guy from throwin' up his hands after you walk a couple guys and give up a three-run bomb?" Says Mulder, "If a guy makes an error behind you, you have to just wear it. The best thing to do is try to let him know it's no big deal. Like, 'Don't worry about it. Next one's coming to you, too.'" Zito? "Nobody feels worse after an error than the guy who booted it," he says. "So there's really no point in piling on. He's probably already swimming in negative thought as it is."

Immediately after Mulder's win over the White Sox, the A's fall into another little funk. Saarloos fails to get out of the 4th inning on July 19 in a 5–3 loss to Toronto, and although the bullpen comes through with 5⅓ scoreless innings in a 1–0 win over the Jays next day, the Oakland offense's inability to score until Miller's game-winning single in the 14th inning leaves Harden with a no-decision, despite 8⅔ innings of two-hit work. Three consecutive losses follow. In the opener of a two-game series in Seattle, Zito gives up five runs in five innings and leaves trailing 5–3, but two innings after the A's tie it in the eighth, Duchscherer gives up a walk-off homer to Mariners rookie Bucky Jacobsen. Redman goes the distance the next day but falls, 4–2, and Mulder allows seven runs on ten hits over six innings the next night at home in an 8–3 loss to Texas that ends his winning streak and gives the Rangers a 4½-game lead in the AL West. Oakland is 51–44.

It's still early, but there's a sense of urgency among the A's now, and they bounce back by ripping off five straight wins. Four shutout innings from the bullpen, including a perfect three-strike-out frame from Dotel, help Saarloos beat the Rangers 6–2 on July 24. Four more shutout innings from the 'pen and four home runs, including Chavez's sixteenth of the year, help Harden beat Texas the next day. Then comes a sweep of Seattle. Zito gives up five runs in six innings of the opener, but he gets fourteen runs of support and three shutout innings from the bullpen to improve to 6–7 on the year. The next day, 2⅔ shutout innings from the bullpen—Dotel strikes out all three batters he faces again—save Redman's seventh win (against eight losses), prompting Mulder to good-naturedly gloat a little about a unit that's thrown 13⅔ scoreless innings over the past four days. "I told you the bullpen was gonna come around," he says before leaving the clubhouse, and he rewards the relievers with a day off in the final game before the big trip. His AL-leading fifth complete game makes him baseball's first fourteen-game winner in a 3–2 victory that Oakland pulls out with single runs in the eighth and ninth innings.

It's not the length of this trip that makes it so grueling. It's the competition. As July 29 dawns, the A's are 20–29 on the road for the year, and the teams they're scheduled to visit are the three AL division leaders—Texas of the West, New York of the East, and Minneapolis of the Central. "I don't want to say it's do-or-die, but if we go out there and lose seven or eight of eleven, it's definitely going to make things tough on us," Zito says before the opener in Texas. "It's kind of cool in a way, though, because this should give us a pretty good idea of how we stack up." A few hours later, Saarloos, in what's expected to be his final start as Hudson's stand-in, gets knocked out in the third inning, but the bullpen has another big night, and the A's rally for a 7–6 win that moves them a half-game ahead of Texas for their first lead in the division since July 6. Harden gets Hudsoned again the next night when Bradford and Lehr give up five runs in the eighth inning to turn a 4–2 lead into a 7–5 loss, but the A's get the division lead right back on a Saturday loaded with positive vibes.

The good news comes in the form of another comeback victory. The great news comes from Northern California, where Hudson comes out of a sixty-four-pitch rehab start at Triple-A Sacramento talking excitedly about his imminent return to the starting rotation. While the A's were digging out of an early four-run hole to beat Texas 9–4, and help Zito improve to 3–0 since the All-Star break, Hudson was testing his strained side muscle with great success.

Neither pitcher's line is particularly eye-popping. Zito allows four runs on five hits and five walks through 5⅓ innings, and Hudson allows two runs on two hits, two walks, and a hit batter over 3 innings against Texas's triple-A club, the Oklahoma Redhawks. But the bottom line is two big wins—one for the standings and one for the A's immediate future. "I felt great out there, I really did," Hudson says by cell phone, while driving from Sacramento to Oakland. "It was a good test for me, man, and I came out of it just the way we all hoped, so I'm pretty excited. My velocity was good, my hip felt great, and I got to get out of some jams. I'm ready to go now." The A's had set a maximum pitch count of seventy-five for Hudson, who breezed through the first two innings on twenty-six pitches. It took him thirty-eight pitches to get out of the third inning, so he fell short of the five innings the A's had hoped to see from him, but he sees the busy frame as a blessing. "It was gamelike, and that's what I wanted it to be," he says. "I struck a guy out on a changeup with the bases loaded and one out, made some other real good pitches in trouble. I'm really happy with the way it went."

As are Hudson's "teammates" in Sacramento, particularly Mike Rose, who was Hudson's catcher for the night. "Everybody was pretty excited to see Huddy pitch," Rose says. "Knowing he was going to be there, guys came out a little earlier, just to watch him work. It was awesome. A great learning experience for all of us, because he's where we want to get, and you could tell that it's a whole different intensity level with these guys." Also impressive to Rose was that Hudson made an effort to blend in. "He was there the day before he pitched, too. He put on the uniform and sat out in the bullpen with the rest of the guys. That showed a lot about his character. And then to watch him pitch, it was just a great night."

Zito is generally happy with the way his night went, too. He's still not conducting symphonies out there, and the formula he's stumbled upon in winning his past two starts isn't something you'd want to patent. But the A's are in no position to nitpick. Five days after getting a win, despite putting his team in a five-run hole after four innings, Zito digs a four-run hole after three innings on Saturday, July 31, but doesn't allow another hit before leaving with two out in the sixth and wins again. "Settling down after they got those early runs is a huge sign for me mentally," Zito says. "I've had some games where something bad would happen and I didn't respond the way I should, but tonight I didn't lose my focus, and that's pretty big."

Hudson, now scheduled to return to action Thursday in New York, says he saw the final score of the A's game (9–4) after

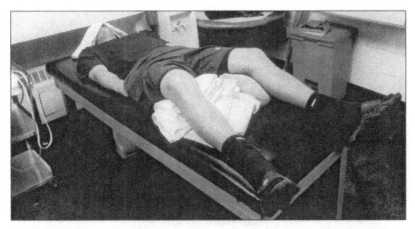

Mulder, relaxing in the trainer's room prior to a 2002 game at Yankee Stadium, isn't one to show much excitement—especially on the days he's pitching.

coming out of the game in Sacramento, and after asking for a few details about Zito's outing, he issues a playful warning to the rest of the AL West. "If Barry's getting it back together and I can get back in there and start contributing again, we might be a handful here the rest of the way," he says. "Things are definitely looking up for us right now." And after padding the division lead to 1½ games Sunday behind seven strong innings from Redman and another save by Dotel, things look even better for the A's. Having taken three of four in the oppressive midsummer heat of Texas, they've won eight of their last nine games as they head for a day off in New York City, before another tussle with the bullies in the Bronx.

Sinatra wasn't singing about baseball players, but his immortal line applies to them as well: If you can make it in New York, particularly at Yankee Stadium, you can make it anywhere. The Big Apple's constantly surging energy overwhelms people from all walks of life, but it can be particularly unforgiving on athletes. Those who play *for* the Yankees and fail to live up to the lofty expectations set by the fans and the press corps of baseball's most storied franchise get torched. Those who play *against* the Yankees and fail to serve up worthy competition get mocked. "It can be brutal," says Hammond, who spent the 2003 season in the Bronx. Now he sits in the visitors' dugout before the series opener August 3. "You need to have pretty thick skin to play here." Mulder—*"I don't give a shit what*

Mulder and rookie shortstop Bobby Crosby (sitting) were housemates during the 2004 season, and they often could be found
together at work, too.

people think of me"—shows the skin of an elephant in the series
opener, shaking off a three-run homer by Posada in the first inning
and a solo shot by Sheffield in the third. He sticks around for seven
innings, and the whole Run Whore thing kicks in yet again as the
A's storm to a 13–4 victory that features several dynamic defensive
plays by Crosby and makes Mulder the first fifteen-game winner in
the big leagues. "It was a total team effort tonight," says Mulder,
who entered the game with a regular-season record of 0–4 and a
9.97 ERA in his career at Yankee Stadium. "Bobby came up huge for
me defensively, and the offense picked me up." The offense has
been picking Mulder up for a while now, and he knows it. His ERA
in July was 5.11, yet he went 4–1. "It's hard to put my finger on it,
but something's a little off right now."

Something's a lot off the next day, and the first clue is in the

A's pregame notes, where the probable starters for the three-game series are listed. Thursday's starter is some guy named "Undecided." The second clue is in left field, several hours before the opener of the series, where Hudson is throwing off flat ground to a catcher before moving into the bullpen to complete a sixty-toss session. About an hour later, the mystery is solved when Macha announces that Zito, not Hudson, will start the series finale Thursday. Hudson will instead start Saturday in Minnesota. Macha explains that while Hudson nearly reached his pitch count in his rehab start, the A's wanted him to go five innings so they could see how his injured side reacted to cooling off and warming up again several times between innings. Thus, Hudson will have to wait another few days. He'll throw another side session Thursday, warming up and cooling down a number of times to simulate game conditions, and face the Twins two days later. "I'm anxious to get back out there," Hudson says, "but this makes some sense for everyone." Statistically, the change makes a lot of sense for the A's. Zito, who pitched Saturday in Texas and now will be working on his regular turn Thursday, has a 2.96 career ERA at Yankee Stadium and is 1–4 with a 4.70 ERA in his career against the Twins. Hudson has a 4.15 career ERA at Yankee Stadium and is 6–1 with a 2.02 ERA against the Twins. Macha says those numbers have nothing to do with the decision, but Hudson isn't so sure. "Barry seems to do pretty well here, man, so let the big dog run," he says. "I've waited this long. I can wait a little more." In that day's game, Harden, who hasn't lost since June 21, gives up four runs on ten hits before leaving with two on, one out, and a 6–4 lead in the seventh inning. But after Macha expertly uses three relievers to mix and match his way to the ninth, Sheffield makes it all moot by crushing a slider for a game-tying two-run homer in the ninth. It's his third homer in fourteen career at-bats against Dotel. "He got me once again," says Dotel, who takes his first blown save in seven chances since the All-Star break. "Normally, he hits my fastball, so I decided to give him something different. . . . That was a hanging slider, right there." Duchscherer gives up a two-run walk-off shot to Rodriguez in the eleventh, and the A's lead is down to a half-game.

Zito has heard all the horror stories about playing in New York, but he's always said he'd like to give it a shot if things don't work out with the A's. The city represents a playground of sorts for Zito, who soaks in as much of it as he can every time he visits. On this trip alone, he's gone out on the town with teammates; popped in on an underwear-line launch party put on by one of his sponsors, Puma; and made a live in-studio appearance on a webcast. "I'd love to play for the Yankees some day," he says, while riding in a town car from MLB.com's Chelsea studios to the Bronx. "I love the energy here, the vibe of the stadium, the vibe of the whole city. I think it'd be cool." Several hours later, while walking through the tunnels under the stadium after Rodriguez's homer off Duchscherer, Zito hears a voice ring out from the other end of the tunnel. Walking in his direction is none other than A-Rod, the $250-millon man, nattily dressed in a blue suit. The sight of Zito, his hair flying every which way, in burnt-orange corduroys and a matching, untucked, striped silk shirt, has Rodriguez smiling from ear to ear. "Oh my gosh, Zito!" he yells. "What a look! You got beef tonight?" *Beef* is player-speak for a date, but Zito does not have one. He never does on the night before a start. That's when he, like Hudson and Mulder and most every other self-respecting starting pitcher, goes into shut-down mode and gets a good night's sleep. But the sight of Rodriguez has Zito temporarily energized. "See what I mean about this place?" he says. "I mean, you walk around a corner and there's A-Rod. How cool is that?"

The only thing cool about August 5 from the A's view is that despite another loss for Zito, who falls below .500 again at 7–8, the question is not *What's wrong with Barry?* It's *How the hell does anyone ever score off Kevin Brown?* Zito's mystifying season continues with another day pocked with brilliance and breakdowns, but a victory would have been tough to come by even if he'd been at his best. In allowing only one runner past second base over eight stifling innings, Brown carves his way to a 5–1 win that drops the A's a half-game behind Texas in the AL West. "It's the best I've ever seen him," Chavez says of Brown. "I felt like I had no chance today." Zito's final line—four earned runs on eleven hits over 6⅔ innings—is nothing to wax poetic about, but were it not for a couple of botched plays by Byrnes in left field, it probably wouldn't have been nearly as bad. Zito rips through a perfect first inning on eight pitches, but Byrnes drops Rodriguez's leadoff liner in the second, and with one out Zito gives up a single to Hideki Matsui, an RBI double to Ruben Sierra, and a two-run double by recently acquired John Olerud. Zito breezes through the third and fourth innings, but Bernie Williams, who led off with a single, scores on a Jeter double when Byrnes, after struggling to corral the carom off the base of the outfield wall, overthrows his cutoff man to the plate. Jeter then steals third, but in his best work of the day, Zito gets Sheffield on a grounder to third and whiffs A-Rod with a high fastball. Crosby then ranges to the right-field side of second base to make his fourth sensational play of the series by throwing out Posada to end the inning. "If I could take the loss for Barry today, I would," Byrnes says dejectedly after the game. "All of his runs were my fault. . . . When you run into a pitcher with stuff like Kevin Brown's and you're not making the plays defensively, it's gonna be tough. I feel bad for Z." Told of Byrnes's self-bashing. Zito insists on taking his share of blame. "I think that's the friend in Byrnes coming out, because he's such a great person," he says. "I have to pick him up after that error." Says Chavez, "Barry's obviously looking better, but he was going up against Superman on the mound today."

Redman and Twins starter Brad Radke both pitch like Superman on Friday night in Minneapolis, but neither factors in the decision. Dotel costs Redman a win by giving up his second game-tying homer in the ninth inning in three days, this one a solo shot by Shannon Stewart that gives the A's nineteen blown saves with fifty-four games left in the regular season. But Dotel stays on for another two innings and the A's reclaim first place when Chavez and Dye drive in runs in the top of the eleventh to give them a 3–1 win and a 5–3 mark on the trip. It's a big win, but it's overshadowed by what's going to happen Saturday. Hudson will take the hill for the first time since June 22, and as he discusses his return, he does his best to downplay his importance to the A's playoff hopes. "I'm just one of twenty-five guys trying to go for the same goal," he says. "It might be a little lift to see me back out there, but we did pretty good while I was out, so I've just gotta come in and try to keep us on that same roll." Mulder begs to differ. "We need Huddy to be Huddy," he says. "He knows that. We all know that. Not to put any pressure on him, but getting him back isn't just some ho-hum thing for us. He's one of the best pitchers in baseball. He's got the best ERA in the league. Of course, it's important. It's very important. It's huge."

Hudson enters the game on a strict eighty-pitch limit, and for fifty-nine pitches he is, in the words of the man catching his darting deliveries, Damian Miller, "as good as he's ever been." But Hudson's day abruptly unravels after he quickly dispatches the first two Twins in the bottom of the sixth. Hudson fails to get an out with his final nineteen pitches, Minnesota mounts a three-run rally, and the A's lose 4–3. "I should be able to get one more out before they score," Hudson says. "So I'm a little bitter about that." In general, though, he's in good spirits. "I still felt strong. I didn't feel like I was getting tired. My command just went to shit. I just wasn't locatin' the ball the way I was earlier." Asked if he felt a little rusty at any time, he even cracks a smile. "Early on, I didn't feel like I missed six weeks," he says. "But after two outs in the sixth, I felt like I missed six months." The rest of the clubhouse is fairly upbeat, too—as upbeat as a losing clubhouse can be, in fact, and the reason is obvious: those first fifty-nine pitches. "If we have that Huddy for the rest of the year," says Miller, "we'll be in pretty good shape." In that sense, the Roadie from Hell is already a success. But as Mulder notes on the eve of his August 8 start at the Metrodome, "Winning at least one of these last two and going home with a winning record on the trip would be huge."

Mulder does little to hurt his status as the frontrunner for the AL's Cy Young Award on Sunday, surrendering three runs on six hits through eight innings, but he could have been done with dinner and two viewings of *Shrek 2* at the team hotel by the time the game ends. He sticks around, though, enduring all eighteen innings of Oakland's crazy 6–5 victory. And while watching it all unfold from the clubhouse with a growing group of teammates who have entered and left the game, Mulder does whatever he can think of to somehow inspire the offense. "It was pretty funny after a while," Mulder says. "First I went Rally Shower. Then I went Rally [clubhouse food] Spread. I was gonna go Rally Beer and Rally Junk Food. I was gonna try everything." Eventually, the A's snap the seemingly endless parade of zeroes on the scoreboard with three runs in the top of the eighteenth, and after giving up a two-run homer in the bottom of the inning, Dotel ends the game about 5½ hours after the first pitch to close out his ninth save with Oakland. "I feel like I pitched yesterday," Mulder cracks. The win, which features ten consecutive scoreless innings by the bullpen after Mulder's departure, moves the A's 1½ games in front of Texas in the West and clinches a winning record on the road trip.

Because he'd pitched in the series finale in New York, Zito doesn't start in Minnesota, and that means four nights to explore the city. But Zito isn't in an exploratory mood after the marathon victory. Instead he wants to hang out—fiddling with his guitar, swapping text messages with a new female friend, watching TV, whatever. "I just want to chill tonight," he says, while kicking back in shorts and a T-shirt in his downtown hotel room a couple of hours after the game. But his most recent start at Yankee Stadium is still fresh in his mind, and when he's asked about pitching to Sheffield, who is on an MVP pace for the Yankees, Zito springs to life. He swoops out of his chair, grabs his rectangular guitar case, and jumps up on his bed like a little kid. The case is large, about five feet long and a couple of feet wide, and he takes it to the head of the bed and leans it, vertically, up against the wall. "This is home plate," he says excitedly, plopping a pillow at the foot of the case. "And dude, I shit you not, this whole area right here—this whole guitar case—is where you can't pitch to Sheffield. That's how big the fucking guy's hitting zone is, from the ground to his shoulders. And I swear to God, if you throw anything in this area, he's going to absolutely crush it. It's a fucking joke how many balls that guy can hit hard." It's the same joke that Anaheim's Vladimir Guerrero takes to the plate, prompting Hudson to say that Guerrero's hitting zone runs from "his toes to his nose." It's part of what scouts call a hitter's "plate coverage," and Sheffield and Guerrero cover the plate as well as anyone in the game. A discerning hitter such as Bonds rarely ventures out of the strike zone to attack a pitch; his ability to lay off what Hudson calls "pitchers' pitches"—anything nasty either just on the edge of, or just off, the plate—is legendary. Free swingers like Sheffield and Guerrero, however, will throw the head of their bat at just about anything.

Given what Zito says about him, it's a wonder anyone gets Sheffield out. But one National League scout says Sheffield can't resist anything inside, even if it's off the plate: "He'll give you two strikes for free if you can get the first couple pitches in on him, because he'll swing and foul it off." To which Zito says, "But then what? He doesn't miss those pitches, either, so if you keep throwing them, he'll keep fouling them off, and that's no good for your pitch count. Eventually, you're probably going to have to throw something in that hitting zone and just hope he gets himself out." And Sheffield doesn't get himself out much against Zito. In sixteen career encounters between the two men, Sheffield is batting .429 with an on-base percentage of .500. And two of his six hits—he also has two walks—are home runs. "The guy's scary-good," Zito says. "You're never scared of any hitters out there, because the great ones represent that great challenge that any competitor wants to take on. But honestly, if you told me I could pick a few guys I'd rather not face, he'd be one of them." For Hudson and Mulder, Giambi is one of those guys. While chatting in the AL clubhouse at the All-Star game, they'd been asked to name the best hitter in the room. Both said, "Jason." Giambi's career average against Hudson is .375; against Mulder, it's .385. "He hits everyone like that, though," Mulder said. "He's just one of those guys that you know you're gonna have a tough time with, even when you're dealing."

Already assured of a winning record on the trip, and with their bullpen maxed out by the marathon victory, the A's have every reason to mail it in Monday afternoon, and deserved days off for starters Dye, Crosby, and Miller don't exactly increase their prospects for success on getaway day. But if there's one label you can fairly affix to the hard-to-define 2004 A's, it's "gritty." They've played through pain and fatigue, they've bounced back well from tough losses, and they've generally gone all-out regardless of circumstance. Thus, their 8–2 victory—Harden pitches into the seventh to improve to 3–0 with a 2.66 ERA in six starts since the All-Star break—surprises nobody in the visitors' clubhouse at the Metrodome. "First game of a trip, last game . . . doesn't matter," says Mark McLemore. "You have to bring it every day when you're in the race, and everyone here knows it. That's how it's gotta be. And when you look at what we did against three teams who were in first place when we got there, it's pretty damn good." The A's have gone 7–4 on the Roadie from Hell, and the following week is looking pretty good, too. Up next on the schedule are six games against Central-division weaklings Detroit and Kansas City in Oakland, where the A's are 36–15. "Let's get back home where we play real good," Macha says, "and see what we can do."

16

FRIENDS, RIVALS, HISTORY

More than all others, baseball is the sport about which virtually everyone thinks he knows a little something. For most American men who grew up before the youth soccer boom, baseball is the sport they played first. On sandlots, on streets, in backyards, and on local diamonds. And its simplicity—hit, run, throw, catch—lends itself to a certain comfort level. By numbers such as attendance and television ratings, football supplanted baseball as the most popular sport in the United States some time ago, but ask the average Joe to explain a "Cover Two" defense and you'll probably get a blank stare in return. Ask the same guy about the suicide squeeze, however, and you'll probably get a discourse that includes a picture-perfect recollection of the bunt he dropped down one glorious day while playing Little League or American Legion or high school ball. In short, it's very difficult to stump someone with a baseball question because most everyone feels informed on the topic. Yet it *is* possible on occasion, even when the person asked is a true baseball lifer like a former big-league player, coach, or scout, and stumping is pretty much a lock when you ask around the game for historical comparisons to Hudson, Mulder, and Zito as a trio.

"Oh, man, that's a tough one," says Ron Washington, Oakland's infield coach who has been around pro ball for roughly thirty years. And that Jim Palmer, the former Baltimore Orioles ace who now works as a broadcaster for the team, had a similar response gives you an indication of just how difficult it is to come up with a comparable staff. "There have been a number of teams that had three—even four—great starters at the same time," says Palmer, who himself anchored one such team. "But I don't know that anyone's had three guys who were as young and accomplished as these Oakland guys. That's very rare. There might not be a precedent in that sense." Palmer's right. His 1971 Orioles made history with four twenty-game winners in the same season, but Palmer was the baby of that group at 25 years old; Dave McNally was 28, Pat Dobson was 29, and Mike Cuellar was 34. The 1949 Cleveland Indians had three twenty-game winners in Bob Lemon, Early Wynn, and Bob Feller, but Lemon was the youngest at 28. The 1970 Mets had a young threesome—Tom Seaver (age 25), Jerry Koosman (age 27), and Nolan Ryan (age 23)—that looks pretty imposing now, but they weren't all aces at the time; Koosman didn't win twenty games in a season until he was 33, and Ryan didn't do it until he was 26, with the California Angels. And as good as the threesome of Jim "Catfish" Hunter, Ken Holtzman, and Vida Blue was, helping to carry the 1972–1974 A's to three consecutive World Series titles, Hunter and Holtzman were 26 when that run started, and Blue went a mere 6–10 as a 22-year-old in 1972. Hudson, Mulder, and Zito haven't yet won twenty games in the same season, but, as noted in chapter 2, they all had a twenty-win season under their belts by the time they were 25. "It's rare," says Art Howe, the former A's manager who was at the helm for each of those three seasons. "Usually, it takes a little while for pitchers, or anybody, to get their feet on the ground—especially pitchers. But they developed very quickly."

But as rare as it is, Howe, who also was at Oakland's helm when each of the Big Three debuted in the big leagues, says he knew immediately that all three were destined for stardom. "Yeah, I had that feeling," he says. "I think what's special about them is their makeup. They're all different, but as far as competing, there was a passion there in addition to the talent. You knew these guys were gonna give you everything they had when they went between the lines, and then just watching them throw the ball, you knew they all had something special. To compete and succeed at such an early age for each and every one of them was incredible. And I think, for some reason, they fed off each other, too. They've got such a great rapport and friendship, it's almost like they feel like they're gonna let each other down if they don't go out and toe the line and do the job that they expect of themselves."

David Justice, who ended his mostly brilliant career as a member of the A's during Zito's Cy Young season in 2002, says the special rapport the Big Three share is something he'd seen before. Justice broke into the big leagues with the Atlanta Braves in 1989 and played with them for eight seasons, and in his final four seasons with the club he played in the outfield behind what many baseball people see as the closest comparison to Oakland's Big Three as there's ever been. From 1993 to 1999, the Braves had the best 1-2-3 punch in baseball: Greg Maddux, Tom Glavine, and John Smoltz. They weren't nearly as young as Hudson, Mulder, and Zito were when they first came together—Maddux and Glavine were twenty-seven in 1993, Smoltz twenty-eight—but they interacted in much the same way. "Hudson, Mulder, and Zito definitely remind me of those three guys, and not just because it's three great pitchers on the same team at the same time," says Justice, who transitioned from playing to the broadcast booth with ESPN. "They interact with each other the same way. Those guys on the Braves, they were friends, they hung out together, they talked a lot. And you see that with the Oakland guys, too. But I think deep down, they all want to kind of beat the other guy out. Not in a bad way, like so they can say, 'I'm better than you,' but in a positive way. I think with guys like that it's more that they want to keep up with the other two." Justice, who quickly became a highly respected clubhouse leader in his one season with the A's, couldn't be more correct.

                  — — —

The professional similarities are amazing. Hudson was called up to the big leagues in 1999 at age 23, and a year later he won 20 games. Mulder was called up in 2000 at age 22, and a year later he won 21 games. Zito came up after Mulder in 2000, also at age 22, and a year after Mulder won 21 games, Zito won 23. Since then, they've taken turns commanding the spotlight every fifth day, trying to top—or, as Justice suggests, simply keep up with—one another. If A's baseball were a comedy club, this would be Eddie Murphy, Chris Rock, and Bernie Mac appearing on the same bill.

"It can be tough," says Hudson, who has traditionally had the luxury of performing first in the pecking order. "If the guy in front of you throws a two-hit shutout, pretty much anything you do isn't going to stack up." On some teams, such a dynamic might breed something of a rivalry. Maybe even a little jealousy. And perhaps, secretly tucked into the darkness of the subconscious mind, a touch of I'd-like-to-see-that-guy-get-lit-up-every-so-often. Then again, few teams have had to worry about such issues. Rivalry? Jealousy? Envy? Bitterness? Leave that to Britney and Christina. Hudson, Mulder, and Zito not only pull for one another, as any good teammates should, but for all of their personal differences, they really do genuinely like one another. "Totally," Zito says. "Can you imagine how lame it would be if we didn't?"

What sustains the friendship? Well, it starts with mutual respect. "I think we all realize that we're in a unique situation as far as being here together," Mulder says. "I don't wanna say we're going to go down as the best staff there's ever been, but I think we're all aware that there's a certain potential here. I mean, individually, each one of us knows he's a pretty good pitcher. And each of us definitely knows that the other two guys are just as good, if not better." Those personal differences help, too. "If we were all the same kind of guy, we might not get along as well," Mulder says. "It sounds kind of weird, but I think we all amuse each other in different ways." And that's the thread that ties the trio together: amusement. They're like little boys—brothers, even—on a field trip, only they're grown men, and the field trip is an annual eight-month tour of the big leagues. "I think that's a pretty good way of putting it; we are like brothers in a lot of ways," Hudson says. "Because we care about each other and probably look out for each other like brothers. If one guy's having a hard time, one of us will be there to try to pick him up and make him feel better about himself. But at the same time, brothers like to give each other a hard time, and if me or Zito does something dumb, Mark'll be the first one to jump in

Zito and Hudson are, in Hudson's words, "closer friends than anyone on the team." They spend a lot of time with each other on and off the field.

and let us know about it. And it's the same thing for all of us. If Z's actin' a fool, I'll hop on and ride him a little, and he'll do the same to me."

One example of such came up during the 2003 season as Mulder was going through "the drill" at his locker, surrounded by reporters and cameras. He'd just gotten out of the shower, and Hudson, at the next locker, noticed that Mulder hadn't yet gotten a chance to do anything with his hair. "Nice 'do," Hudson chirped, and when Mulder pretended not to hear, Hudson made a prediction. "Watch him," Hudson whispered to Zito, who was two lockers down. "You know how important Mulder's hair is to him. It's killing him right now that it's messed up and the cameras are on. Watch, he'll run his fingers through it or something; give it a quick hand-salon deal." As Hudson and Zito burst into giggles, Mulder glanced over at them and rolled his eyes in the middle of an answer. "Wait for it," Zito said. "Oh, it's comin'," Hudson said. "You know it's comin'." And sure enough, five seconds later, up went Mulder's arm, and through the hair his fingers went as he listened to the next question. "There it is! There it is!" Zito cried, as he and Hudson cracked up. "Attaboy, Mulder," Hudson yelled. "Still looks like shit, though."

Do they have their moments of discord? Of course, they do. What brothers don't? The baseball season is a marathon of a grind, and even the best of friends get on each other's nerves when they share close quarters for too long. Mulder's acerbic wit, for instance, can be piercing, and Zito's sensitive soul doesn't take kindly to clubhouse criticism, so the two of them aren't nearly as close away from the game as are Hudson and Zito. "Mulder and I see the world through totally different lenses," Zito says. "That doesn't mean we don't get along or like each other. We do. But as far as spending a lot of time together on the road or in the off-season or whatever, that doesn't really happen because we have totally different interests. We'll go out on the road, but not all the time, and it's almost always in a group. Me and Huddy, we'll go out just the two of us sometimes. I just vibe a little bit better with Huddy overall, I guess." Hudson's take on Mulder and Zito? "They're just different guys who like to do different things," he says. "Mulder, he could be happy just sittin' around playin' video games. Barry's not like that. He's a little more high-strung, so he always has to be doing something. And I'm a little on the high-strung side, too, so that's probably why Z and I hang out a little more. But we're all close, no doubt about it. I mean, if you look into the dugout on the days none of us are pitching, more often than not you're going to find the three of us together. We have a lot of fun."

Even when the grind starts to grate, at the end of the day Hudson, Mulder, and Zito are friends. And while they might fret over having such tough acts to follow, each will continue to want the other to kill whenever they're on stage. "*Rivalry* is the wrong word for it," Mulder says. "It's more of . . . I don't know if there is a word for it, but it's just more that we push each other. I mean, if Zito goes eight innings, five hits, I want to go eight innings, four hits. And then Huddy'll want to go eight innings, three hits. It's not to outdo the other guy. It's just to push each other, to make each other better. Nobody wants to be the weak link. So to me, I think it's good. I think it's great."

Zito, a photography buff, set his camera up in advance to capture this shot of the Big Three killing time in front of a TV during the 2002 playoffs in Minnesota.

If you really want to know what somebody is like, ask his mother. Dad tends to let parental pride get in the way just a little bit more than Mom, so his view is going to be a tad skewed. Mom tells it like it is, warts and all. Sue Hudson, Kathy Mulder, and Roberta Zito are no exceptions. And as the mothers of the Big Three open up about their sons, one thing comes through loud and clear: these women are as different—and as similar—as the pitchers themselves.

Sue Hudson had to be talked into an interview by Tim's wife, Kim. A shy sort, she spoke from Kim and Tim's in-season home in the Bay Area—after changing the diaper of granddaughter Kennedie—in the same soft southern drawl that Tim employs. But just as Hudson has slowly grown into the role of clubhouse leader, Sue, over the course of the interview, grew slowly at ease with detailing the young life and times of the boy she still calls "Timmy" to this day. "Our relationship is real close and always has been," she says. "We've always had a very tight family, and that hasn't changed one bit. I've got two other boys, and Timmy's the baby, and he's the same Timmy that he's always been. Timmy will never change."

Kathy Mulder was in the process of packing up for a move from Illinois to Arizona when she was interviewed about her son, but she showed the same kind of poise her son shows on the mound in handling questions, while worrying about what's in what box. Pleasant but measured at first, she opened up more and more as time went by, just as Mark has done with the media. "We're a close family," she says, "but just like any young man who goes off to college and into a career, they mature and become more independent. I can already tell that's happened with Mark. Before he would call for a little more advice, but now that he's been doing it for a while, phone calls are a little fewer and far between. He's just doing more things on his own now, and that's natural."

Roberta Zito spoke happily from a hospital bed in Southern California. At the time she was battling a bout of bronchitis, and because she's had a liver transplant, the doctors kept her for a couple of days as a precaution. No big deal, she insisted, before waxing joyfully about her only son. To say that Barry is the light of her life seems a massive understatement. "I would describe our relationship as very special and very different because of Barry's particular nature," she says. "His complete self-acceptance and the freedom he gives himself to just be himself has always surprised me. The only thing that's changed is I just don't see him as much. But we still talk all the time, and sometimes he'll call in the middle of night just to ask for prayer. Our relationship is still very special and open. He doesn't consider me an authoritarian, but more of a friend."

Baseball has always been part of the Hudson family fabric. "Yes. It's just baseball with us, nothing else," Sue says. "Timmy's brothers, Ronnie Jr. and Keith, were good ballplayers, too. And there's an eleven-year difference between Keith and Timmy, so by the time Timmy was getting started in T-ball, we'd been in baseball for a long time." Perhaps that's why Sue and her husband, Ronnie Sr., knew right away that they had something special on their hands when Tim first picked up the game. "Timmy was always a little bit hyper, but he always had a ball and a glove in his hands, and he was real good even then," she says. "Even at eight, nine, ten years old. He was always such a tiny little boy, but Timmy would knock 'em out. The other moms would wonder how he did it, but size don't mean nothin', and Tim and I, we had a secret. We'd stop by the store on the way to the game and get him some chocolate candy. That's the only candy he'd ever get because he was sort of hyper, but he'd eat that candy bar and just go knock those bigger boys out." Hearing that his mother outed him on their secret weapon, Hudson cracks up. "She told you that?" he says with mock disgust. "Great, now other teams are gonna come into our club-house and try to steal all the candy bars." Sue, though, knows that it wasn't the candy that set Tim apart. His talent did. "His father and I both knew God had given him a really special gift from the time he started. All through the years he was doing well from one level to another, so there was never any one moment. But I guess once he got to Auburn and started doing it against that level of competition, we were pretty sure he'd be a professional. In my heart, I really didn't have any doubt. . . . I always told him, 'Timmy, one day you're gonna be mom's little major leaguer.'"

Kathy Mulder says her oldest son wasn't really any different as a youngster from the way he is now. "You can't change your person-ality too much," she says. "He had a lot of energy, but he didn't waste his energy on things he didn't feel were worth it. But he was always involved in everything. Little League, soccer, basketball—he was always into something active. And Mark just loved to tease his brothers and play tricks on them. Finally, my middle son just ignored him, so Mark left him alone and said he was no fun. But the younger one would get so mad, and the madder he got, the more Mark would come after him and egg him on." The confidence was there at an early age, too. "Mark was always the all-star, and he always wanted the big moments," Kathy says. "I remember in one game, his team got down to the last out and the coach needed a pinch-hitter, but Mark had just batted, and none of the rest of the kids wanted any part of it. Mark was so mad. He said, 'I can't believe none of them wanted to go out there. I would have given anything to get out there and take a whack at it!'. . . He was always pretty successful, and it seemed like he was just built for it. He's always had that athletic build. He was never pudgy; we could never keep his pants on his hips, and he was always taking slim sizes. And we had a good friend of ours who used to coach Little League, and he always talked about how good Mark was. There wasn't one thing. We just knew all along that he was a good athlete." And yet Mark's success as a big leaguer did catch Kathy by surprise. "It's just kind of happened so fast. He was drafted, spent one month in the fall league, then all of a sudden they wanted him at triple-A. Then suddenly the next year he's in the major leagues and we thought, "Okay, they're gonna give him a shot.' So, yeah, it has surprised us. But when it comes to athletics, things have always come rather easy for Mark. I'm not sure if that's a blessing or a curse. . . . We just keep reminding ourselves that this cool that he has about him on the mound, he kind of carries that into real life, too. He's never real uptight or real upset about anything until he has to be."

Roberta Zito doesn't really believe in curses, but she knows that her only son is blessed. She's known it for a long time, too, in part because Barry didn't go through the "brat phase" that most young boys go through. "Never," she says. "We were constantly amazed by that, too, my two daughters and I. Even when he was a teenager, he and I had a regular date, and we'd go to the movies every weekend. We'd trade off—one week we'd go to one of his boy action movies, and the next week we'd go to what he called one of my 'chick movies.' And as he got older, I'd say, 'But Barry, it's Friday night. Don't you want to be with your friends? Aren't you embarrassed to be seen with your mom?' He'd say, 'No way,' and just put his arm around me. He's just somebody very special. My girls are nine and thirteen years older than Barry, and while I love all of my children equally, we just always considered that Barry was an extra special gift to our family. . . . He just carried the sameness of personality wherever he went that he has now. So cool. Just unaffected in everything. Just calmness." Unlike Kathy Mulder, Roberta wasn't surprised when her son hit it big. "No," she says. "It was surprising for him to be up so quick, but it didn't surprise me that he made it because we always felt that he would. That was always his goal, and we just knew he'd achieve it. I think he always knew, and I always knew, and my husband always knew. But how many coaches will tell you, 'What are the chances?' Well, I always said that 'chances' have nothing to do with Barry."

Mothers aren't just honest about their children. They're perceptive as well, and Kathy Mulder makes the same point that David

Justice makes about the relationships among members of the Big Three, while discussing Mark's relationship with his brothers. "Mark's very competitive at everything, and like I said, he loves to tease his brothers," she says. "He always has, and there's still this healthy competition between them, just like there is between Mark and Hudson and Zito. If one of them does this or does that, the other wants to do it better."

It's not just difficult to find historical comparisons for the Big Three as a group. It's tough to find historical comparisons for them as individuals, too. A group of seventy-five people who work in baseball—players, coaches, executives, and sportswriters—were asked to weigh in on the topic over the course of the 2004 season, and not one of them had an immediate answer that conveyed total conviction. "I think there's a variety of reasons for that," says Fosse, who caught that great A's staff of the early '70s. "For one thing, guys have more pitches these days than most of the studs from the past did. You didn't have a lot of guys throwing cutters or splitters back then. There were a lot more three-pitch guys, even two-pitch guys."

Zito, until he picked up the two-seam fastball from Randy Jones, was a three-pitch guy. But his curveball is so special that even he represents a challenge, as far as historical comparisons go. "I've never heard anybody compare me to anyone else," he says. "I guess I'm kind of unique in that sense. And I didn't really pattern myself against anyone when I was younger, because as soon as I figured out that my curve was probably a little better than most people's, I just stuck with that. I never really needed anything but fastball-curve when I was younger. Obviously, as you progress and move up to higher levels of the game, you have to add a changeup, and it took me a while to get completely comfortable with that. But once I got that, it was like, 'Okay, these three pitches are enough to get guys out. Why change anything?'"

Fosse says Zito reminds him a bit of Holtzman, who made his big-league debut when he was 19 and went on to win 174 games over 15 years. "Kenny was a three-pitch guy, and he came right over the top with everything like Barry," Fosse says. "And just as the case is with Barry, he threw such a good curve that when it was on, you just went to it. It was money in the bank." Holtzman never had a monster season like the one Zito put together in 2002, but like Zito, he was good at a relatively early age, winning 17 games as a 23-year-old with the Chicago Cubs in 1969 and 17 more the following year. He joined the A's in 1972, and during Oakland's dynastic run of three consecutive world titles, Holtzman won 19, 21, and 19 games, respectively. He won 18 games in 1975, at age 29, and retired after the 1979 season with a career ERA of 3.49. "Wow," Zito says. "That's a pretty sick career." Not as sick as the one Zito hopes to put together, though. "You know what one of the things I hate about this game is? It's that if you're totally open and honest about your goals, people try to crush you. If you come out and say, 'I want to be one of the best pitchers of all time. I want to be a Hall of Famer,' people think you're being arrogant or unrealistic and get on you about it," he says. "That's so lame to me. Why wouldn't you want to be the best of all time at what you do? If you don't, why are you even doing it? Hell yeah, I want to be the best of all time. Hell yeah, I want to go to the Hall of Fame. And anyone who tells me that it's unrealistic, I don't want any part of that person. I look at everything—in baseball, music, relationships, whatever—thinking that if I really want to achieve something, I'm going to achieve it. It goes back to that power-of-the-mind thing. If I want to make something happen, I really believe I have it in me to get it done."

Finding anyone with a solid historical comparison to Hudson and Mulder proved fruitless. The name that came up most often in reference to Hudson was Pedro Martinez, also slight of build and fiercely competitive, and Hudson says he did indeed look up to Martinez, who made his big-league debut when Hudson was seventeen years old. Mulder was most often compared to Mike Mussina, another tall, poised, athletic pitcher with excellent command, but Mulder never looked up to Mussina, who is eleven years his senior. "I always wanted to be a hitter, so I didn't pattern myself after anyone," Mulder says. "Until probably my last year of college ball, I always put a lot more thought into hitting than pitching." And while Martinez, who had won three Cy Young Awards going into the 2004 season, and Mussina, who finished in the top ten in Cy

Young voting eight times between 1992 and 2001, are great pitchers, they're not historical comparisons at all. They're contemporaries. "There weren't really any guys like Huddy and Mulder when I played," Fosse says. "They both have so many weapons. You just didn't see a lot of that in the old days."

Hudson and Mulder would have been freaks in 1970. Each of them throws seven pitches. Four-seam fastball, two-seam fastball, split-fingered fastball, cut fastball, curveball, slider, and changeup. And because Hudson drops down and throws two of them sidearm on occasion, he actually has nine pitches. You might think that would create problems for a catcher, who only has five fingers with which to call pitches. And you'd be right. For Hudson's four-seam fastball, the catcher puts down one finger. For the two-seamer, he puts down one finger and wiggles it from side to side. Two fingers calls for the cutter. Two fingers wiggling calls for a slider. With a lefty at the plate, two fingers wiggling just inside the catcher's thigh that's farthest away from the batter calls for a curveball. If they're wiggling and tucked in toward the batter, it's a slider. Against a right-handed batter, two fingers wiggling away is a slider, two wiggling in is a curveball. Three fingers is a split-fingered fastball. One finger turned to the side is a sidearm fastball—two- or four-seams. Two fingers turned to the side is a sidearm slider. Nine signs. "It's not as hard as it sounds," Hudson insists, "but I can see why people would think it is." He's matter-of-fact when discussing his repertoire, but don't be fooled. Nine pitches is a lot. Seven is a lot. Even today, most pitchers have no more than five. "Right," Mulder says. "And most games, I won't use more than five. But you never know. Maybe one day you don't have a good feel on your slider, so you ditch it and go with your curve more. Huddy, I know, hardly ever uses his split. But the thing is, it's nice to have those options in case you all of a sudden lose your feel for a couple of pitches out of the five you're using that day. It's like you have a backup plan." Says Hudson, "That's exactly it; you always have a little something extra. It gives you options. You can just show a pitch to a guy early in the game to give him something else to think about, and never use it again. Or you can bust it out on him late in a game when he hasn't seen it all day. Or you can not use it at all, but he probably knows you've got it somewhere, and maybe he's thinking about that." He laughs at the thought of how an even-more expanded arsenal might play with a hitter's head. "Just wait," he says. "I might just bust out with some knuckle-curve shit someday, and I'll drop down sidearm with that, too. Then they're really gonna be fucked up."

So there really aren't any historical comparisons for the Big Three, as a trio or on their own. Perhaps, Howe suggests, they will be on the other end of such comparisons at some point. Perhaps there are three Little Leaguers out there right now—say, one from Kentucky, one from New York City, and the other from San Francisco—who are destined to pitch together with great early success in the majors and be the impetus for such a search. "The three guys in Oakland, I hope some day I'm going to their Hall of Fame induction, if I'm still living," Howe says. "That's the kind of ability those three guys have. They've got a chance, if they stay healthy, to do something real special in the game."

17

"GO TIME"

If the A's of recent vintage have become known as second-half monsters, they've been particularly scary in August. From 2001 to 2003, they went 66–20 in the month; the next-best team over that span was the Houston Astros, at 52–33. And from 1999 to 2003, Oakland had the best record at home in the big leagues, so the six-game home stand that follows the Roadie from Hell looks promising, with the lowly Detroit Tigers and the Kansas City Royals coming to town. The Tigers, who threatened a record for single-season futility while losing 119 games in 2003, come first, but Macha does all he can to keep his charges suitably inspired. "There are no easy games," he says. "None. Zero." He points out that the Tigers are much improved, and the off-season addition of catcher Ivan "Pudge" Rodriguez gives Detroit a middle-of-the-order threat with Hall of Fame credentials. Rodriguez, however, isn't much of a factor in Oakland's series-opening win, which Zito earns by bouncing back from his beating in New York with seven solid innings to improve to 4–1 over his past five starts. Chavez hits his eighth home run since returning from the disabled list, and Dotel gets his tenth save since the trade, but Zito, like Hudson and

Mulder, is a huge part of the story every time he pitches. Despite the win, his ERA over the last three starts is a whopping 5.59, but he continues to insist that the way he feels is more important than the numbers.

"Stats are so pliable to people," Zito says, while walking out to his car, a modestly appointed black Dodge Durango. "Sometimes I wish they didn't keep stats at all. It'd be nice to just go out and play baseball, and let people decide with their eyes whether or not they think this or that is good or something they like. At this point, I don't really care about the numbers. I can't. It's August and I have eight wins, so it's not like I'm going to have the twenty-win season people seem to expect. My ERA is pretty high, so I'm not going to get real low there no matter what I do. So now I have to just focus on what's happening out there when I'm out there, and in that sense, I feel good about the way I'm throwing the ball. I've given up some runs in my past three starts, but I don't think it's indicative of how I felt, because my stuff's been crisp the last three games." Not much is crisp about the second game of the series on August 10. Redman, who has been as bad at home as his team has been good, gets pounded for six earned runs over four innings of an 11–3 loss that leaves him with a 1–4 record and an 8.42 ERA in day games in Oakland.

The next day, Hudson waits for the media to clear out of the clubhouse before expressing his glee about the Detroit lineup that's just been posted for the series finale. He's naturally pumped up to make his first start at home since coming off the disabled list; he's 4–0 with a 1.34 ERA in Oakland this year, and he's 9–2 with a 3.04 ERA lifetime against the Tigers. But he's especially excited because Rodriguez isn't playing tonight. In twenty-four career at-bats against Hudson, he has eleven hits (.458), including a triple and a home run, with seven RBIs. "Pudge isn't in the lineup?!" Hudson booms before squealing, "Yippee!" and jumping up and down like . . . well, like a Little Leaguer whose mother just let him tear into a block of chocolate before a big game. "I oughta send a nice bottle of whiskey over to him in their club-house and tell him to start drinkin' now," he says. "That way he won't be able to pinch-hit late in the game." Unfortunately, Hudson isn't around by the time the late innings come. Still concerned about his arm strength, the A's have him on a short leash, and though he holds the Tigers to two runs on six hits through five innings, a slew of foul balls and deep counts forces him to take a seat with his pitch count at ninety. "My arm felt great," he says. "My strength was fine. I definitely could have gone back out there, but I understand that they want to pull the reins back on me a little. If it was up to me, I'd go and go and go, but that's probably not the smart way to go about it at this point. Hopefully, I can go a little deeper next time so we can give the ball to the bullpen a little later." The score is tied at 2–2 when Hudson exits, leaving him with another no-decision, and Duchscherer gives up two home runs in the sixth. The A's fall 5–3, so for the first time all year, they've dropped a series at home to a sub-.500 team. "I don't think anyone expects us to win every series the rest of the year, but this is usually a good time for us," Hudson says. "We just showed on the road trip that we can hang with the big boys, and now we've got a little bit of a soft spot on the schedule, so we have to make a move and get some momentum going heading into the stretch drive."

The stretch drive essentially starts September 6, and it's not going to be an easy path for the A's. The month opens on the road in Chicago, and after a stop in Toronto, they go home to face the two teams who have given them the most trouble this year— Boston and Cleveland. Then the real fun starts: the last twenty games of the regular season are against the rest of the American League West, and it all ends with a three-game series in Oakland against the Angels. "I've been looking at that last series for a while," Hudson says. "I wouldn't be surprised if it all comes down to that." First, though, the A's have to do what good teams do, and that's to kick sand in the faces of the weaklings. After hosting the Royals for three games, Oakland's final thirteen games before the trip to Chicago are against the Tampa Bay Devil Rays and the Baltimore Orioles, who fell out of contention not long after the games started counting. "It's go time," Hudson says. "Time to win a bunch of games and build that lead." The A's, at 64–50 for the year, lead the AL West by 1½ games.

Nobody seemed to notice in July because he went 4–1, not including his win in the All-Star game, but Mulder wasn't nearly as sharp
in July as he'd been the previous three months. In April and May,
his ERA was 3.00, and in June, it dropped to 2.74. In July, it was
5.11, but after he gets tagged for seven runs over seven innings in
a shocking 10–3 loss in the opener of the Kansas City series on
August 13, he's not even close to being ready to admit that something might be seriously wrong. "I made one bad pitch, really,"
Mulder says, referring to a sixth-inning grand slam by rookie
Abraham Nuñez. "It lost the game for us, but otherwise, I felt
really good out there. It's just that the one bad pitch killed me."
Mulder's all-time record against the Royals was 8–0 with a 1.72
ERA going in, including 5–0 with a 0.68 ERA at home, so his
becoming the first sixteen-game winner in the big leagues looked
like a lock. But after throwing five shutout innings, he gives up
his first career grand slam to Nuñez, followed by a two-run shot by
Joe Randa in the eighth. "Yeah, it's disappointing," Macha says.
"You've got your number one guy out there leading the league
in wins, you're expecting a good ball game, and you get pounded."
The disappointment fades the next day when Harden allows a
run through six innings and picks up his fourth straight victory
since the All-Star break, and it's a particularly encouraging day
because Mecir, Lehr, and Dotel combine for three perfect innings
of relief. But on August 15, the A's, their bullpen, and Zito hit some
new lows.

Zito pitches beautifully for 6⅔ innings, striking out a season-
high nine while looking as dominant as he's looked all season, but
the A's offense is in the middle of one of its funks. And when Zito
is pulled with runners at second and third with two out and Oakland leading 1–0, you can practically feel what's about to happen.
And it does. Ricardo Rincon, brought in specifically for his efficiency against left-handed hitters, comes on and hits the only batter he faces—lefty David DeJesus—on an 0–2 pitch to load the
bases. Duchscherer enters and gives up a three-run double to
Randa. Kansas City scores two more runs in the eighth and another
in the ninth for a 6–1 victory that ends a baffling 2–4 home stand.
"We haven't played well the past few days," Macha says, earning
immediate induction into the National Duh Hall of Fame. "I think

there might have been a little bit of a hangover after that road trip. Hopefully, we've fought through the period of being drained physically and mentally."

Zito takes an incredibly tough loss, but at first he focuses on the positives. "My changeup's been a better pitch for me the last couple games, the curveball's more consistent, and the fastball's on both sides of the plate," he says. "I've been looking at some tapes, and I feel like I look basically the same as I did in 2002." Then he admits that the day's events left a bit of a sour taste in his mouth. He's less than thrilled that Macha didn't give him a chance to get out of his own jam. Macha, who had waved in Rincon before he even got to the mound to give Zito the hook, defends himself by pointing to Zito's pitch count of 114 and noting that lefties have hit Zito hard this year. "Rincon's been outstanding against left-handers; they're hitting two hundred points less than what they are off Zito," he says, and he's about right. Lefties were hitting .183 against Rincon and .367 against Zito going into the game. But Zito, who had struck out DeJesus twice and walked him once in the game, would have liked to at least have been allowed to plead his case. "There wasn't a physical problem with me having to come out," he says. "If [Macha] came out and said, 'How do you feel?' I would've said, 'This guy's out, I've got him.' But the decision was already made." Macha says that 114 pitches "was enough. Barry did his job. The bullpen just didn't get it done." Fortunately, the ensuing road trip is to Baltimore and Tampa Bay, and those teams prove to be the Advil and the Aleve to whatever's been ailing the A's.

Fittingly, the road trip starts with another gem from Redman, who, after easily handling the Orioles, has the league's second-highest home ERA (6.37) but the fourth-best road ERA (3.04). "I told Billy [Beane] that I should get it put in my contract that I only pitch on the road, because I've been stinking it up at home," Redman says, after Dotel's eleventh save enables Oakland to cling to what is now a half-game lead in the division. "I just need to carry this back to Oakland." The next night, August 17, Hudson carries the A's to an 11–0 drubbing. Free to exceed the 100-pitch mark for the first time since being activated, he needs only 97 to spin a five-hit shutout, making the scads of support he received after Jermaine Dye's solo homer in the fifth window dressing. "He was awesome," says Orioles third baseman Melvin Mora. "He was nasty. He was incredible." Specifically, Hudson went to a three-ball count only twice, never allowed a runner past first base and retired twenty-three of the last twenty-six batters he faced. "And it's not like he did it against just anybody," says Byrnes, who hit the third of Oakland's four home runs. "That's a really, really, really, really good hitting team. . . . Four reallys." Baltimore had entered the game batting .283 as a team, good for second in the AL, but they bat .167 (5-for-30) on the night against Hudson, who lowers his AL-best ERA to 2.95. "He was still throwing ninety-three [mph] in that last inning," Macha says. "That was a dominating performance. Maybe the best of his career." In response to Macha's claim, Hudson stops to think for a moment. He did, after all, enter the season with the third-best winning percentage of all time among pitchers with at least fifty wins—at .708 (80–33), he was right behind Pedro Martinez's .712 (166–67) and Spud Chandler's .717 (109–43). There are many great performances to ponder. "I'd say it's definitely up there," Hudson finally says. "It was just one of those nights. I wish you could bottle it up." Minutes later, backup catcher Adam Melhuse, who has become a regular behind the plate during Hudson's starts for no reason other than offensive matchups, says something that underscores the extremely high standards the A's have for their right-handed ace. Asked if what he'd just seen was especially impressive, given Hudson's layoff, Melhuse says, "Impressive for someone new to the league, maybe. Not for him."

A couple of hours before Hudson's gem, Mulder is sitting in front of his locker in the visitors' clubhouse at Baltimore's Camden Yards. He's wearing the casual garb that he wears before most games—a gray, long-sleeved T-shirt and some long white Michigan State basketball shorts—and he's in a talkative mood because he's been asked to talk about pitching, and that's a topic he's always eager to discuss. He lights up when he does it, too, leaving the listener with the impression that there's a lot more passion beneath the cool-breeze veneer than people might assume. "I don't consider myself a power pitcher," he says. "I mean, if you consider someone a power-sinker guy, maybe. But I don't think people look at me as a sinker ball pitcher like they would Huddy, and I think that that has a lot to do with the camera angle. I mean, you see the camera angles, and it looks like Huddy's ball moves eight feet. And it does, don't get me wrong, but the way they have cameras set up behind the pitcher, off to one side, you can't see a lefty's movement as much as you see a righty's. Like, sometimes Zito's ball cuts really good, and mine sinks, but you just can't see it. But if you asked hitters, they'd probably say it sinks a lot when I'm going good. As for being considered a power pitcher, I think it's a little different just because I'm so much bigger than Huddy, so people think I'm more of a power guy. But I wouldn't consider myself a power pitcher just for the simple fact that I don't try to strike guys out."

That's not to say Mulder considers himself a finesse pitcher, though. "I'm a little of both," he says. "And that's what I mean by more of a power-sinker guy, if I have to classify it. And really, I think Huddy's in the same class, even though there's some differences in how we use our stuff. He's got a better slider, I can throw a better cutter. Our sinkers are probably similar. We don't really get fly balls, we don't get pop-ups. That's why it cracks me up when people are like, 'Oh, it must be great having all that foul ground in Oakland.' Well yeah, but I never use it. I barely ever get pop-ups in foul ground. It's just the way I pitch, so it doesn't really benefit me that much."

Asked now about Zito's willingness to add a two-seam fastball so that he has a pitch with more movement, Mulder disputes the notion that Zito didn't have movement before he added the pitch. "It's not that his ball doesn't move. It's that his ball doesn't sink," Mulder says. "His ball actually runs a lot, and that's what makes him so effective, because it runs so much. I was talking to Melhuse one day and I said, 'When Barry goes in [on a hitter], does his ball stay straight?' And he said, 'It runs this much,' and he held his hands out, like, a foot apart. And I'll be up there watching him pitch, and he'll throw a fastball in, and it almost hits the guy as he starts to swing. So I start to think, 'How does that happen?' Any time I throw a ball in to a righty, they never swing if it's in, if it's a good pitch in and if it's up. But that's because my ball starts outside and comes back, and his starts over the middle of the plate and runs totally off the plate. That's what makes him so good at coming in at righties."

Still chatty, Mulder flashes some of that brotherly love when talking about what it's been like to watch Zito's struggles. "It's very tough, because you don't know what to say," he says. "You want to try to do something to help him, but it's not really my place to do that. Something I go and tell him isn't just going to make him go, 'Oh, yeah, now I'm better.' And the thing is, everything got so blown up about him pitching poorly, and I know he wasn't pitching well, but I didn't really think he was pitching all that bad. It's just that it seemed like if something *could've* gone wrong for him, it did. If he had second and third and two outs and he jams a guy, where in the past it was caught, now it fell in for a hit. If he threw a pitch off the plate, the guy stuck his bat out and hit a line drive right over the bag. It just seemed like if it could've gone wrong, if he could've made one bad pitch at the wrong time, he did. . . . I didn't really think that it was something where they know what's coming, or he's tipping his pitches. I didn't see that. Everybody had something to say about it, but I'd sit there and watch it, and it just seemed like it was just bad luck. I know there were some pitches he was leaving pitches up, but I didn't see a difference in his style. There were times where he thought he was tipping pitches, and I said, 'Dude, I watched, I didn't see anything.' I wanted to almost reinforce to him that 'Don't think that's what it is, because I don't think it is.' But it was definitely tough to watch that happen. It's like I almost feel bad that everybody was giving him their opinion on why and this and that, and I wanted to tell people, 'You know what? Just quit talking to him. Quit telling him you think it's this, or quit telling him you think it's that. Just let him worry about going out and doing his thing and he'll be fine.'"

And finally, he's asked to submit yet another opinion on Zito, only this time in reference to what's gone right over the past couple of weeks. "I see a little more confidence out there," he says. "You can tell when Barry's feeling it. You can see it in the look on his face, like, 'Okay, bitch, come and get me.' And you see that more now. Plus, it just seems like the pitches that were just over the plate are now a little bit more in, and he's getting the jam shot and it's not dropping in. So his bad luck has turned a little. But mainly, I think it's just confidence."

Confidence, of course, has never been much of an issue for

Mulder. "I think it's been a problem with Barry this year, maybe as far as the way he prepares," he says. "He wants to know guys' weaknesses, and maybe he could use a little less of that and just trust his stuff, because he's got great stuff. Personally, when I go into a start, I want to know who swings early, who bunts, and who swings early with runners in scoring position. That's all I want to know, because I'm gonna pitch my game no matter who's there in the box. My stuff isn't exactly like anybody else's, and neither is Barry's. I'm pitching my game no matter what."

Backed by a career-high three home runs from Durazo, the last of which is a tie-breaking solo blast in the eighth inning, Mulder gets his MLB-leading sixteenth win on August 18. The start of the game is delayed by rain for fifty-seven minutes, and though Mulder later insists that it hadn't affected him, he allows four runs on five hits in the first three innings before settling in. Baltimore manages just one hit thereafter, and with the help of two double plays and a perfect pick-off move that gets him a big out in the fifth inning, Mulder faces the minimum fifteen batters over his final five innings before handing off to Dotel for the ninth. Nonetheless, his confidence actually sounds a bit shaken a day after he'd discussed Zito's occasional need for more of it. He'd thrown only ninety-one pitches over eight innings, which is good. But he'd thrown forty-one balls, which for him is bad. "That's not him," says Macha, and Mulder knows it. "It seemed like I was 2–0 on everybody," he says. "But then I'd throw a pretty good pitch and get a big out. . . . I think Chavvy described it best. He said, 'Dude, you've become effectively wild.'. . . I was just battling, trying to stick around long enough to let the offense come around." Later in the night he's more candid, expanding on what's become a bit of a theme with him after games. "Something still doesn't feel . . . I don't know . . . *right*," he says. "I feel like I'm getting away with something right now with all these wins, because something's fucked up. I'm not sure what it is, but it's there."

The rest of the A's don't seem concerned about anything at this point. It's go time, and they're going nuts. After a day off in Tampa to enjoy their sweep of the Orioles, they beat the Devil Rays in the opener of a three-game series at the bad joke that is the dome over Tropicana Field. Harden gets his fifth consecutive win, Chavez hits two homers to give him twenty-three for the year, and Rhodes retires all four batters he faces in his return from the disabled list as four Oakland relievers combine on 3⅔ innings of one-hit work. A day later comes an even more welcome sight: Zito throws eight shutout innings as the A's extend their winning streak to five games, improving to 70–52 on the year, while still clinging to a half-game lead in the division. "This is the best I've felt in a long time," Zito says, after scattering four hits. "I can't remember the last time I've felt this good." And when Zito feels good, his teammates feel even better. He's 5–2 since the All-Star break, and he has a 2.08 ERA over his last three starts. "He's throwing the ball so well, and we really need him right now," Chavez says. "He's really stepping up. He looks great. Last week he got a bum deal at home, but I told him he would be the key for us down the stretch. He'll be right back on the map with what he's doing."

Now 9–9 on the year, Zito says the reasons for his improvement are many. (1) He's throwing his curveball for strikes with more consistency, so he's getting ahead in the count. (2) The two-seam fastball is hell on lefties. (3) He's thinking less, enjoying the purity of the game more. And finally, what he says might be the most significant reason of all: (4) He's throwing his changeup harder. "People were sitting on my changeup because even though I wasn't tipping it with my grip or my glove or whatever everyone was saying, it was almost like I was tipping it because I was taking so much off it," he says. "It had gotten to the point where it was, like, fifteen miles an hour slower than my fastball, and that's too much, because it gives guys time to recognize it and reload their swings. Now it's more like ten miles an hour slower, which is perfect. . . . I'm just being more violent on the arm action, and that lets me get away with leaving it up more; it gets fouled off more."

Redman loses the finale of the Tampa Bay series, but that does little to slow the A's, who head home with a 5–2 record on the road trip or seven more games against the overmatched Orioles and Rays. Everything is clicking now, and not even Tejada's first appearance in Oakland as an opponent can take the focus off how well the A's are playing. Down 3–1 going into the bottom of the sixth inning of the home stand opener, they score three runs to get Hudson a win, which is secured by spotless relief from Rincon and Dotel. Mulder follows that with his seventeenth win, but he walks three and hits two batters while allowing two runs on four hits through six innings. So he's again unimpressed with his performance when recounting a conversation he'd had in the dugout with Bradford, who had gotten two big outs to end the seventh inning. "Chad came off the field and I said, 'Nice job.' He says, 'You, too,' and I said, 'Yeah, right. Four hits, three walks, and I hit two guys.' He says, 'Dude, six innings, two runs.'" Mulder shrugs. "He's right to an extent. I mean, six innings and two runs is fine. But nine base runners in six innings, to me, isn't."

The wins just keep coming. The A's are on their typical August roll, and the Orioles, the Devil Rays, and the White Sox are in the way. Harden throws eight shutout innings and Scutaro hits a three-run homer in the bottom of the ninth on August 25, and an undernourished Zito completes the sweep of Baltimore the next day. "I felt good, but I was thinking back, and my nutrition wasn't right," Zito says to the bemused media. "I had a protein shake [Wednesday night] and hadn't really had a meal since. . . . I was so spaced out. I was really spacey out there for the first three innings, and then the last two innings I really made myself calm down. I couldn't focus, so I attribute that to the lack of eating right." To which Susan Slusser, the veteran *San Francisco Chronicle* beat writer, later says, "The old Barry is back, on the field and off. He's back to being weird and funny, and he's back to pitching great. I think there's a connection."

So in come the Devil Rays, and the A's win three more, including Hudson's tenth win of the year in the series finale. Then Harden extends the winning streak to eight games by beating Chicago in the opener of the last trip of the month. It's also the last game of August, giving Oakland another twenty-win month. "I don't know what it is about us and August," Hudson says. "But I like it." There's more to like in early September, too. Though Zito gets Hudsoned on the first day of the month when the bullpen blows his 4–2 lead in the seventh inning, Redman shines on the road again in the series finale to become the fourth member of the starting rotation with at least ten wins, and the A's take the first two of three at Toronto. Hudson gets his eleventh win in the opener against the Jays, despite allowing his first home run since May 8, and Oakland shakes off another mysteriously mortal outing by Mulder, who quietly got away with another sub-par month in August (5.14 ERA) by going 3–1. He gives up ten hits and leaves after six innings trailing 5–2, but the offense explodes late for a 9–5 win. Mulder, whose ERA is up to 3.90, gets the kind of no-decision a pitcher doesn't mind. "This was huge," says Byrnes. "So often this year Mulder has picked us up, and it's nice to kind of return the favor for a change."

Harden, pitching in his native country for the first time as a big-leaguer, gets hammered for seven runs in four-plus innings as his six-game winning streak ends in the finale of the Toronto series. But as the A's head home from Canada on September 5 for the start of the stretch run, they're winners of fifteen of their last eighteen games and on top of the division by three games. And everyone's looking forward to the challenge that awaits in the form of the Red Sox, who have won seventeen of nineteen. "This," Hudson says, "is gonna be fun. This is what we play for."

18

CRUNCH TIME

The obvious angle as the Red Sox roll into town for a three-game series is that it's a potential preview of a postseason rematch of the 2003 ALDS. The phrase *"If the playoffs were to start today . . ."* can be found in virtually every series preview, noting that the A's and Boston, the AL wild card leaders, would be squaring off in the first round. "But they don't start today," Macha says before the opener. "After today we have twenty-five games left, and I believe they've got twenty-six. We play the Angels and Rangers a bunch more times. They play the Yankees a bunch more times. I think people temporarily lose sight of all that." Thus, Macha says he's treating the series not as a playoff preview but as just another hurdle on the path to the playoffs, and his players follow suit. "There's so much baseball left," says Chavez. "I know people want to make this a 'statement series' or whatever, but whoever wins this series could still end up out of the playoffs, and whoever loses it could end up in." Adds Hudson, "It's excitin' when you play another one of the big-time teams like this, but there's a lot of meat left on the bone here in this race. I'm sure there's gonna be a playoff atmosphere here, but it ain't the playoffs."

Good thing, too. If it were a playoff series, it would have been Oakland's most embarrassing exit. Dating to the 2003 ALDS, the Red Sox entered the series having won eight of their last nine games against the A's—and five of six this year, by the cumulative score of 53–33. They leave the series with a sweep, by a cumulative score of 23–7, and only the opener of the series is even close.

Zito is sharp for much of his Monday-night outing, holding Boston to two runs through the first six innings. But the runs come on back-to-back homers by Manny Ramirez and David Ortiz in the fourth inning, wiping out a 2–0 lead while pushing Zito's career-high total for homers allowed in a season to twenty-six. "I'm not the first guy to give up homers to those guys," Zito says of Boston's dual MVP candidates. "But that doesn't mean it's not frustrating. You work your ass off to get those guys out." The Red Sox—all of them—make Zito work for everything. His pitch count is at 34 by the end of the second inning, 65 through the fourth, and 106 after the sixth. A single and two doubles chase Zito with one out in the top of the seventh, the Oakland bullpen gives up four runs—three come on a bases-loaded double by Ortiz off Rhodes—while getting the next eight outs, and the 8–3 loss brings to light an interesting statistic. In Zito's ten losses thus far, the A's offense has scored a total of twelve runs while he's been in the game. "I thought Barry threw the ball very well," says Macha. "He continues to pitch well and has nothing to show for it." Told of the lack of run support he's received in his losses, Zito admits that he's noticed it but insists he's not bothered by it. "Right now, I'm so locked in on what little there is that I can control in this game, I can't let that even enter my thought process. All I can really control is the way I'm pitching, and I'm pretty happy about what I've been able to do in the second half."

Redman gets even less support in the second game of the series; the A's score their only run when Miller grounds into a third-inning double play. But as far as story lines go, the lack of offense takes a backseat to Redman's struggles at home. In allowing six earned runs over 5⅔ innings, he sees his ERA in Oakland jump from 7.04 to 7.25 on the year. And when he's asked if it's weighing on his mind, he once again spits out the sourness that separates him from the Big Three and even Harden, who at twenty-two seems to already have learned how beneficial—and easy—it can be to make nice with the media. "I think it's more on *your* mind," Redman says. "Next question."

What's on everybody's mind even before Redman's latest disaster is Hudson's much-hyped start on Wednesday, September 8, against Pedro Martinez in the series finale. So as he dresses for batting practice Tuesday, Hudson stops a reporter's question about the matchup and calls out to the rest of the scribes, who are killing time with small talk near the clubhouse stereo. "Hey, media," Hudson yells, playfully waving everyone over. "If y'all got Pedro questions, get over here now. This is the last time I'm gonna talk about it." But after the pack heads for the daily skull session with Macha in the dugout, Hudson agrees to another brief conversation on the topic and expresses a measure of disdain. "How come it's always, 'What's it like to face Pedro?'" he asks. "How come nobody's over there [in the Boston clubhouse] asking Pedro what it's like to face me? I've pitched against the guy a bunch of times already, and I've beaten him more than he's beaten me, you know." Sure enough, Hudson is 2–1 in three regular-season meetings with Martinez heading into the game, including a two-hit shutout in August 2003. "I'm not saying I'm better than him, but gimme a break," Hudson says. "The guy's human." And so, quite obviously, is Hudson—especially against these Red Sox.

When Hudson is painting the black borders of home plate, twenty-six pitches get him through three innings. Maybe even four. In the first inning Wednesday, twenty-six pitches get him one out. When Hudson is burying sinkers in the lower half of the strike zone, the other team's leadoff man doesn't get his third at-bat until the sixth inning. On Wednesday, Boston's Johnny Damon gets his third at-bat with one out in the third. And when Hudson is at his bulldog best, he rises to the challenge of facing another ace and spins the kind of gem that stops losing streaks and leaves base runners stranded and purists in awe. On Wednesday, instead of locking horns with the mighty Martinez, who holds up his end of the deal with six innings of two-hit work, Hudson turns in one of the worst performances of his career as the A's lose their fourth in a row, 8–3.

The most startling aspect of Hudson's performance comes when he walks the first three batters of the game. "I don't think I've ever seen him do that," Macha says, and he hasn't. "Definitely not in the big leagues," Hudson says. "Maybe in Little League." In lasting a season-low three innings, Hudson gives up six hits and a season-high five walks, hits a guy, and surrenders a season-high seven earned runs. Going into the game, his ERA was the best in the American League, at 2.95. Now it's up by more than a third of a run, to 3.30. "I just wasn't very good," he says. "I just didn't make any pitches. . . . I've got no excuses. Got nobody to blame but myself. We needed me to come up big and I didn't, and that's what sucks. This team counts on me, and usually I'm able to come through. This time I didn't." Hudson also dismisses the suggestion that he might have been too geeked up for the game, resulting in that flattened out sinker. He says his emotions were well in check, and while his pride has taken a hit, his sense of humor remains very much intact. "Actually, I was pretty calm out there," he says in private. "Calmly gettin' my ass kicked."

Enter the Indians, who haven't exactly cowered in the presence of Oakland's aces this year, either. And as evidenced by a column that runs in the *Chronicle* the day after Hudson's loss to the Red Sox, alarms are sounding. "Don't look now," writes Glenn Dickey, "but the A's starting rotation, which should be their strength, has developed some serious holes." Dickey, understand, generally shows up for about ten games a year in Oakland, so he's hardly an expert. But his premise is unassailable, and the biggest hole in the rotation has become the spot occupied by Mulder, whose 5.14 ERA in August suggested that his 5.11 in July was no fluke. Dickey makes the case that Mulder's mechanics are the problem, and that case is based on Young's assertion that Mulder's arm angle has dropped slightly, preventing him from getting "on top" of his pitches and causing them to "run" through the strike zone horizontally, rather than sink through it vertically. But a day after giving up a game-tying homer to Tribe leadoff man Coco Crisp in the eighth inning of what became a 4–3 loss in eleven innings, Mulder says mechanics have become the least of his problems.

No doubt because he'd held the Indians to three runs over

seven-plus innings, Mulder refers to his second-half struggles in the past tense. Yet his guard is clearly down, and while autographing a box of baseballs, he occasionally slips into the present tense while making what, for him, is a jaw-dropping admission. Mark Mulder, who had cruised through the first 4½ years of his big-league career coolly meeting his stated goal of not thinking on the mound while letting his bevy of physical gifts guide him, says he's been thinking *too much.*

"It wasn't as much mechanical as it was in my own head," he says of his funk. "And that's so rare for me, which is why it's so frustrating. Anything I've ever done in sports or anything like that, when there's something wrong, I've been able to correct it like that." He snaps his fingers for effect. "It was no big deal. It was, 'Make an adjustment, I'll fix it.' But this is the first time I've actually dealt with something that I couldn't just fix, to where my release point and things like that started getting into my own head. That's just not me. I kept thinking to myself, 'This doesn't happen to me.' And that's what became so frustrating, because I've never had to deal with anything like this. . . . You could show me a new pitch, and within two starts, I'll be like, 'Okay, I got it.' I can just pick things up real quick. I can make adjustments between starts, between innings, between pitches, whatever. This is the first time where I can't do it, or I can't do it quickly. So I've tried to take a different mind-set of, 'OK, this might not be an overnight thing this time.' Two weeks ago, I walked six guys [against Tampa Bay], and that was probably as frustrated as I've ever been in my entire pro career, and things like that, shit I've been dealing with over the past month or two, I've never dealt with any of it."

Suddenly and inexplicably, Mulder knows what it's like to be the other guy. The guy who has doubts. The guy whose confidence disappears from time to time. The guy for whom the very difficult game of baseball has never been, and never will be, easy. "It's changed my mind-set," he says. "What I'm going through has nothing to do with working hard. You know, it's not like I can work a little harder or do a little extra and I'm fixed. It's not like that. Me throwing eighty pitches in a side is not going to fix it. It's getting the right mind-set. It's getting the confidence. It's getting the stupid stuff out of your head, the stuff that I've never thought of in my entire life when I'm out on the mound. I mean, there's been times during this when I've actually been worried about where my hands are in my delivery *while* I'm throwing a pitch. Are you kidding me? I don't think about that. Screw that. I'm normally like, 'Here it is. Try to hit it.'. . . I've never been like this, and now all of a sudden I am? Why? That's the whole thing. Why, all of a sudden, am I thinking so much? I have no idea."

Much like Zito making a concession to the physical side of the game by adding a new pitch at the All-Star break, this is Mulder making a rare concession to the mental side of the game. And in doing so, he makes another fairly shocking—and extremely amusing—admission. In search of answers that might help him win this first foray into the head games so many other elite athletes play, Mulder has turned to the grand master of head games. *Paging Dr. Zito.*

"You know what? I talked to him about it when we were in Chicago. I talked to him for probably thirty, forty minutes in the dugout about it," Mulder says. "And he joked around with me, 'See, now you know what I go through every day.' And I kind of looked at him and laughed. He said, 'So the shit that's going on in your head right now, it's never crossed your mind?' And I'm like, 'No.' He said, 'Dude, I've been dealing with this since I was ten.' That's what he said to me. . . . It was funny in a way, but it actually helped me to relax because I was so worried about it, thinking, 'Why can't we fix this?' In a weird way, him saying to me, 'Dude, I deal with this every day,' it helped me. You realize that this is not that bad. This is not something you can't overcome, or get rid of. It was a funny conversation, but in the long run it helped."

Reminded that, earlier in the season, he had said he avoids discussing pitching with Zito, Mulder laughs. "I know. I know that's what I said," he admits. "But we weren't talking about pitching, really. It was just, 'Why am I thinking too much?' That's why I asked him, because I wanted to know if this is what he was talking about when he says he thinks too much. And in a way it was. It was so comical. The things I was explaining to him about what's going through my head, he was just listening and going, 'Yeah. . . . Uh-huh. . . . Yeah. . . . Welcome to my world.' Then he said, 'You've never thought of this? You've never doubted yourself?' I said, 'Never,' and that's the truth. Never once have I had these bad thoughts going through my head when I'm out on the mound—*ever*! I don't do that in anything I do. I'm not one to worry about stuff. I don't *do* this. This isn't me. I'm like, 'This doesn't happen to me. This *shouldn't* happen to me.' But it *was* happening to me, and yeah, it freaked me out a little."

Recalling the conversation with Mulder in Chicago, Zito, too, laughs. "Oh, you mean 'the Talk'?" Zito says. "Pretty ironic, isn't it, Mulder coming to me? But I thought it was great. He said, 'Z, I wanna talk to you, because I've got some stuff going on in my head,' and he asked me a couple of questions about, you know, how to just deal with all of it. And a lot of what he said really amazes me, because he said that only recently has it ever been this way for him. I was like, 'Wow. That's incredible, dude.' Because where he was before this, that's where I'm trying to get: to *not* think. I was just kind of being an ear for him more than giving advice. Just let him get some shit out, let him talk about it and try to help him as much as I could by being there for him."

And in doing that, Zito felt a connection he'd never before felt. "I think it'll make us closer," he says. "Because contrary to what some people might think, a lot of players don't talk to other guys about what goes on in their heads. It's a manly thing. Nobody wants to give up their edge, or whatever they think their edge might be. With me personally, I don't mind. A lot of people let ego get in the way and don't want to be vulnerable, but I'll go up to Huddy all the time and ask him what he thinks about this or that. It's just good to get a fresh opinion from someone who's got a more objective look at you. So from that perspective, I thought it was cool that Mark wanted to talk about some of these things. It's a big step for him. And not that I wasn't pulling for him before, but knowing what a guy's dealing with out there, and being able to relate to that because you've fought some of those same battles, I think it's only human to make you want to see him do that much better."

~ ~ ~

Mulder's loss to the Tribe was Oakland's fifth in a row, and the division lead is down to one game as Harden takes the hill for the second game of the series on September 11. And when he leaves the game trailing by four runs after the seventh inning, it looks like a dark day for the A's. But with three runs in the bottom of the seventh, back-to-back homers by Crosby and fellow rookie Nick Swisher in the eighth, and a fine performance from the bullpen (Dotel's nineteenth save in twenty-four chances with Oakland caps it), the A's take a thrilling a 5–4 victory that snaps the losing streak and gives them an instant jolt of much-needed confidence. "It's huge," says Crosby, whose nineteenth homer of the year pulls him into a fourth-place tie with Ernie Banks (1954) for most homers by a rookie shortstop. "A loss today would have been tough to swallow." Instead, the A's get a victory that pushes the division lead back to two games, ensuring that when a twenty-game push to the end of the regular season starts Monday with a visit from Texas, they'll still be atop the AL West. "It's unbelievable," says Swisher, who'd been called up from triple-A Sacramento the previous weekend in Toronto. "To be here and helping these guys in a pennant race is so far beyond my wildest dreams, it's ridiculous."

Better still, Zito and the bullpen have another fine day Sunday, Durazo's career-high twenty-second homer is enough for a 1–0 win, and when the Indians leave town, they take with them a lot of bad juju for the A's. Against the Tribe, the Red Sox, and the Yankees this year, Oakland is 6–21, for a winning percentage of .222. The A's are 23–15 (.605) thus far against the teams they'll play over the final twenty games of the year, the AL West's Angels, Rangers, and Mariners. "We couldn't ask for anything more," says Zito, who improves to 7–3 since the All-Star break by scattering five hits and two walks, while striking out a season-high ten over seven innings. "This is what it's all about. That's what you look forward to from the first day of spring training, that chance to be right there down the stretch." That Zito's masterpiece comes in front of a national television audience doesn't escape the notice of Byrnes, who says he expected nothing less than a great night from his good friend. "Z's a performer, man, and what performer doesn't love a big stage?" Byrnes gushes. "He was awesome." Macha has a similar sentiment; three hours before the first pitch, he'd predicted a "big game" from Zito, and sure enough, only two runners had gotten past first base against him. "It was a clutch performance when we needed it," Macha says afterward, and particularly clutch was Zito's final inning. With his previous outing against Boston on his mind, he'd lobbied hard to stay in the game, despite having thrown 108 pitches through six innings. "He came in and said, 'Let me go out there for one more inning,'" Macha says. Two strikeouts and a foul pop-up later, Zito walked off the field to a standing ovation and chants of "Barry! Barry!" from a crowd of more than 29,000. "I thought it was important that I prove to Macha that I can go out there after a hundred-plus pitches and throw a quality inning," Zito says. "So yeah, that was big. For me and for the team." The bullpen makes its share of clutch pitches, too, with Hammond and Bradford tag-teaming a dicey eighth and Dotel striking out Crisp to end the game with two on in the ninth. "It was a pitching coach's dream," Macha says. Little did he know that a nightmare was about to unfold.

As the twenty-game stretch drive opens, the A's marketing department hands out T-shirts emblazoned with "Crunch Time" at the opener of a four-game series with the Rangers, who arrive in Oakland five games off the division lead and in danger of slipping out of the race. And though an embarrassingly small crowd of 15,535 shows up, the teams on the field put on an absolute show. Not a pretty show but a show nonetheless. Not long after Texas blows the first save of the night by coughing up three runs in the bottom of the eighth, Mecir gives up Alfonso Soriano's second homer of the night to blow a save for Oakland—Hudson is the victim—with two out in the top of the ninth. And then it gets a little crazy. As Texas third baseman Hank Blalock steps in to face Rincon, who'd followed Mecir into the game, a scuffle erupts between some Rangers relievers and a group of fans down the right-field line. It's a mess that gains national attention, featuring Texas rookie Frank Francisco hitting a woman in the face with a thrown chair, and it delays the game for about twenty minutes. Once order is restored, the Rangers take another lead with a run in the top of the tenth, but Francisco Cordero sticks Texas with its second blown save of the night, and Chavez's two-out single up the middle in the bottom of the inning gives the A's a crazy 7–6 win that keeps their lead over the Angels at two games, while dropping the Rangers six back. "I know everyone's gonna focus on the fight down there, but the game was all that mattered," says Hudson, who'd worked eight solid innings and would have picked up his twelve win of the year had Mecir retired Soriano. "What some dummy does when a fan gets under his skin don't matter. . . . I would have been sick if we'd have lost that game. But we battled, man. We battled, and we won a big one."

And then they lose two big ones. Looking to change his luck at home, Redman essentially admits that he, too, is in his own dome when he switches his uniform number from 55 to 18 before the second game of the series. And change his luck it does. From bad to worse. Redman suffers his sixth loss in nine decisions at home, allowing seven runs on six hits, four walks, and a hit batter over 3⅓ innings in a 12–9 loss. But Redman being awful in Oakland is almost expected by now; he's 3–6 with a 7.81 mark at home. Far more disturbing is that Mulder, who had felt so good about his previous outing against Cleveland, looks like he's still a bit of a head case the next night, allowing a season-high eight runs over six innings of a 10–3 loss that pushes his ERA to a season-high 4.13. The Angels lose, too, so the A's lead stays at two games, but that's of little comfort in the clubhouse, where Mulder's problems are getting more and more difficult to sweep under the rug. He's 8–3 since June 27, but his ERA in that span is 5.57, he's winless in his past four starts, and he's allowed twenty runs over twenty-five innings in those starts. The Cy Young Award is slipping away fast. And so the chorus starts: *What's wrong with Mark?*

Most of the same people who'd spent the first half dissecting Zito are now poking and prodding Mulder, but there aren't nearly as many theories. The main one is that he's hurt. His velocity is down, from 92–94 mph to a consistent 88, so the assumption is that his arm is injured, fatigued, or both. Mulder dismisses the many health questions that come his way, insisting that he's physically sound, and he also dismisses the idea that the dip in velocity has much to do with what he's going through. "Zito pitches at 88, 89 every day, and he won a Cy Young," Mulder notes. "Jamie Moyer throws in the low- to mid-80s, and he won twenty games last year. Velocity is overrated; that's why I have the radar gun turned off when I pitch at home. I don't *want* to know how hard I'm throwing, because that doesn't make a difference to me. What matters is making pitches, and for whatever reason, I'm not making pitches right now. My ball's not moving the way it normally moves, so when I don't hit the spot I'm trying to hit, when I get a ball up, instead of a guy maybe fouling it off, he hits it out or off the wall. I'm just not getting away with any mistakes whatsoever right now."

—   —   —

Harden gets the A's back into the win column by beating Texas in the series finale, getting 2⅔ innings of shutout help from the bullpen in the process, and his victory makes a little bit of Oakland history. It's Harden's tenth win of the year, giving the A's five starters who have at least ten wins for the first time since the franchise moved from Kansas City to California in 1968. It's a nice little nugget, but the only nuggets the A's are concerned with at the moment are the sparkling ones that would encrust a World Series ring, and with Boston running away with the wild card race, it's clear that the only team from the AL West that will get a shot at those rings will have to win the division. So as the A's pack up for their final road trip of the year, a ten-day jaunt on which they'll play three games in Seattle, three in Texas, and three in Anaheim, the mood in the clubhouse is far more serious than it is after a typical win. "We've always kind of had that wild card to fall back on, but now it's pretty much gone," Hudson says. "It's win this bitch or get ready for some TV-watchin' in October."

Gentlemen, start your flat screens. On the heels of his genius against Cleveland, Zito allows a run on four hits over six mostly dominant innings in the series opener in Seattle on September 17, but Macha doesn't let him take the mound for the seventh, in which three relievers give up five runs to turn a 3–1 lead into a 6–3 loss that cuts the division lead to one. Zito had thrown 125 pitches against Cleveland, the second-most of his career, and Macha cites Zito's pitch count of 106 through six innings against Seattle as the main reason for pulling him. Zito doesn't openly question the move, but he does make a fairly forceful point when asked about it. "I think pitch counts are important; you want to keep guys healthy," he says. "But there should be less attention on them when you're in a pennant race in September." It starts the road trip on a sour note, but two days later, life is sweet again.

In the second game of the series, Dye returns from a two-week absence from the lineup necessitated by a fractured thumb suffered in Minnesota and helps Hudson, who admits to having less than his best stuff, pick up his twelfth win. "I was terrible in the bullpen," Hudson says after getting fifteen ground-ball outs while allowing three runs on eight hits over eight innings. "But I had a decent sinker, so I just kept flippin' it up there and hopin' they'd keep beatin' it into the ground." A day later, Redman makes another case for a name change to Roadman—he's 8–6 with a 2.88 ERA away from home—by allowing a run over 6⅔ innings, and three relievers take care of business from there to post a 2–1 victory that pushes Oakland's division lead to three games with thirteen games to play. Bret Boone, Seattle's star second baseman, essentially tells the *Chronicle* that the race might be over. "The A's have three legitimate number one starters—who else has that? Nobody," he says. "There's a reason they have that many wins. Guys like that, even if they don't have their best stuff, they give you a chance to win every time."

Mulder, however, doesn't give the A's a chance to win the opener in Texas. He gives up three runs in the first inning and four in the fourth, and he can't get an out before being yanked in the fifth. The A's lose 9–4, and although Macha says Mulder is "still our number one guy," Mulder sounds like anything but that after the game. His ERA is up to 4.25, his private admission to struggling with the mental side of the game goes public for the first time, and he's unrelenting in ripping himself. "It was horrible, embarrassing," he says. "It's been like this for a while. I need to do something. I'm not doing the team any good. It's ridiculous. I feel like a hitter who's gone 0-for-100." And now he's saying of himself what he was saying in Baltimore when talking about Zito's first-half problems. "If I have a chance to make a good pitch, I don't. . . . If there's a spot where I can't make a bad pitch, I do. I'm making bad pitches, and guys are hitting doubles . . . It's not one particular thing, and that's why it's so frustrating." Mulder reiterates that he's 100 percent healthy, but a few minutes later, over in another corner of the near-silent clubhouse, Chavez isn't so sure.

"You look at his velocity and it makes you nervous," Chavez says. "Maybe all those complete games are starting to catch up with him, I don't know. But when you see a guy who typically throws 92–94 dropping down to 88, it makes you wonder. I don't care about his control or whatever else is going on. You watch the hitters. They'll tell you everything, and right now I see a lot of loud outs and a lot of hard-hit balls. That's a little scary to see with Mark up there, definitely." Adds Miller, the veteran catcher who's handled so many great pitchers over the years, "I wish I had an answer for what Mark's going through, but I don't." He does, however, suggest that Mulder is "babying" his pitches in an effort to find the right arm slot. "That's just the way this game goes," he says. "Everything clicked for Mark in the first half, but right now nothing's clicking. Once you think you've got it figured out, the game comes back to bite you. . . . He's got two more starts to work it out, though, so we'll just keep plugging along."

Chavez gets something else off his chest while dressing, too. Lowering his voice to a near whisper, he says something nobody else in the organization will say: the Big Three miss Peterson. "Anyone who says they don't is in denial," he insists. "Say what you want about Rick, and I know some people don't like him, but you don't have to like him to know what a great job he did when he was here. Look at what's happened. All three guys are off a little. How can anyone honestly say that Rick wouldn't have been able to help? Nothing against Curt, but if you think these pitchers don't miss Rick, I think you're stupid. It's obvious."

The pall cast by the loss carries over into the next two games. Needing a sweep to stay alive, the Rangers pull it off, and they do it by becoming the only team not based in the Bronx to sweep three games started by Oakland's Big Three. Zito enters the second game of the series with a 3.12 ERA for the month and gives up seven hits, four walks, and five runs in five innings before being lifted with a pitch count of 117. "I was trying to be too fine," he says after falling to 11–11. "I was trying to paint the black instead of going right after guys." Over the last sixteen games, in which the A's are 6–10, the starting pitchers are 4–8 with a 6.60 ERA. "Obviously, it stands out as a red flag, because this staff has had a lot of success on the mound," says center fielder Mark Kotsay, who has quietly put together a career year at the plate. "But we're still leading the division. Everybody is chasing us." Hudson enters the

Series finale with a 6.23 ERA in four September starts but pitches well, leaving with a 3–2 lead after seven innings, and Crosby homers in the top of the ninth for a big insurance run. Dotel, though, gives up three runs in the bottom of the ninth, and the A's walk off losers, 5–4. "This one hurts real bad, man," Dotel says after Hudson is Hudsoned yet again. "The worst of the year? Yeah, I'd say so. For me, anyway. We had this game won, and I lost it. These guys count on me, and I didn't do it. It's a tough loss. Really tough." Asked about the latest bullpen blowup, Hudson refuses to beat the dead horse, which has already been beaten beyond recognition. "It ain't just the bullpen," he says. "It's all of us. We're stinkin' it up right now."

Fortunately for the A's, the Angels have turned cold, too. And when Harden—8–1 since the All-Star break—comes to the rescue by winning the opener in Anaheim, Oakland's lead in the West is three games with ten to play. In the history of major league baseball, only five teams have been in that position and not won the race. "After the series we had in Texas, I think some guys might have been feeling a little pressure," Harden says. "This should take a little pressure off."

Uh, no. Redman pitches okay on Saturday, but the bullpen allows two runs in the eighth, and the A's fall 5–3. The next day is much worse. Mulder reaches another new low, getting the hook after allowing four runs in 3⅔ innings of a 6–2 loss that sends the A's back home for the final week of the season—four against the last-place Mariners, three against the fast-closing Angels—desperately looking for positives. They've lost thirteen of their last twenty games, the lead is down to one, and Mulder is in a two-month freefall. But as usual, they cling to the notion that they're still the chased, not the chasers. And the chasers will have to do their chasing in Oakland, where the A's are 49–24 this year. "If you'd have told me back in spring training that we'd have a one-game lead going into the last seven at home, I'd say those are pretty good odds," says Hatteberg. "If I was a betting man, I'd say it's going to go down to the final three games."

19

FITTING FINALE

Sitting at his locker on Monday, September 27, before the A's open their final home stand of the year with the first of four games against Seattle, Damian Miller expresses amazement at the courtesy extended to Mulder the night before by the group of beat writers who follow the A's. After most games, the manager is the first person with whom the media speaks, followed by a scrum with that night's starting pitcher. That's how it had gone Sunday, too, and here's what Ken Macha, when asked if Mulder would get the ball again the following Friday in the opener of what's expected to be a winner-take-all series with the Angels, had said: "I'm sure there'll be a discussion on the situation. That's an extremely difficult decision to make. This guy's our horse. We relied on him all year, and there were some games earlier in the year when he picked everybody up because of an overworked bullpen or whatever. So it's tough. The kid does nothing but give you all he's got out there. I'm not gonna be committal one way or another. I'll talk directly to Mark. . . . I don't want to make it a big issue right now."

Taking that last sentence to heart, most of the A's writers had decided, independently, to refrain from asking Mulder about

Macha's comments until after the two had a chance to discuss the situation in private. After all, Mulder hadn't won since August 24, he had a whopping 8.10 ERA in five September starts, he'd lost the last three of those, and the A's were staggering home from a 3–6 road trip. It's not like the writers didn't already have plenty of material for the night. So Mulder had fielded just one question about the once-unthinkable possibility of his turn in the rotation being skipped, and his response—"Why *wouldn't* I want the ball?"—was predictable.

"If Macha had said that in New York or Boston or Philadelphia or Chicago, Mulder would have been crushed right then and there," says Miller. "That's all he'd have been asked about. 'Macha says you might not start. What do you say to that? Does it piss you off?' It would have been nonstop, a huge shitstorm." Instead, it's not that much of a storm at all, but it's clear on Monday that Macha's request that the topic not become an issue has fallen on deaf ears in the Bay Area. It's not just an issue. It's *the* issue, and after reiterating about six thousand times before batting practice what he'd said Sunday, Mulder knows it. "I expected it," he says of the questions. "I mean, it's not like I don't know that I've been shitty. This is the most important time of the year, and I've been awful. But do I think I can turn it around? Of course, I do. This is my time. I love this time of year. This is why I play baseball, to pitch this time of year and to pitch in the playoffs. It's why I love it so much."

Earlier in the year, when Zito was battling his own demons, never did his teammates express anything less than complete confidence in his ability to bounce back. "Even when Barry was pitching poorly, he'd have flashes of brilliance," Eric Byrnes says. "Whether you saw it in one inning, or one start, or even one batter, you knew that it was still there, and that it was just a matter of time before he really got it going." With Mulder struggling, though, it's a little bit different. Nobody out and out rips him, but nobody's particularly shy about expressing the depth of his concern. "He lost the magic touch out there with the movement he has on the baseball," Young said, after the Sunday loss in Anaheim. Added Scott Hatteberg, "It's no secret how long it's been. He's just not the same guy he was in the first half." Chavez, of course, had already weighed in with his thoughts, and even Hudson admits that Mulder's woes have him baffled. "Performance-wise, when Barry was strugglin', there were signs of the Cy Young Barry Zito," he says, echoing Byrnes. "But it seems like when Mulder started struggling, it was like his golf game. It was here one day and gone the next, with no signs of where it went."

Mulder agrees. He sees the obvious similarities between his funk and Zito's, but he sees the differences, too. "Mine was way worse than his," he says. "For one thing, I think that mine was way more magnified because it was during the stretch run. But I still think that mine was worse than his. He was bad, then pretty good, then bad, then good. He was just inconsistent, more than anything. I was consistent. Consistently bad." That he's again referring to his funk as though it's in the past seems to suggest that his confidence is coming back, and he insists that it has. One reason for that, he says in private, was a brief visit from Billy Beane, who'd gone to him earlier in the day with an uplifting message. "He said, 'I wouldn't care if you were 0–15. You'd *still* be starting," Mulder says. "And you know what? That's what really matters. People can say or write whatever they want, and that's their jobs. I understand that. But it's people like Billy, people who know the game and know me and know what I'm capable of, who you worry about what they think. And for him to come and tell me that, that's all I need to hear."

Not long after Mulder talks about the vote of confidence he'd gotten from Beane, Macha, speaking with reporters during batting practice, makes it official: Mulder, who has failed in six consecutive bids for his eighteenth win of the year and fallen hard out of Cy Young consideration, will get one more chance. Following him in the Angels series will be Zito and Hudson, so if Hatteberg is right, and the race does indeed all go down to the final series against the Angels, the three biggest games of Oakland's season will be in the hands of the Big Three. "It's been that way for the past four years, if you think about it," Mulder says. "Maybe not right down to the end, but it usually comes down to what me and Zito and Huddy can do. We've done what we've done as a team for a reason, and this is our time to go out and get the job done. There's no time for excuses. There's no time for anything. We're the ones the team needs to step up, and it's on our shoulders. And it's not that I say it's always just the three of us. It's Rich, it's Redman, and everybody's gotta step up.

But more than anything, the fans and the media look at me and Zito and Huddy to do that. And that's part of it. It's been like that since we got here. We're used to that. We're okay with that."

— — —

Zito throws 111 pitches Monday night, and most of them seem lifted off a highlight reel of his Cy Young season. He spots both of his fastballs well, his changeup gives the Mariners fits for most of the night, and his trademark curveball is so good that it buckles even Edgar Martinez, one of the great hitters of this generation. "I didn't even notice that," Zito says of Martinez's mini-limbo move. "I was feeling it. I was totally locked in." But with the A's leading 5–2 with one out and two runners on in the top of the seventh inning, Zito uncorks a pitch that spoils everything positive that came prior. Willie Bloomquist, Seattle's number nine hitter, tags a three-run, game-tying homer. Crosby wins the game for Oakland with a sacrifice fly in the bottom of the ninth, and it's a huge win; the Angels' win in Texas had already been posted on the out-of-town scoreboard. But that one pitch to Bloomquist leaves Zito so pissed off that he does something he's never before done in his career: he ducks out without taking questions from the media. "I just couldn't hang," Zito says by cell phone on the drive back to his apartment in San Francisco. "I was like, 'You've gotta be shitting me.' One bad changeup, and it's like the whole night was a waste. . . . I just didn't want to talk to anyone. I feel bad now because that's not like me, but I just had to get out of there. . . . Thank God we won the game." If Bloomquist's homer, only his second of the year, had been an isolated incident, Zito probably wouldn't have been so upset. But it wasn't. In Zito's previous start, at Texas, Eric Young hit his *first* homer of the year, also a three-run shot on a changeup, to snap a 2–2 tie. "Two starts in a row now I've felt great, and one bad changeup fucks everything up," Zito says. By Tuesday, though, his frustration is gone. And he notes that this particular kind of frustration is far different from what he was feeling during his miserable first half. "Back then I was just plain shitty," he says. "It wasn't one bad pitch back then. It was a bunch of bad pitches. Now at least I know, when I step back, that I threw a pretty good game, and that makes a huge difference mentally. I'm throwing the ball well now, and I know it."

A few hours later, Hudson has the opposite feeling. He gives seven runs on eleven hits over six innings, pushing his ERA (3.57) higher than it's been since his first start of the season, and the A's never really have a chance in a loss that drops them into a first-place tie with the Angels. Ichiro Suzuki, chasing George Sisler's 1920 major league record of 257 hits in a season, doubles to open the game and start a three-run rally that proves to be all the offense the Mariners need in a 7–2 victory. "Any time you give up three first-inning runs and put that kind of pressure on the offense, it's gonna be a tough night," Hudson says. "I take the blame for this one tonight." So Hatteberg *was* right: the AL West race will be decided this weekend. No matter what happens over the next two days between the A's and the Mariners—or the Rangers and the Angels, for that matter—nothing can change that. "It's a tough loss, especially with a guy like Hudson on the mound," Hatteberg says. "But I think there's still a lot of fight left in this team."

Wednesday, September 29: another day, another step backward toward the Showdown. Clinging to a 2–1 lead, Harden gets the first out in the top of the eighth by winning an epic thirteen-pitch battle with Suzuki, but the next batter, Randy Winn, singles off Harden's leg, and Boone follows with a double. Rincon comes on to strike out Raul Ibanez and heighten the tension, but then Mecir comes out of the bullpen to a quiet chorus of boos from a crowd that's seen this same scenario turn out ugly too many times. Jolbert Cabrera strokes a two-run single. Another run scores on an error. Oakland loses 4–2, and the Angels take a one-game lead in the division with an extra-innings win in Texas. The A's are in second place for the first time since August 5, and now Anaheim will need no more than two wins in the final series to claim the crown. "Tonight I didn't get it done," says Mecir, who gets a friendly pat on the back from Harden as he eats in the quiet A's clubhouse. "But we've got four games left, and we just have to go out and do it." What they have to do is win three of their final four games, and there isn't much to suggest that it's possible at this point. They've lost four games in the standings in five days, and Redman, of all people, is the man who the A's need to come through in the Seattle series finale. There really isn't much reason to be upbeat about anything, but Hudson, bouncing out of the clubhouse on his way to the field Thursday morning before Redman's start, says he has another one of his good feelings.

Never mind Redman's dismal numbers at home, he says. Never mind Oakland's seven losses in the last nine games. Never mind yesterday. "Watch," Hudson says. "Redman's gonna pitch great today, the bullpen's gonna be great, we're gonna win on a walk-off homer, and we're gonna win two out of three this weekend. Watch." A few hours later, after the Angels lose in Texas, Redman gives the A's 5⅔ clutch innings (two earned runs). Four relievers shut the Mariners out for 3⅓ innings. And after Crosby's walk-off homer in the bottom of the ninth gives the A's a 3–2 win and another tie in the AL West, Hudson does his best to suppress the urge to gloat over the first half of his prediction coming true. "Just lucky, I guess," he says with a smile. "But I did have a feelin' about all that stuff." The second half of his prediction—winning two of three over the weekend to win the division—is, of course, the part that matters most, and it all comes down to the Big Three. Harden, who is 11–7 with a 3.99 ERA, is the hottest pitcher on the team, but he will pitch only in relief, if at all, over the weekend.

Mark Mulder on Friday, Barry Zito on Saturday, Tim Hudson on Sunday. With everything on the line. "Those are our horses," Macha says. "Mulder, Hudson, and Zito? They have absolutely been the people who have put this organization on the map. I don't think you could have drawn it up any better." Says Dye, "This gives us a lot of confidence. . . . We've got our Big Three going. A couple of them have been struggling lately, but it's time to put all of that behind, give it our all, and see what happens."

For Hudson, still smiling at it all, the weekend can't come soon enough. Having to sit and watch Friday and Saturday, he says, will be a form of torture. But if it leads to everything being on his shoulders come Sunday afternoon, he'll happily bear that weight. "Let's call this what it is, man. This is a playoff series. It's the playoffs before the playoffs," he says. "And it's set up so perfectly, too, with the three of us goin' out there back-to-back-to-back. I can't wait, man. I can't wait to get out there and kick some ass, because everybody's talking about the Big Three chokin', and when we pull this off, it'll be the biggest 'Fuck you' ever."

Can one game provide redemption for three months of frustration? Three months of ineffectiveness? Three months of coping with the unfamiliar sensation of inadequacy? For Mulder it can. Beat the Angels on the first day of October, and all is forgiven. "It would definitely change the way I feel about how much I've contributed in the second half," Mulder says on the eve of his final start, and he certainly isn't the only one who'll feel that way. Beat the Angels, and *What's wrong with Mark?* disappears in the media. Beat the Angels, and the fans stop wringing their hands. Most important, beat the Angels and start getting ready for the postseason. "If I pitch well and we win, I can't see Zito and Huddy both losing the next two days," Mulder says. "So yeah, there's pressure. But it's a good kind of pressure. Honestly. I don't mind it. It's something I can use." As is his history in playoff situations; his ERA in four postseason starts is a stingy 2.25. "It helps, but you can't live off the past," he says. "It's not that you can't use that. 'Okay, I've been in this situation before, I can do it again.' But last year is last year, two years ago is two years ago. You can't live off that. This is a new year."

Is it ever. The sign being paraded around the concourse as a sellout crowd of more than 47,000 pours into the Coliseum for the series opener against the Angels—"Mulder Magic"—is a symbol of hope and optimism, but two innings into the game, the sign and the optimism are gone. And so is Mulder. There is no magic. Mulder's bag of tricks, once so full of devilishly darting pitches, is all but empty against Anaheim, and whatever momentum might have been generated by Crosby's walk-off homer against the Mariners is gone. *Poof!*

Mulder gets through the first inning on thirteen pitches but not before allowing a couple of hard-hit balls. Chavez makes a diving play to rob leadoff man Chone Figgins of a double, but it's one of those "loud outs" of which Chavez spoke back in Texas. After Vladimir Guerrero, in the midst of a late-season MVP push, laces a two-out single to center, another loud out comes in the form of a line drive by Troy Glaus that lands in the glove of Dye in right field. As Mulder walks off the mound, the hopeful crowd salutes him, but the same walk back to the dugout after the top of the second inning is his last walk of the night. Maybe of the season.

It all starts with a pretty good pitch to Garret Anderson, who bounces it into no-man's land between the mound and first base. Mulder, an exceptional fielder who has fielded several ground balls up the middle *behind his back* during his career, usually makes this play, but he can't quite get there in time. Anderson, hobbled by tendinitis in his left knee, hustles his way to an infield single, and it ends up being the snowflake that causes an avalanche. Adam Riggs follows with a ringing double to left-center field, pushing Anderson to third, after which Mulder makes another good pitch to David Eckstein, who grounds it to the right side of the infield. Marco Scutaro throws home in an attempt to nail Anderson, who is laboring down the line, but home plate umpire Brian Runge calls Anderson safe after a high tag from Melhuse, who is catching because Miller has a bruised thumb. Replays show that the tag was applied before Anderson's foot found the plate. "I haven't seen the replay," Mulder says later, "but I've had people tell me he was out. It was a big play in the game."

Jose Molina follows with an RBI single. Another run scores on a double-play ball—another good pitch. But that pitch is followed by a bad one, a flat sinker that Figgins sends into right-center field for a triple. And then comes the play that sums up Mulder's second half. Trying to get a handle on a perfectly placed bunt between the mound and first by Darin Erstad, Mulder stumbles, and as he falls to the turf, his attempt to flip to Hatteberg for the inning-ending out goes awry. He loses his grip on the ball, it squirts harmlessly out of his hand, Figgins scores, and Erstad is safe with another infield single. Mulder quickly bounces off the grass and retires Guerrero on a ground ball to end the inning, but the enduring image of his night has been burned into memory in that second or two that he spent splayed out. Back in the dugout, with the A's down 4–0, Young goes to Mulder and breaks the news: rookie right-hander Joe Blanton, recently called up from triple-A and seen by many as the next ace in Oakland, is taking over to start the third. "Of course, I was surprised," Mulder says. "But you have to look at it both ways. I don't have so big an ego that I want to stay in when I'm hurting the team." Blanton gives up a grand slam to .155-hitting Alfredo Amezaga in the sixth inning of what turns into an embarrassing 10–0 loss, and Bartolo Colon gets the win by holding Oakland to three hits over seven innings. On three days of rest.

After the game, Mulder isn't nearly as dejected as he's been after most of his recent starts. Hudson says he'd heard that Mulder was being clocked at 90–91 on the radar gun, and Melhuse confirms that Mulder's velocity was good, adding that the sinking two-seam fastball on which Mulder relies had shown signs of life. But all of that just makes the night more vexing for Mulder, who again is peppered with questions about his health. "There's no physical problems whatsoever," he says. "I've been saying that forever now. If there was, that'd be a good excuse." So it must be mental, right? "It's not mental anymore, either," he insists. "I felt great out there, and I made some really good pitches." But making "some" good pitches doesn't get the job done. "I made at least three pretty bad ones, too," Mulder admits, "and they hit every one of them hard." Only once before in his career has Mulder gotten the hook so early, and it came during his rookie campaign of 2000, when he left an August start against the Yankees after two innings. "It's tough," he says softly. "These are the situations I love. I want to be that person to go out there and win the big game. It's been a struggle. . . . I feel like I'm letting everyone down."

As Mulder searches for words to further express his disappointment, Hudson comes to his defense. "I know he's gonna take some abuse again, but people better not forget that we got shut out tonight," he says. "Mulder could have thrown a complete game and given up one run tonight and we'd have still lost, so don't put it all on him." Mulder doesn't hear that, and after the crowd of reporters at his locker leaves, he does exactly what Hudson doesn't want anyone to do. He blames himself, and not just for the night. In his seven starts since August 24, Mulder is 0–4 with a 7.27 ERA. He's allowed 28 earned runs while giving up 16 doubles, 7 homers, and a triple over 34⅔ innings. "It sucks," he says. "Barry's been pitching a lot better in the second half. Huddy's gotten his wins. Rich has been great. Even Redman came up big yesterday. And I haven't done anything. If I win just two of my past seven starts, we're in the playoffs already. Two. Two out of seven. And I get none. Nice. Way to go, Mulder. Way to fuck everything up."

Redemption? No. Not even close. But hope? Still flickering.

The two wins Oakland needs to make the playoffs for a fifth consecutive season are still out there to be had. Zito, the performer, takes the stage Saturday, and Hudson, the warrior, is practically frothing at the mouth in anticipation of what could be an all-the-marbles Sunday. "I know it doesn't look good right now," Mulder says. "But we've got two games left, and we've got two great pitchers going."

Scribbled in blue ink on a white greaseboard next to the cork bulletin board in the Oakland clubhouse is the acronym "WOGH"—win or go home. It's been there for the last week, but now it applies quite literally for the first time. Yes, there will be a game Sunday, but it will be a glorified exhibition unless the A's win Saturday. As early as Wednesday, Zito had a feeling that it might come to this, but he was typically philosophical on the subject. "If that's what happens, I don't look at it as having the weight of the world on my shoulders," he says. "I look at it as having to go out and win a baseball game, and that's something I know how to do. I've been doing this my whole life, so it's not like it's going to freak me out all of a sudden. There's a baseball game, I'm pitching, and we need to win. If I pitch well, we will. Pretty simple, really." Not exactly. Nothing has been simple for the A's all season, and Saturday, October 2, is no exception.

Zito enters the game averaging 17.3 pitches an inning, second-highest in the AL, and it takes him 19 pitches to get through the first inning. But after a leadoff single by Anderson in the second, he doesn't give up another hit until the sixth. "I felt really sharp," Zito says. "Spotted my fastball, good curveball. I didn't throw a lot of changeups, but the ones I threw were good. Everything felt great." Angels starter Kelvim Escobar appears to be feeling pretty spry, too, though, and several of his fastballs hit 98 on the radar gun early on. But the A's nearly match their total of four hits from Friday while taking the lead in the bottom of the third, getting singles by Kotsay and Byrnes in front of a two-run double by badass Chavez. Zito responds with a huge top of the fourth; facing the menacing heart of Anaheim's order, he retires Guerrero, Glaus, and Anderson on twelve pitches before walking off the mound to his second standing ovation of the day.

The first standing ovation had come after the third, mostly in appreciation for Zito's ability to handle the extra work forced upon him by sloppy defense. In the second inning, a two-out error by Crosby required Zito to make nine extra pitches to get out of the inning, and a dropped foul pop-up by Hatteberg in the third led to five extra pitches. After Zito rips through a perfect fifth, earning yet another standing O, his pitch count is at eighty-three. Without the errors, it would have been an economical sixty-nine. "After the fifth I felt okay," Zito says. "The sixth and seventh were a bitch."

Guerrero, who'd entered the game on a 16-for-25 tear, was the focus of Oakland's pre-series pitchers' meeting. "He's the guy we didn't want to hurt us," Zito says. Oops. Guerrero tags a game-tying, two-out, two-run homer in the top of the sixth, threatening to leave Zito with yet another outing spoiled by one swing. "Yeah, that probably crossed my mind," Zito says. But the A's won't let it happen. Dye singles to open the bottom of the sixth, and with one out, Miller, playing through the pain in his thumb, doubles him home. Angels manager Mike Scioscia turns to his stellar bullpen in what's normally the kiss of death for opponents, especially an opponent who entered the game with the lowest batting average with runners in scoring position (.259) in the American League. But after Brendan Donnelly strikes out Crosby, Scutaro pokes an RBI single into right field that gives Zito another two-run lead. And when Zito sets the Angels down in order on ten pitches in the top of the seventh, the crowd again explodes. "That's when I thought, 'Okay, we got it,'" Hudson says.

Zito, who has thrown 114 pitches, is thinking the same thing as he makes the toughest decision of his baseball life. While the A's are batting in the bottom of the seventh, he goes to Young and tells him he's done for the day. "My legs were tightening up out there, and I was starting to labor," Zito explains after the game. "I know I was getting outs, but I felt like in that seventh inning, I got lucky. I got away with some pitches that weren't very good. . . . I just didn't have that fluidity in my core that I'd had earlier in the game.

It had nothing to do with my pitch count. I felt like I was wearing down, and the last thing I wanted to do was go back out there feeling funky and fuck it up for everyone else in here."

If Mulder's face-plant on Friday was a microcosm of his second half, what happens after Zito's exit is a microcosm of Oakland's entire season. As Mecir takes the mound to start the eighth inning, an uneasy buzz runs through the Coliseum. Mecir hasn't allowed an earned run in thirty-five of his last thirty-six outings, but his blown save earlier in the week against the Mariners is obviously a fairly fresh wound for A's fans, and Bengie Molina's leadoff single picks at the scab. Mecir strikes out pinch hitter Curtis Pride, but Figgins singles. The buzz having turned to boos, Macha replaces Mecir with Rincon, and all hell breaks loose. Erstad jumps on the first pitch Rincon throws and sends it high off the fifteen-foot wall in right-center field for a game-tying double and blown save number twenty-eight of the season for the Oakland bullpen. Macha orders Guerrero intentionally walked and replaces Rincon with Dotel, who gets Glaus on a fly ball to left before Anderson provides the dagger. He caps Anaheim's comeback with an RBI single to right. The A's get a leadoff walk from Dye in the eighth, but Francisco Rodriguez strikes out the next three batters, and Angels closer Troy Percival works a perfect bottom of the ninth. Anaheim 5, Oakland 4. Angels win the West. "We've certainly had some lows in the bullpen," Macha says, while a celebration rages in the visitors' clubhouse. "It caught up with us again today."

After getting a hug from his father, Joe, who whispers, "You did your job," into his crestfallen son's ear, Zito stands in front of his locker to face the media, eyes ringed with red. Trying to get his head around the idea that he's not going to the playoffs for the first time in his career, he's immediately hit with wave after wave of questions regarding his decision to leave the game. And there's no denying that with some of the questions comes the implication that he bailed on his teammates. That he couldn't handle the heat. That he didn't want the pressure that would have come with going back out for the eighth. He patiently explains his decision a few times, but, eventually, he snaps.

Zito rarely gets truly angry at anything, but this is one of those times. "Look," he says, "I don't want to debate this. Don't you think I'd want to go out there and bust my ass for this team? That's what I'm paid for. It shouldn't be an issue. If you feel your stuff is starting to wear out, it's up to you to decide if you're going to be able to go out and help the team or not. I didn't think I could. That's the decision I made. Obviously, the way it worked out, I'm the ass in here."

A few minutes later, Byrnes gets wind of the accusations against Zito, and now he's plenty pissed off, too. "That's ridiculous if anyone is going to criticize Barry after today," he says. "Look at what that guy did today. Biggest game of the year, everything on the line, and he was awesome. He did everything he had to do. Seven great innings, two-run lead when he left. You can't say enough about what he did. We just didn't get it done. That's it. *We* didn't get it done. Barry did his job, plain and simple."

But the bullpen did not, and there's a cruel symmetry to it all. It isn't just Zito who has been Hudsoned this time. Hudson, who has been robbed of glory by the bullpen more than any other A's pitcher over the last few years, is a victim again, too. He's still pitching Sunday, but instead of the "everything" game he'd so hoped it would be, it's a nothing game. Meaningless. His prediction didn't pan out, and the season is essentially over.

20

HOLD 'EM OR FOLD 'EM?

C*hokeland A's?* Tough to argue against it in the immediate aftermath. The September surge on which the team had grown to rely never happened; the A's went 12–16 for the month. The Big Three went 3–8 after August 24. And there's absolutely no disputing that blowing a three-game lead with nine to play by losing six of the first eight ranks right up there with the biggest regular-season pratfalls in history. But again, the word *choke* is a harsh one. For one thing, it dismisses the fact that on the other side of every alleged choke job is usually a brilliant comeback. When the Yankees blew a three-game lead over the Red Sox in the 2004 American League Championship Series, for example, they were immediately labeled the worst postseason chokers of all time. Even in Boston. But that takes something away from the fact that the Red Sox put together an unbelievable series of clutch performances on their way to the World Series. There's this, too: the Red Sox were the better team. Yes, the Yankees won the division, but Boston won the season series with New York and eventually proved their superiority across the board during the ALCS. And where were they most superior? On the mound—particularly in the bullpen. Just as the

Angels, who got swept by the Red Sox in the ALDS, were superior to the A's.

The word *choke* also implies gross underachievement, and a case can be made that the 2004 A's overachieved by winning ninety-one games and extending their streak of ninety or more wins to five seasons. Their most dangerous hitter, Chavez, missed six weeks. Their most reliable starter and team leader, Hudson, missed six weeks, too. Several key players were running on fumes physically down the stretch, including Dye (thumb), Durazo (wrist), Kotsay (knee), Miller (thumb), and McLemore (knee), and the A's used the disabled list eleven times, resulting in a total of 516 games missed by various players. From June 28 to July 9 alone, they had seven players on the disabled list, including projected starting second baseman Mark Ellis, who missed the entire year. But as Macha said countless times over the course of the season, "Injuries are part of the game." And Zito, when presented with all that went wrong for the A's, including his first-half funk and the inexplicable demise of Mulder in the final months, waves it all off as material for an excuse machine that he

In homage to the latter's midseason stint on the disabled list, Harden (left) and Hudson (right) form a human "DL."

won't crank up. "You'll just drive yourself crazy with that kind of shit," he says. "I mean, you can always say, 'What if?' You can say that about everything in your life. But the bottom line is that you've just gotta play the hand you're dealt. Right now, we're not going to the playoffs, and we have to deal with it."

Of course, the biggest "What if?" relates to the bullpen. Zito, as part of his explanation for coming out of that last start against the Angels, tried to express his confidence in the team's relievers by saying, "Nine times out of ten, the bullpen goes out and gets it done, and we're not having this conversation." It's the kind of thing a good teammate has to say, but statistically, it's way off the mark. He'd have been more accurate if he'd said, "Five and a half times out of ten . . . "

Had Oakland's bullpen converted nine of every ten save opportunities in 2004, it would have had about fifty-six saves and the A's would have won the division by twenty games. That's not a realistic hypothetical, though, because even the best bullpens don't convert 90 percent of their save opportunities. The Los Angeles Dodgers led big-league ball with a conversion rate of 85 percent in 2004, and the Angels, as deep as they were in the bullpen, ranked sixth at 75 percent. Had the A's converted 75 percent of their save chances, they'd have had about forty-seven saves and won the division by eleven games. Had they been in line with the league average of just over 64 percent, they'd have finished with forty saves and won the division by four games. Even at the same 62 percent conversion rate that ultimately cost a playoff spot for the Giants, who ranked twentieth among thirty teams, they'd have had thirty-nine saves and won the division by three games. A dismal 60 percent would have given the A's a two-game cushion when it was all said and done. But the Oakland bullpen converted just 55.6 percent of its save chances—only Cleveland (53), Kansas City (53), and Colorado (51), were worse. "The bullpen," Beane conceded on the final Saturday of the season, "didn't work." Added Mecir, "I haven't seen anything like it."

So the bullpen is to blame, right? Not so fast. Of all people, it's Hudson—even with the lengthy stint on the disabled list, he had nine no-decisions, and he left six of those games with a lead—who comes to the relief corps' defense. "Our bullpen's taken a lot of heat, but we had some pretty good arms down there," he says. "They've taken a lot of heat, but they were constantly put in situations where there was zero margin for error. And it's tough to ask a bullpen to hold a one-run lead for two or three innings against quality teams. It's not easy. I pitch against those lineups six or seven innings a night. I know it's not easy. And then you bring a guy into a situation where there's runners on base, and if he gives up a hit, it's gonna be a tie ball game, it's not fun. And it seems like they were always in those situations."

The suggestion, backed by Beane and Macha shortly after the season ended, is that despite some pretty good numbers by the offense, which set an Oakland record with 1,545 hits and tied another Oakland record with a .270 team batting average, it has to shoulder some of the blame, too. Chavez spent much of the season telling anyone who would listen that the A's were never going to "beat up on anybody," and he was right. The A's played fifty-two games decided by one run, the most in the majors. They played eighty games decided by one or two runs. They played nineteen extra-inning games; only the Indians (twenty-three) played more. They played sixty-two games decided in the seventh inning or later, and forty-seven of those were decided in the winning team's final inning at the plate. Offensively, they were ninth among the American League's fourteen teams in runs scored (793) and hit .260 with runners in scoring position; only Toronto's .259 was worse. They led the league in runners left on base. They stole an AL-low forty-seven bases, and their twenty-five sacrifice hits were fourth fewest in the league. "Nobody stole bases, nobody hit and run, nobody bunted," Chavez said after the A's were eliminated. "We didn't blow a lot of teams out, so we had to be able to do other things to win, and we didn't do enough of them."

The starting pitching can't be excused, either. Like the offense, the rotation put up some decent numbers. With a 4.24 ERA and a .266 opponents' batting average, it ranked second in the league. It led the AL in complete games (ten), innings pitched, and fewest home runs allowed. Five starters won at least ten games. But there was an ugly side, too, and it was ugliest down the stretch. The A's were 81–54 and had a four-game lead in the division entering play on September 5, and over the final twenty-seven games of the season, the starters were 5–12 with a 5.82 ERA, while lasting no more than six innings fourteen times. As for the Big Three? Same deal. They went a respectable 40–25 with a 4.17 ERA in ninety-four starts, and they didn't get a lot of help, either. They left only twenty of those starts with a lead of more than two runs, and they got Hudsoned a total of fourteen times. But they deserve some blame, too. Twice they went fourteen consecutive starts without recording a win, including from September 9 through the end of the season. That's why you won't hear Hudson throwing a blanket of blame over the bullpen.

"I don't want to throw *anyone* under the bus, because we had a bunch of problems," he says. "For me, it was inconsistent offense in big games. An inconsistent bullpen in big games. We were streaky, just like we've been for the past few years, only this time one of our bad streaks came at the end instead of one of the big finishes we've had. And then, when it really came down to it, the security blanket of this organization, which has been our starting pitching down the stretch, wasn't there. People talk about the book *Moneyball*, and the A's philosophy and how it was really good, and how they've always been able to plug in holes on a shoestring budget or whatever, but it was all dependent on our starting pitching and the Big Three. It all looked good on paper, it all looked good in the book, but this year showed that it don't matter who was on that field if the starting pitching didn't do what everyone expects us to do, year in and year out. If the starters weren't damn near perfect, it wasn't gonna happen for us. And obviously, this year, we were far from perfect."

A week after the fact, Zito is still a little bit chafed by the criticism he took after handing that 4–2 lead to the bullpen on the final Saturday of the season. As much as he claims to blow off what people say about him, he doesn't always succeed. To blow it off would require a certain amount of insensitivity, and part of what makes Barry Zito such an interesting person is his sensitivity. Insensitive people don't really see the whole picture. They see what's right in front of them. Zito uses a wide-angle lens. Some would argue that he might benefit from a little more tunnel vision, but that's just not him. He wants to see and feel everything. So, yes, the criticism stings a little, even though he feels it's unjust. But he insists that he won't ever succumb to what would seem to be a natural temptation to wonder if he made the right call. "It was definitely the right call," he says, while sifting through a pile of photographic slides at a friend's San Francisco flat. And with that, he stands up and makes an admission. He did, in fact, feel the weight of the world on his shoulders as he took the mound against the Angels with the season on the line. "This is what that game was like," he says, pantomiming the lifting of a giant globe onto his back. "Every inning, as I left the dugout, it was like that." He picks up another imaginary globe and trudges toward an imaginary mound. "I'm telling you, those seven innings took more out of me than any other start I've made in my life, including the playoffs, and I gave it every ounce of energy I had. I'm the only one who knows what my body was going through, and I knew I was done. So, no, I don't have any regrets at all."

Nor should he, says Hudson, who had approached Zito in the dugout after the Angels tied the game. "You know me and Barry. We're the closest friends of anybody on the team," Hudson says. "So I just asked him, 'You couldn't have gone one more?' And he said, 'Nope. To be honest with you, I felt like I was done. I felt like I was spent.' He said, 'Obviously, if I'd have known *this* was going to happen, I'd have gone out there and tried. But I felt like it was better to get a fresh arm in there.' And I would have, too. There's been times when I've done that. I've said, 'Listen, I'm done. I can go back out there if you want me to, but I don't think it's a great idea.'" As for the criticism? "That's horseshit," Hudson says. "Those are guys who just don't understand what we go through. I didn't hear a single player with a problem with what Z did. It's the guys who've probably never played the game of baseball and don't know what it's like to go out there for seven innings and bust your balls and mentally go through the grind of pitching in a playoff situation. They have no idea what it's like to be out there."

Zito looks at it all the same way he looks at the season as a whole: a valuable learning experience. The common perception will be that he pitched poorly in the first half, when he went 4–7, and much better in the second half, when he went 7–4. But the reality is that he had highs and lows throughout the season. His highest single-month ERA, for instance, came in April (6.83). His lowest came in May (3.18). In June it was 3.65, in July it shot up to 5.97, in August it dropped to 3.48, and in September it was 4.54. In that lone October start it was 2.28. The final numbers—11–11 with a 4.48 ERA and a team-high twelve no-decisions in thirty-four starts—matter less to him than the final feeling.

As various media folk weighed in on the state of the A's after their season came to a close, much was made of the fact that after going 47–17 with a 3.04 ERA in his first three seasons, Zito is 25–23 and 3.87 ERA over the last two. "People can say what they want, like, 'Oh, Zito's had two bad years in a row now,'" he says, "but I've learned that that's what comes with something like winning a Cy Young. And even though Mulder and Huddy haven't won one—yet—they have to deal with the same thing. We basically all came onto the scene and had a lot of success right away, so that's where we're supposed to be all the time. But what we did in those first few years is unusual. With most pitchers, it takes a few years to kind of figure things out. So maybe that's what we're going through right now, at least me and Mulder. Huddy, he's been good all along. He might never go through what Mulder and I have. But maybe Mulder and I, we figured it out early, and now we kind of have to re-figure it out. And personally, I feel like I'm on my way. . . . I feel like I grew a lot this year."

Looking back at the season and forward to an uncertain future, Zito insists that he's again at peace. His home in the Hollywood Hills is being remodeled in a style he describes as "straight out of the movie *Blow*," which essentially means the guy who dresses like a '70s porn star will be living in a house that could be owned by a '70s cocaine dealer, and that's his primary focus at the moment. He knows that he was the subject of trade talks during the season, and less than a week after the Red Sox won the World Series, Zito trade rumors were again in the news. He knows that people think he missed Peterson more than anyone (some of the rumors had Zito headed to the Mets for a reunion with his one-time mentor), and he knows that some people still might be wondering *What's wrong with Barry?* That's fine, he says. To each his own. "Everyone wants to blame why I struggled on something tangible, because they can't comprehend what it's like to be in this game," he says. "And I don't wanna *say* what it's like to be in this game, because everyone has a different experience, because they're seeing the world out of their own eyes. What it's like to be in my consciousness, in my head, with my learning and my level of intelligence, nobody knows that but me."

Well, maybe one other person knows. Actress Alyssa Milano, the former child star of *Who's the Boss?* turned grown-up vixen, started showing up at A's games over the final few months of the season, and rumors of a relationship with Zito ran wild. Zito denied the rumors publicly during the season, but privately, within a week after he'd met her, he was telling friends that he'd finally found a woman with whom he could truly "go deep" without fear of coming off as a freak. They share many passions, including Zito's new-found love for photography, and shortly after the season ended, they decided to ditch the secrecy and started making appearances in public together. "Alyssa's the coolest chick I've ever met," he said in early August. "I mean, she's amazingly beautiful and sexy and a star and all that, but that's surface shit. She's a million times more amazing inside, and it's been great to have someone like that to talk to, someone who gets what I'm saying. She's like, 'I can't believe that you think the way you do and you're in this game that's all statistical and result-oriented.' She's like, 'You need to be an artist. You need to do something with no form to it.' She's the only person who really gets that and understands why I go through the things I do in baseball."

The way Zito sees it, though, he already is an artist. And he's still working at mastering the craft. "I would say pitching is definitely an art," he says. "And that's always what my deal is, to erase all the shit that fills our heads—you know, stats, expectations, media, coaches, teams, what I have to do—and just say to yourself, 'You know what? This is an empty palette today. And I don't know what's going to happen, but I'm not gonna feel bad about myself if the palette's not painted correctly. I'm just going to paint and not care.' And I'm kind of getting to that point lately, where I'm like, if shit happens, I can deal. If I give up runs, I can deal. If I have a los-ing record, I can deal. If the media hates me, I can deal. If I get sent down to triple-A, I can deal. If I get traded or sent out of baseball, I can deal. So you go down through every, quote, fear that you've ever had, and you realize that even if the worst of the worst happens, I'll be all right. I'll do anything I want in life and accomplish what I can.

"So that's the mind-set that I've started taking to the mound with me now. And then, when it comes back to the moment of making the pitch, you don't care anymore. If you want to hit me, hit me. And then look what happens. More often than not, they won't hit you. It's a trip, man. This game is a trip."

Relaxed and reflective while packing up some of his belongings in the clubhouse a couple of days after his final start, Mulder says that his head, so clear for so long before it suddenly turned into a muddled mess midway through the season, is clear again as he discusses his latest shocking revelation. For someone who entered the season with what seemed to be unshakable confidence, admitting to thinking too much on the mound was big. Admitting to asking Zito for help with it was bigger. This one might be the biggest: in an effort to right himself down the stretch, he'd been talking to a shrink.

He doesn't use the word *shrink*, of course. That's one pool of vulnerability into which he isn't ready to dive. "Honestly, I don't know what you'd classify him as," Mulder says. What the rest of the world classifies "him" as is a famous sports psychologist. Harvey Dorfman has written four books on the cerebral side of baseball, including *The Mental ABC's of Pitching*, and he was employed by the A's from 1984 to 1993. Curt Young was a pitcher for the A's during nine of Dorfman's ten years with the team. "Curt's actually the one who mentioned it to me," Mulder says.

There was no couch involved, he notes. The conversations took place over the phone. "It was basically him wanting me to tell him what I'm out there thinking and what I'm out there doing, and what's going on," Mulder says. "Basically, it was him telling me, 'Look, this isn't what you think it is. You're making it more than it really is in your head.' And it just kind of showed me how powerful it can be, how something in your mind can take over and affect what you're doing physically. Like, say you go back and watch an old game, like I do with the Arizona game. I'd do that to look at my mechanics, but he said, 'I don't want you going back and looking at your mechanics or your release point or anything.' He said to go back and try to remember what was going on in my head at that moment. 'What are you thinking about while you're out there dealing? What's your focus right now? What's going on in your head right there?' Well, there's not a whole lot going through my head when I'm right. That's where I want to be, where I was before all of this started.

"But when it was bad, it was more where I got something in my head because something felt funny. I didn't feel right. So I lost focus about the process of it all." Imagine that. *The process.* Mulder using Zito-speak. "Instead of just focusing on the simple things, like, 'Hey, let's execute this pitch. Make the pitch,' I was worrying about where my knee was, where my arm was, where my head was, where my back was, where my shoulder was—as opposed to the way I used to be, like, 'Who cares about your mechanics? Make the pitch. Focus on executing the pitch and putting it where you want it.' Because when I'd be playing catch, just playing catch in the out- field before batting practice or whatever, I'd feel great. When I'm just playing catch, I'm not thinking about anything. It's just a game of catch. I'm just throwing it the way I have my whole life. But when I got on the mound, I'd start thinking about all that stu- pid stuff, and that's what hurts you." And now? "Since I've started talking to him, I've gotten over all that thinking about my mechanics. That was kind of going away, anyway, as I started talk- ing to him, but I think he's helped. Certain things he's told me, try- ing to get me in a different mind-set when I'm out there, it definitely helped. But even he said to me, 'It's a process. It's not nearly as bad as you think it is, but it's a process.'"

Looking back at the Big Three's 2004, Mulder is careful in trying to come up with the right words. "It's been a . . . *different* kind of year," he says. "Huddy pitched well, but he got hurt and missed a bunch of time in the middle. I did well in the first half and then struggled. Zito struggled at the beginning and then did well. So it's kind of been an off year, you might say, for the three of us." On his own year, which ended with a 17–8 record and a 4.43 ERA in thirty-three starts, he's more blunt. "I think despite my record, it wasn't very good. That's just what I feel inside, and it's not because of the ERA. I could have a 4.00 and still be happy with the way I'm pitching, even though a 4.00 isn't that great. It's just the way it all happened. The first two months, first two and a half months, I was very happy with the way I threw. After that, I wasn't pleased at all. At all." And not just because of the second-half slide. Even before things turned ugly for Mulder, before the wins stopped coming at a breakneck pace, he was growing less and less satisfied. "It's just my standards," he says. "I know what I'm capable of doing, and I didn't do it enough. You look at the numbers: okay, seventeen wins. That's pretty good. They look okay. But whether I get wins personally for my record, that's irrelevant. I don't care. I just want to pitch better. And if I go seven innings and give up three runs, which is a so-called quality start, if I give up a homer in the eighth inning, that homer just fucked it all up. Just ruined it for me. It takes away from walking away from a game with a really, really good feeling, and I did that twice this year, even before it got really bad at the end of the year. Those are just the little things where I hold myself up to a higher standard than that. I always take pride in going deep into games and holding a 1–0 lead, holding a 2–1 lead, but I've had games this year where I've given up runs in the seventh or eighth inning to let teams go ahead or tie it, and I never do that. Or I *shouldn't* do that. It's going to happen, but it shouldn't, is the way I look at it. I'm better than that. I know I am."

In late October, Mulder is speaking by phone from Arizona, and his confidence seems to be back. He's golfing again, and he says he recently shot 74 at the TPC of Scottsdale, the same course at which the PGA plays the Phoenix Open. He even jokes when it's noted that at spring training 2005, *What's wrong with Mark?* will be a factor until he returns to his old dominant ways. "Yeah," he agrees. "Wear it." But despite his late-season problems, he doesn't plan to radically change his off-season approach. "The only thing is that I'll start a little later," he says. "Last year, we wanted to make sure the hip was okay, so we got going a little earlier." And he's finally willing to admit that he might have been fatigued as the season came to a close. "You know, I was talking with Chavvy and Ellis the other day, and one thing Chavvy pointed out was that there was a time during the season when every time I went out there, I *had* to win that game. I'm talking about when Huddy was hurt and Zito was struggling and Rich hadn't quite caught fire yet. I had to win every game, and that takes a lot out of you. And so does the complete games I was throwing to save the bullpen. I'm not complaining or making excuses; my job is to win and get deep into games. But I think there was a combination of things that might have piled up on me and worn me down a little."

On the possibility that the Big Three might not exist much longer, Mulder sounds like he's not ready for it to happen. He's heard the Zito trade rumors, but he knows that he could be dealt, too, and he's particularly animated when it's mentioned that the team could very well decide to trade Hudson, who will be in the last year of his deal in 2005, if an extension can't be agreed upon. "That would be weird," he says. "I mean, I just can't see them trading Huddy. He's the guy who started all of this. He was the first one to get to the big leagues. He was the first one to dominate. He was the first one to win twenty games." Reminded that the A's traded Mark McGwire once upon a time, he says, "True. And with all the guys they've let leave, obviously nobody's untouchable. But still, man. Without Huddy here, it would be really weird." Weird enough to make you think differently about staying in Oakland? "Definitely, but you know what? Something else Chavvy said the other day is true. He said, 'Everyone thinks the grass is always greener, but it's not.' Look at Jason [Giambi]. He's not exactly having a great time in New York. Look at Miggy. He was out of the race in a hurry in Baltimore. And yeah, it'd be nice to see the team spend some money on offense and the bullpen like they did in Atlanta when they had that great starting pitching, but here in Oakland, we're still a good team. And we'll be good for a while. So would I like for us to stay together? Obviously. I love pitching with these guys. But I don't have a say in it. All I can do is get ready for next season and try to apply what I've learned this year to next year and the years that come after that, wherever I am."

And wherever he is, the memory of 2004 will be with him. In a three-start stretch in May, Mulder went 3–0 with three complete games and a 1.33 ERA. In his last three starts, his longest outing being four innings, he went 0–3 with an 11.17 ERA. The experience,

Hudson, feeding his daughter, Kennedie, in a hotel lobby during the 2001 playoffs in New York, is the only husband and father among the Big Three.

he says, changed the way he looks at the game and his gift to play it at the highest level. And there *is* a certain vulnerability in Mark Mulder that didn't exist when the season began. "I think *humbling* is a good word for this season. I think it's definitely done that," he offers. "It's given me a look at the bad side, if you know what I mean. Never in a million years did I think I'd have to deal with something like this, but you know what? It's not that easy, what we do. It's not always going to happen that you're as good as you think you are. But will I have confidence in that happening the next time I take a mound? Yeah. You'd better have that confidence. If you don't, you're done. Trust me. I know that now."

More than a few pro ballplayers will tell you that when their season is over, they want to get as far away from the game as possible. Hudson is not one of them. Family and baseball are everything to him, so a week after the season ends, he's sitting in the family room of his modest in-season home in the hills of San Ramon, California. Boxes are cluttering the room, soon to be filled for shipping back to the Hudsons' off-season home in Florida. His oldest daughter, Kennedie, is climbing in and out of his lap. His youngest daughter, Tess, is nodding off in a swing. His wife, Kim, is offering a guest a bottle of water. Hudson, meanwhile, is staring intently at the huge television in front of him. The playoffs are on, and the St. Louis Cardinals are hitting. "Now that's a complete team right there. That's the kind of team I want to play for," he says, pointing to the screen. "That's a playoff team, a championship-caliber team."

The 2004 A's, he says, were not. And when asked if not making the playoffs hurts more than losing in the first round four years running, he drops his head and stares at the floor for a few seconds. When he lifts his head, there's that Hudson fire in his eyes. A nerve has been touched. "The way this team was goin', it's probably better that we didn't make the playoffs this year, because we would have gotten our ass beat again," he says. "And to do that to our fans, to do that to us, emotionally, it just wouldn't have been right. We fought to the end, and everybody wanted to win, but the way we were playing, and the way things were going, we wouldn't have been able to compete with some of those teams that are clicking right now. Those teams that got in, they did what you're supposed to do to make the playoffs: they started playing their best ball at the end of the year. We didn't. We didn't deserve to go. The way our team was going, it wouldn't have been good, and then it would have been, 'Oh, there the A's go. Five years in a row they can't get out of the first round.' How's that going to look?"

Not good. And at this moment, Hudson doesn't have the most optimistic view of the 2005 A's, either. Shortly after the season ended, the A's announced that they were declining their option for next year on Dye, one of their few power threats. Talk of trading Zito had started. Durazo, Byrnes, and Dotel are expected to get huge raises in arbitration, and there's no guarantee that they'll be back. Miller is a free agent. In short, it'll be another off-season of massive turnover, and Beane has already said that the A's payroll, which was about $60 million in 2004, won't be much higher any time soon. Hudson's agent, Paul Cohen, and the A's have had little in the way of any substatial talks about a possible contract extension, and right now Hudson is far from sure that his status as the Big Story next spring will have the happy ending the Chavez saga had.

"Every single year, the off-season's all about how are we gonna replace this guy or that guy? We can't afford this, we can't afford that," he says. "Do I want to be a part of that every single year, the rest of my career? No, man. No. There needs to be a serious facelift with this organization, all the way around."

He's back in a New York state of mind, thinking about money and winning and how the two intersect. He's thinking about former teammates. About having to make do with less. About the twenty-six career wins he's seen disappear with a blown save. About the inconsistent offenses. About the pressure placed on the Big Three to keep the A's afloat in one of the game's most competitive divisions. He's agitated now, and there's no doubling back to diplomacy this time. The gloves are off.

"It's been bubbling to a head for the last couple of years, just seeing all the guys have to leave," he says. "From 2001, seeing Giambi leave, seeing Miggy leave, seeing Foulke leave, seeing Izzy leave, seeing Johnny Damon leave. All these great players being let go, when if we'd have just kept some of these guys, we'd be a great team. So it's time to get off your fuckin' wallet, pay these guys, keep 'em around, and win championships. Instead of tryin' to go the cheap way and sign and develop all these young guys in the minors, and hope that the Big Three is gonna carry the team to a championship. Stop ridin' our fuckin' shoulders, man. We're not supermen. We're not gonna be there every year. This year was a perfect example. The Big Three struggled a little bit, and you know what? As a team, we fell flat on our ass because of it, because there's nobody to make up for anything less than having the three of us at the top of our games all the time. There's gonna be years when other guys are gonna have to pick the strength of your team up. Whether it's the offense or the bullpen or whatever, you can't rely so much on one aspect of the organization to win every single year. And that's been the case. And luckily, up to now, we've been really good. We've been able to do it. We've had just enough offense and just enough bullpen to get the job done. But you know what? This year we didn't have the bullpen, we didn't have the offense, we didn't have the starting pitching, and we got our ass beat. We almost made it, but we didn't. And whose fault is it? It's not the players. We go out there and bust our ass. We just fell short one time.

"So get off your wallet and pay the guys. Let's go win some shit. We've got a great base laid down with us pitchers; even better now that Harden's comin' into his own. Now let's try to get some good free agents. So it's gonna cost you a little bit of money. Well, you know what? If you want to win—if you *really* want to win—it's gonna cost you. . . . It's like the owners are satisfied with just con-tendin', and I just don't get it. And when I hear, 'Oh, we can't afford to keep the Big Three together,' it really pisses me off. You gotta be shittin' me, man. They're sittin' on a gold mine right here, man. Keep us together, keep Rich, go get us some help, and we'll dominate for years to come."

With domination would come something Hudson and Cohen have talked about as they formulate a strategy for negotiations. "Paul asked me, 'How important is the Hall of Fame to you? Because those are things we need to think about,'" Hudson says. "And he's right. Where you play, the number of games you win, the championships you win, that's the kind of stuff that goes into the Hall of Fame, and that's definitely a goal of mine. Championships first, but hell yeah, I wanna be in the Hall of Fame. You win cham-pionships and make the Hall of Fame, that means you've been on top as a team and on top as an individual. You've kicked this game's ass, and that's the ultimate payback for how many times the game kicks *your* ass."

Thanks to Cohen, whose job it is to research such things, Hud-son has an idea of what he'd be worth on the free-agent market, and $50 million over four years would be a reasonable starting point for his next deal. "If I was on a big-market team like the Yan-kees, they'd give me at least thirteen or fourteen [million] a year. At least. With the way their pitching is right now?" And don't even get him started on the concept of a hometown discount. Even if Hudson is back with the A's in 2005, he'll be making less than he would have with more support around him in 2004. An escalator clause in his contract would have paid him an extra $1 million in 2005 had he finished in the top three in 2004 Cy Young voting, and the no-decision he took in the final game of the season—he left with the game tied at 2–2 after seven innings of four-hit work—

left him with a 12–6 record (and 3.53 ERA) that didn't impress many voters. "Let's leave that alone," he says of the clause. But he's more than willing to talk about his unwillingness to sign for much less than his market value.

"First of all, I should have twenty-five to thirty more wins in my career than I already have, okay? So why should I want to come back to somewhere that *maybe* I'm gonna get three or four runs a game most of the time? Maybe not even that," he says. "And when I come out, it's probably gonna be a one-run lead, okay? And probably half of the time, after I come out, the game's gonna get tied up and I'm gonna get another no-decision. Right? Why should I take less money for that, you know what I'm sayin'? Why should I want to come back and take less money for that?"

And, suddenly, he catches himself. He hates talking about his own salary. He hates the idea of sounding greedy, of sounding

The Big Three, here being posed at spring training 2003 by famous sports photographer Walter Iooss Jr., have long been the collective face of the A's.

like an individual, rather than a member of a team. He wants to make one thing very clear. "Look," he says. "It's not about money. I'm not gonna need tons of money. I've got plenty, and I'd go to a place like St. Louis for less. Why? Because I know they want to win championships. They have a great offense, they have a great bullpen, they have a great closer. They want to win it all, man. So yeah, I'd take less to go there. And the A's are probably gonna say, 'Well, if it's not about money, then take less and stay here and we'll win.' But you know what? If I take less, that's not gonna guarantee that we're gonna win. It's not gonna guarantee that our owners are gonna spend any money on other free agents. Besides, by not paying me an extra two-to-three million a year, that two-to-three million they don't spend on me isn't gonna be enough to go out and get the players we need, anyway. They have to open their pockets up more than that, and I need to know that this team is headed in the right direction. Right now, we're not headed in the right direction. Bottom line, I'm not gonna deal with what I've dealt with for the past four years for the next four years."

He falls silent for a moment, until the silence is broken by one final question. Are you really ready to leave Oakland—and the potential legacy of the Big Three—behind? "I'm ready to win," he says. "I'm ready to go somewhere we're gonna win. I hope it's here.

"God, I hope it's here."

EPILOGUE

"COMPLETE AND UTTER SHOCK"

Two weeks into the off-season, Tim Hudson is frustrated and confused. He and his agent, Paul Cohen, haven't heard a word from the A's, and they decide to force the issue.

So as not to take any of the focus off its showcase event, major league baseball executives request that its clubs not make any significant announcements during the World Series. What the commish *can't* do is put a muzzle on players or agents, so Hudson and Cohen prepare to make their own announcement during the World Series, setting a March 1 deadline for Oakland to get a contract extension done. If the deadline passes, Hudson will play out the last year of his deal and enter free agency. "Each day that we don't hear from them pisses me off a little more," Hudson says a few days before the Fall Classic. "I mean, if they wanna do what they did with Miguel [Tejada] and say, 'We can't afford to re-sign you,' fine. I'd respect that, and I'll just pitch my ass off for them next season and then go somewhere else. No hard feelings. But not knowin' what's goin' on . . . fuck it. We'll make a big splash. Let everyone know they're draggin' their feet."

It seems out of character for Hudson, this idea of making a big splash, because he's not one to make waves. And sure enough, two days later he changes his mind. "We're gonna give 'em some more time," he says. "The last thing I want to do is look like an asshole, 'cause that ain't me. But it's frustratin', man, just sittin' around wonderin' what they're thinkin'."

So he waits for another month. But all he hears out of Oakland, aside from the news that Jermaine Dye is leaving as a free agent, is that GM Billy Beane, on November 27, has acquired three-time All-Star catcher Jason Kendall from the Pirates in exchange for Arthur Rhodes and Mark Redman. (Damian Miller is allowed to leave as a free agent.) "I think it's a great deal," Hudson says. "It's definitely an upgrade offensively. I think it's a good statement [by ownership] to the players that they're looking to win right now, and that's exciting."

Mark Mulder is excited, too, and not just because of Kendall's offensive skills. He sees addition by subtraction. After Rhodes publicly ripped into Hudson and Mulder through the media in June, Mulder and Rhodes didn't exchange another word. "Rhodes didn't want to be here, anyway," Mulder says. "It was time for him to go." Nobody laments the loss of Redman, either. "I like Red," Mulder says. "But it just seemed like he never really fit in." The scout who predicted frequent address changes for Redman was right. He's on to his fifth team in five years. So much for the continuity in the rotation that his three-year deal appeared to bring.

Hudson's enthusiasm about the Kendall trade fades when he realizes that Kendall is scheduled to make $10 million in 2005. "Now you don't know if adding his salary means they want to cut somewhere else by trading someone like me," he says. And over the next three days, he hears plenty of rumors about just such a trade. But he doesn't hear from the A's. So on December 1, Cohen issues the March 1 ultimatum—with a sudden, unexpected twist.

The night before the announcement, Hudson says if he ends up playing for Oakland in 2005 without an extension, the door will remain open on a return: "I still want to be there if the situation's right, but they'll have to get in line with everyone else." The next day, however, Cohen says that if the deadline isn't met, Hudson will *not* entertain offers from Oakland after the season. "The window to sign Tim is open now," Cohen says. "After March 1, the window is closed." Blindsided, Beane reacts with bemused disdain: "So if I offer them $30 million a year on March 2, they won't take it?"

Hudson's motive is simple: "I just want to get 'em to talk to us. Tell me what's goin' on." To that end, it works. Sort of. Beane does indeed contact Hudson, but he doesn't exactly provide clarity. "It was a good conversation," Hudson says, "but he didn't say I wasn't gonna be traded. He said he didn't *want* to trade me, but he also said he might have to. So I didn't get that assurance one way or another. Nothing concrete, that's for sure."

Prior to going to baseball's annual winter meetings, held December 10–13 in Southern California, Beane lets it be known that he'll listen to offers for all three of his aces. Once there, he does, and Hudson's name comes up in rumors involving the St. Louis Cardinals, the Atlanta Braves, the Baltimore Orioles, the New York Mets, the Cincinnati Reds, the Philadelphia Phillies, the Boston Red Sox, and the Florida Marlins. Cohen tells him not to pay attention to any of it, but Hudson can't help himself. From his home in Florida, he has roughly twenty telephone conversations with one of the writers at the meetings (me). "What the hell's goin' on out there?" he asks at one point. "Every day I'm going to a different city. What the fuck?" He also says he's heard that the Braves have been poking around at Auburn, asking people who know him about his hip and his character.

The meetings end with him still in limbo, though, and a day later he's fed up. "Hell, if they don't send me to the Atlanta, which would make it easy on my family because we're from out there, I don't wanna go anywhere," Hudson says. "Just let me play in Oakland next year, and we'll go from there."

Two nights later, Beane calls him again. To tell him he's been traded to the Braves. The Big Three is down to two. How's that for concrete?

—   —   —

The Braves have won thirteen consecutive division championships, so Hudson is getting his wish as far as playing for a legitimate title contender. And having grown up about ninety minutes outside of Atlanta, he's long dreamed of donning the red, white, and blue of the Braves. "I remember doin' the Tomahawk Chop in our livin' room," he says. "Now people will be doin' it for me, and that's pretty cool." But even a return to his southern roots doesn't take much sting out of that final conversation with Beane.

"I was pretty emotional, man. More than anything, it was sad," Hudson says. "I mean, it's not like it was unexpected, with all the talk the last couple of weeks. But hearin' it come out of Billy's mouth, makin' it real, that's when it really just hits you in the face. You just kind of realize, 'Man, it's really over.' All the relationships I've built with teammates, with the fans, with people in the organization—it's hard to think that it's never going to be the same. They're not gonna be a part of your everyday life the way they've been for so long. And this affects Kim, too. The whole family got traded, man, and she's got a lot of friends in Oakland, too. It's just really sad.

"I feel like I just got dumped by my ninth-grade girlfriend."

Not long after he gets word of the trade, Hudson speaks with Mulder, who has a similarly emotional reaction. "It fucking sucks," Mulder says. "Fuck. That's pretty much all you can say. Fuck, fuck, fuck. And not so much because we're losing a great pitcher, even though that's a big part of it, but it's more knowing that this guy who's become such a good friend over the years isn't going to be around. Huddy's locker has been right next to mine ever since I came up to the big leagues, and now he's not going to be there. So yeah, it's sad. It's definitely sad."

Barry Zito, Hudson's best friend on the team, has a hard time putting his feelings into words: "Wow, man. I guess we all had a feeling this might happen, but wow. Huddy's gone. What a trip. He's been such a big part of this team for so long. He's been a big part of *my life* for so long. This is sad, man. Wow."

The next day, Hudson is playing big brother for Mulder and Zito one last time, trying to put a happy face on everything while driving to his first press conference as a Brave. "In a perfect world, I'd have been able to play in Oakland forever, and me and Mark and Barry would always be the Big Three. But it ain't a perfect world. It's a business. But everyone's gonna be fine, man. They've still got each other, and Harden's gonna be great, so who knows? Maybe we'll all meet up again in the World Series."

Two days later, that scenario becomes impossible when Beane makes another tough call. To Mulder. To tell him that he's been traded to the Cardinals. The Big Three is down to one. One in Atlanta, one in St. Louis, one in Oakland.

Mulder is actually on an Arizona golf course when he first hears the news. He's golfing with Eric Chavez, who gets a call from his agent, former A's ace Dave Stewart. "Stew says you're going to the Cardinals," Chavez tells Mulder, and when Mulder gets back to his house, his mother, Kathy, is on the phone. "It's Billy," she tells him. Mulder doesn't recall much of either that conversation—or the one that follows with St. Louis GM Walt Jocketty. "It was just complete and utter shock," Mulder says. "I mean, I didn't really hear a word either one of them said. I just had a million things running through my head. I'm thinking, 'I gotta get a place in Florida for spring training. I gotta get a place in St. Louis. I gotta do this, I gotta do that.' And my parents are right there, on the verge of tears. My head was absolutely swimming. . . . When Huddy got traded, we kind of saw it coming, and it was like, all right, this sucks, but we're still a pretty good team. And then this? I had no idea this was coming. Playing in St. Louis and getting to hit again will be great, but this sucks."

Beane faces vicious backlash in the Bay Area for trading two-thirds of what he'd often called his brain. But he insists that the moves were needed to keep the A's competitive long term. Among the six players he got in return for Hudson and Mulder are Dan Meyer, one of Atlanta's top pitching prospects, and Danny Haren, one of St. Louis' top pitching prospects, and they might have to step right into the rotation along with Joe Blanton, Oakland's top pitching prospect. But barring the acquisition of a cheap veteran, that would leave Zito, whom Beane says "will not be traded," as the grizzled veteran of the staff at age twenty-six. The only other starter with more than a year of experience will be Harden. "I'm actually looking forward to it," Zito says. "It's another challenge for me.

Now I'm going to be the leader of the staff, and it's gonna be cool to take on that role for the first time." Hudson says Zito is perfect for the role: "I can't think of anyone better," he says. "Barry loves to talk about pitching and share ideas, and that's something those young guys are gonna need."

By early January, the shock has worn off. Hudson, Mulder, and Zito are getting used to the idea of being apart. Hudson and Mulder are already making bets on who'll hit a home run first, and Hudson, aware that the A's and the Braves will square off during interleague play in June, is warning Mulder, Zito, and Harden to be careful if they face him. "If they throw me somethin' I can hit, that's what they'll get from me," he says with a laugh. "But if I see their nasty shit, I'll fuckin' bury 'em."

The sadness lingers, of course, and it's put into perspective beautifully by Zito when he's asked if there's any sense of unfinished business. "Yes and no," he says. "The goal was to win a World Series together, and we didn't do it, so in that sense, yeah. But it takes more than three guys to win a championship, so it's not like we're failures in any way. We did the best we could as a team and came up short. The important thing is that we had that time together, and it's something none of us will ever forget. To start our careers together with the success we did have and with the friendships we made, nobody can ever take that away.

"We're in different places now, but in my mind, we'll always be the Big Three."

AFTERWORD

"STRANGER THINGS HAVE HAPPENED"

Zito was right. They'll always be the "Big Three." At least in Oakland, anyway. He's reminded of that every day of spring training 2005. With Hudson and his contractual situation out of the picture, Zito is the Big Story at the A's camp. Virtually every reporter who sets foot on the grounds at Phoenix's Papago Park, where Oakland's pitchers and catchers report for work every February, approaches Zito for the same obligatory round of questions.

"The first one is usually, 'How does it feel to be the "Big One"?'" he says on March 1 from the comfort of his rented town house in nearby Scottsdale. One of his favorite DVDs, the movie *Happiness*, is playing on the living room TV at the moment, but that title doesn't exactly describe what he's feeling at this particular time. There is no movie titled *Resignation*. Says Zito, "The next questions are like, 'What kind of leader do you think you're gonna be?' or, 'Do you feel any added pressure?' It's all the same, basically, and I get it. I totally get it. I mean, breaking us up was a big deal. And obviously people want to know what I think of it. But I'd be lying if I didn't say it was tired already. And what sucks is that I can't exactly come out and say, 'You know what? I'm not going to talk about the Big Three any more. It's over. Let's move on.' I can't do that because part of being a leader, at least in my mind, is handling the media. You know, being one of the go-to guys. I've pretty much been that my whole career, but so were Huddy and Mulder, and it's like I have to pick up the slack for them now."

There's a certain edge to Zito now that's difficult to decipher. Part of it, no doubt, comes from the fact that in the wake of the Hudson and Mulder deals, there was no shortage of opinions shared, by fans and media alike, that the A's had kept the wrong guy. Zito claims to be oblivious to such information, but every now and then he'll say something that suggests otherwise.

"I guess some people kind of looked at me as the number three guy among us," he volunteers one March night, while drawing cartoon figures on a chalkboard across from the bar at Frasher's, the laid-back Scottsdale watering hole and restaurant he's begun to frequent. "Whatever. That's just something I can use as fuel."

So, too, might be the notion that even with Hudson and Mulder gone, Zito still isn't even the number one in Oakland. Rich Harden's performances started catching up with his potential in the second half of 2004, when he went 8–2 with a 3.49 ERA after the All-Star break, and more than a few "experts" have him pegged as the ace of the new-look A's.

"You know what? That's fine with me," Zito insists. "I've never been a big numbers guy, anyway, as far as who's the number one guy or number two guy or whatever. It's not like I went to camp in '03 [after winning the '02 Cy Young] and considered myself the number one guy. That's never been the case with me, and it shouldn't be with anyone unless it's when you're actually on the mound in a game. That's the only time you should think of yourself as that guy, because that's the mind-set you need to be that guy. But in the clubhouse, or talking to the media, you're just one of five starting pitchers, part of a twenty-five-man team."

Asked directly about this new edge a few days before starting Oakland's season opener in Baltimore, Zito finally comes up with his own word for it: *maturity*. "Not that I was immature before, but this deal here, being the salty vet, flying solo, surrounded by all these young guys, it's a responsibility I haven't really had before," he says. "And I take it seriously."

A week before leaving for the Cardinals' camp, Mulder is finally at peace with the notion of joining a new organization and a new league. The frustration of his late-season fade is nonexistent, replaced by sheer excitement. "What we had in Oakland was awesome, and I wouldn't change a minute of my time there," he says from his off-season home in Arizona. "But now we're all in different places, and I think it's going to be a good thing for everyone. You just have to turn the page and start fresh."

Mulder, by absolutely no choice of his own, is still trying to do just that—start fresh—with the Cardinals, and by March, with a couple of weeks of work at camp under his belt, he claims to be doing so with surprising success. He's been welcomed in the Cardinals' clubhouse with open arms. His arm feels strong, his mind clear. He's virtually unaffected. And yet, on the eve of his spring training debut as a Cardinal, Mulder is still just a tiny bit freaked out.

"Everything is even better than I expected it to be here, and I can't tell you how much I love this team," Mulder says. "But I have to admit it: I'm still getting used to the red shoes. The first couple times it felt like I had neon lights on my feet. I'd be in the middle of my leg kick and see this red flash out of the corner of my eye, and I'd be like, 'What the hell is that?'"

Spoiled for years by the freedom of expression that's always flowed in Oakland's traditionally young clubhouse, Mulder figured it might take some time to be accepted among the comparatively staid veteran Cards. "But it ended up being the total opposite," he says. "Even though I'm not a guy like Larry Walker or Scott Rolen or some of the other guys here who've been in the big leagues for a long time and have that respect that comes with it, I'm treated the same way they are, and it was that way the second I walked in the door." Walker and Rolen are two of the many reasons Mulder is feeling so cozy. Jim Edmonds, Albert Pujols, and the rest of the powerful St. Louis offense are among them, too.

"I can't wait to pitch for this team," Mulder says. "Even if this team is down 3–2, 4–1, 4–2 in the sixth or seventh inning, you know they're not done. They're gonna score more runs before it's over, and that means you're gonna be in a position to win just about every single game." The Cardinals can't possibly expect Mulder to win every game, but they are expecting him to be their ace. He is, whether he likes it or not, viewed by many as the missing piece of a championship puzzle.

The Cardinals team that reached the 2004 World Series had one glaring weakness—the starting rotation—when it was swept by the Red Sox, and Mulder is seen as a major part of the strengthening program. Like Zito, though, he's fighting the notion of being The Man.

"I know everyone's making a big deal out of me being the number one guy, and it's flattering, but I'm not looking at it in those terms. I never have," he says. "Maybe it's because in Oakland I was always one of three guys who could be the ace, but more than that, I just don't think having or being a number one guy is what matters. It takes five good starters to be a great team, and we have that. I'm just one of the five guys." Unfortunately for him, the St. Louis press doesn't see it that way. And they don't just see his terrific record over the past four years. They see the second-half numbers from 2004 and want answers. "Yeah, all the questions I was getting while it was happening, I'm getting them all over again here," Mulder says with a sigh. "I know everyone has a job to do, but I can't wait for the subject to change. I honestly can't wait to be asked about the bomb I just gave up instead of about what happened last year."

Hudson, of course, has been getting a healthy dose of the media this spring, too. And he quickly came to the same realization that former Athletics such as Johnny Damon and Jason Giambi came to not long after leaving Oakland. "Man, we had it easy in the Bay Area," he says a few days after attending Camp Leo, an annual pre–spring training gathering of Braves hurlers run by pitching coach Leo Mazzone. "I've talked to a lot of guys who have left [the A's] who said the same thing, the grass ain't necessarily greener and all that, but you don't really realize how true it is until you see it for yourself. For a big media market, the Bay Area is pretty tame, man. It's definitely different here, though. There just seems to be a totally different level of interest in the team." The tip-off? "The second I got on the mound [at Camp Leo], there were cameras up my ass," he says with a laugh. "I mean, they're right on you, to the point you think you might hit someone on your follow-through or somethin'."

Working with Mazzone represents something of a challenge for Hudson, who'd become understandably set in the Oakland way of training arms. The biggest difference in Atlanta is that the long toss, a staple for the A's, isn't part Mazzone's program. Throwing every day in the bullpen is. "It's not that I'm resisting the way they do things here," Hudson says a week after reporting to camp in Florida. "I'd have to be an idiot to do that, with all the success they've had here. But I swear, man, not bein' able to long toss is killin' me. I don't know if it's mental or what, but I'm already startin' to feel like my arm's weaker than it was. I'm seriously thinkin' about payin' one of the kids in the clubhouse to sneak off to a high school field with me after practice." There's one other thing that bugs Hudson a little about Mazzone. "They never stop talkin' about Greg Maddux here, man," he says. "I swear, it's 'Maddux did this, Maddux did that.' I'm like, 'Hey, man, I know Maddux is a Hall of Famer and all, but last time I checked the back of my jersey, it said 'Hudson.'"

A week later, Mazzone and Maddux are the last things on Hudson's mind. Less than a month after his agent, Paul Cohen, informed the Braves that there remained a March deadline for getting his client signed to a contract extension, Atlanta announces that a deal has been reached: four years, $47 million. "It's a bigger relief than I expected it to be," Hudson says. "The main thing, like I've said all along, is knowin' where me and my family are gonna be. Free agency has a certain appeal to it when you see guys gettin' wined and dined and all that, but the bottom line is stability at home. I don't wanna be one of those guys whose wife and kids have to pack up and move every year or two."

With a week left in spring training, Hudson's putting some thought into something far less pleasant, and it represents a little déjà vu. Atlanta's bullpen has been awful in Florida. "It's only spring, but I don't know, man. We're not lookin' too good down there yet. We've got some great arms, but we've had some problems," he says. Then he laughs. "I'm startin' to think it's me now. Maybe that's gonna be my thing: I'm the guy who gets fucked by the bullpen. It's gonna just follow me around wherever I go."

On April 12, Hudson leaves his first start of the season at Atlanta's Turner Field after eight innings of six-hit work. He has a 3–1 lead . . . and promptly gets Hudsoned. New closer Danny Kolb, brought in so John Smoltz could join Hudson—Atlanta's Big Three of the '90s meets Oakland's of the '00s— in the starting rotation, gives up three runs in the ninth, and the Braves lose, 4–3. Five days later, Hudson throws nine shutout innings but takes another no-decision because Atlanta gets shut out through nine innings, too. Through three starts, his ERA is 0.82, and he has two NDs. "It's kinda funny, man," he says. "It's like, 'Haven't I already seen this movie?'"

Zito's season gets off to a rocky start. On opening day, he gives up four earned runs in six innings as the A's are shut out, 4–0. Five days later, he has the worst statistical day of his career, giving up 11 runs in 3⅓ innings at lowly Tampa Bay, dropping him to 0–2 with an 11.57 ERA. He bounces back with eight innings of four-hit work against the Angels, who are heavily favored to repeat as AL West champs, but in a theme-setter for Zito's season, the A's give him one run of support and he falls to 0–3. By the end of April, he's 0–4 with a 6.60 ERA and still looking for his first winning April as a big leaguer. "Obviously, this isn't the way I wanted to come out of the chute," he says. "But I don't know, I don't feel like I'm pitching as bad as my numbers say I am. Tampa Bay was bad, but since then I've felt pretty crisp. That's why I'm not down on myself the way I've been in the past when things aren't happening for me. I feel like I'm right there, like things are going to turn around for me any day."

His first start in May justifies those feelings; he holds the Mariners to two runs on five hits over seven innings and gets his first win. He pitches well during the rest of May, too, allowing three runs or less in four of his next five starts and posting a 3.49 ERA for the month, but the A's offense isn't much help. On May 27 at Cleveland, for instance, Zito gives up a run on two hits while striking out seven over six innings . . . and loses to fall to 1–6 on the year. "Am I frustrated? Yeah, for the team," he says. "Not for me. This isn't about me at all. What kind of example would that set for the young guys in here if I'm worried about anything individual? That's the last thing they need to see."

The A's are losing a lot of games—32 of their first 49, to be exact, dropping them 15 games under .500 and 12½ behind the division-leading Angels. That 2004 AL Rookie of the Year Bobby Crosby went on the disabled list with fractured ribs on opening day and hasn't played yet hasn't helped, nor has the strained oblique muscle that sent Harden to the DL in mid-May. And Zito's impact on the young starting rotation appears minimal. Through his first ten starts, rookie Joe Blanton is 0–5 with a 6.66 ERA. Dan Haren, one of the players acquired for Mulder and also in his first season as a big-league starter, is 1–7 with a 4.87 ERA. "It's my job to pick these guys up, guys like

Blanton and Haren, and there are two ways to do that," Zito says. "One is to start winning. The other is to stay positive. I know it looks bleak right now, but I honestly believe in this team. If we get healthy and stay positive, we can turn this around. There's no doubt in my mind. We can do this."

Over the next eighty-two games, starting May 30, the A's follow Zito's script beautifully. They win fifty-eight games in one of the most dramatic in-season turnarounds in baseball history. Never before had an AL team gone from fifteen under to at least fifteen over in the same season, but on August 30, the A's are nineteen over and two games *ahead* of the Angels atop the AL West. The return of Crosby and Harden are significant factors, but Zito certainly does his part. He goes 3–2—the A's score a total of two runs in his two losses—with a 3.02 ERA in June, and in July he finally starts getting some support, going 6–0 with a 2.51 ERA on his way to AL Pitcher of the Month honors. He's even better in August, putting up a 2.13 ERA, but thanks to an offense that again loses Crosby to injury during the month, he wins only one of his final five starts of the month; the A's score a total of seven runs in those five games. Nevertheless, he's 12–6 with a 2.77 ERA over the last four months, and that includes the less-than-stellar May.

As usual, Zito's physics-defying curveball has been a big factor in his return to dominance. "When Barry's hook is on, it's not just the hitter who buckles," says A's catcher Jason Kendall. "The umpire buckles. I buckle. People in the first few rows buckle. It's that good." But now that big breaker, along with his old four-seam fastball, changeup, and the two-seamer that helped him get back on track in the second half of 2004, is complemented by two more additions to the arsenal. He's been dabbling with a cut fastball, and he's unveiled a slider, giving him twice as many pitches as he used in 2002. "The slider is the big one," Zito says. "I used to be reluctant to throw it because I thought it would throw my mechanics out of whack, but it really hasn't. And it gives me a totally different look." After facing the new-look Zito for the first time in 2005, then-Seattle second baseman Bret Boone had shaken his head and said, "It's like facing someone you haven't seen before."

"I don't know that I'm all that different of a pitcher physically," Zito says on September 1, on the eve of the stretch run. "I'm still basically the same fastball-curveball-changeup guy. The difference for me is mental. I'm back to pounding the strike zone. I'm committed to every pitch. For whatever reason, I lost that for a while in 2004. Now I'm back to just acting like I own it out there. Like there's nobody better." That's as close to self-hype as you'll hear from the 2005 Zito, who would much rather talk about Oakland's about-face. "It's pretty gratifying," he says. "Me getting wins, that's great. But it's great because it means we're scoring runs, we're playing good defense, and the bullpen is getting it done. The whole team is clicking, and it's just such a satisfying thing. No matter what happens from here, I'm so proud to be part of this team."

He's not just a *part* of the team. He is, to the surprise of those who have mistaken his eccentricities for flakiness over the years, every bit the leader in Oakland that Hudson was. And about that, Hudson, who predicted that Zito would thrive in '05, happily crows. "People see Z and his candles and pillows and guitar and whatever you want to call his hair, and they think he's out there," Hudson says. "And don't get me wrong—he is. But not when it comes to baseball. I knew he was gonna kick ass this year. He's got a lot of pride, and no way was he gonna have a bad year with all those young guys looking up to him."

Truth be told, not everyone in the A's clubhouse believed in the team the way Zito did. Haren certainly didn't think he possessed the wherewithal to bounce back so well, but he went 13–5 with a 3.33 ERA in his final twenty-four starts of the season to establish himself as one of the best young pitchers in the league. And he gives most of the credit to Zito's steadying influence. "I honestly thought I was going to be sent to triple-A when I was struggling," Haren says. "And when I lost confidence early in the season, he's the guy who picked me up and got me turned around. He had more faith in me than I did, and that just meant so much to me. Especially early, when things weren't going well for him, either. To kind of put his own situation aside and take care of me, to show concern for where my head was at, that's something I'll never forget."

Zito has found a kindred spirit in Haren, a sensitive, soft-spoken, but brutally honest and fun-loving sort who quickly replaced Hudson as Zito's best friend on the A's. Another close new buddy is rookie Huston Street, who took over for injured closer Octavio Dotel and stormed his way to the 2005 AL Rookie of the Year with twenty-three saves, including eighteen in a row after the All-Star

STRANGER THINGS HAVE HAPPENED"   281

break. "I pick his brain every chance I get," says Street. "And he's just an incredible, giving person, on and off the baseball field."

Blanton stages quite a turnaround of his own, despite getting even less offensive support than Zito. In nineteen of Blanton's thirty-three starts, he gets two runs or less, but, taking a cue from Zito, he never seems bothered by what he can't control. Blanton goes 7–5 with a 2.65 ERA after the All-Star break—his 1.17 ERA in August earned him his second AL Rookie of the Month award—to finish 12–12 with a 3.53 ERA. "Just watching how he prepares and handles himself, and knowing what he's already accomplished, you learn what it takes at this level," Blanton says. Adds Kendall, "He's the leader of the staff, no question about it. Harden has incredible talent, but Barry's the number one guy here. On the mound and in the clubhouse."

＊＊＊

Between the December night he was traded and the end of spring training, Mulder speaks to Zito once, on the phone. The conversation is short, and here's what Zito takes away from it: "Mulder misses Scottsdale, big-time." Scottsdale fits Mulder like the Catwoman suit fit Halle Berry. Pretty much perfect. And that's one of the many things that initially pained Mulder about being traded. Scottsdale is the vibrant, sun-splashed focal point of spring training in Arizona, where twelve MLB teams work out and eight are within a short drive of one another. The Cardinals train in Florida, where you might be looking for sunscreen one minute and scrambling for an umbrella the next. The Grapefruit League is, quite literally, all over the map, and Jupiter, Florida, where the Cardinals are based, is anything but vibrant. "I swear, the worst place to go at night in Scottsdale would be the best place in Jupiter," Mulder says. "One of the guys took me out and said, 'This place is great.' We got there and there's, like, thirty people, and half of them are sixty years old."

Hudson misses Arizona, too. While the Cardinals are preparing for the season in Jupiter, the Braves are 180 miles upstate in Orlando. But Hudson has a home in Florida. Home for Mulder is Arizona, and to a lesser extent—still—Oakland is his home. When St. Louis played in San Francisco during the 2005 season, Mulder got permission to stay on the "other side" of the Bay Bridge so he could hang out with some members of the A's clubhouse staff.

"It's been tough," Mulder admits. "I mean, I think it's natural to miss something that was such a big part of you for so long. I have a lot of friends in Oakland. . . . I don't know if I'd say I've been lonely in St. Louis; I have plenty of friends on the team. But not like in Oakland."

Others, though, do get the impression that Mulder is a bit lonely, including equipment manager Steve Vucinich, to whom Mulder speaks at least once a week by phone for much of the season. "He called me twenty minutes after the trade, and I talked to him twice that day," Vucinich says. "I'm in contact with a lot of players who have left here, but it usually fades off after a while. For example, I still talk to Jason [Giambi], but not as much as I used to. With Mark, it hasn't faded."

It needs to be noted that this is a two-way street. When Crosby, with whom Mulder shared a house during the 2004 season, was photographed sporting a $15,000 watch on the red carpet of a Hollywood-style spring training bash in Scottsdale, Vucinich faxed Mulder the newspaper article. Mulder immediately left Crosby a voicemail razzing him for being quoted as saying, among other things, "I always wear Paper Denim Jeans," and, "I'm very single, and I can't wait to get inside." Says Mulder, "Oh my god. I thought I taught him better than that. That was awful." Counters Crosby, "That's a bunch of shit and Mulder knows it. He'd have done the exact same thing. . . . I'll tell you what, though, he knows everything we're doing. And anything he doesn't, I fill him in. We talk at least twice a week. . . . Is he lonely? Maybe a little bit. All his best friends are here."

If Vucinich or Crosby aren't available, Mulder gets his green-and-gold fix elsewhere. "Ohhhh, yeah. He pays attention [to the A's]," says St. Louis closer Jason (Izzy) Isringhausen, who played in Oakland from 1999 to 2001. "Whenever he can get them on the TV, he's watching. So we get on him about cutting the cord." Mulder insists that Isringhausen is overplaying things: "It's not about cutting the cord or letting it go. It's that some of those people in Oakland—Crosby, [Mark] Ellis—are my best friends. And what person traded to a new team doesn't get their balls busted about cutting the cord? [Jason] Marquis has been here two years, and they still get on him about missing Atlanta." Still, when asked to rank in order which of the three would find his comfort zone with a new team the quickest, Crosby and several other A's answered: Hudson, Zito, Mulder. "Izzy is a piece of Oakland for Mark," Vucinich says. "If it weren't for Izzy, Mark might be a lost soul for a little while."

Mulder's season is similar to Zito's: not so great early on (4.34 ERA before the All-Star break) and very, very good later (2.77 after the break). But the first-half number is skewed by a particularly bad June, in which his 7.18 ERA had some people wondering if he was "losing it" again. Mulder, though, says the self-doubt that haunted him in 2004 was never a factor during his first rough patch with the Cards. "This time, I knew exactly what it was," he says. "It was a couple of little mechanical things that I just needed to get straightened out, and it took me a few starts to do it, but mentally, it was night and day from last year. Last year I had no clue. This year, I had a clue. And so did Dunc [Cardinals pitching coach Dave Duncan], so we just worked it out and moved on."

Mulder says he thoroughly enjoys working with Duncan, and he marvels at the intensity of St. Louis manager Tony LaRussa. But nobody impresses him more than Albert Pujols. Mulder turns into an awestruck teenager when talking about the Cardinals' superstar first baseman. "It's hard to even put into words how unbelievably awesome Albert is," he gushes. "I mean, you hear about guys that you haven't seen much, how great they are, and whatever. Sure, he's great. But getting to watch Albert day in and day out, you're like, 'This guy is ridiculous.' I remember one time in spring training, some guy gets him out, and Albert comes back into the dugout and says, 'He better not throw me that again.' Now, believe me, you'll hear a lot of guys say that, so I'm used to it, but when Albert said it, a couple guys on the team told me he only does that three, four times a year, and when he does say it, he almost always hits a homer the next time up. So I'm not missing that next at-bat for anything in the world, and sure enough, Albert hits an absolute bomb. But he doesn't pimp his trot, he doesn't come back into the dugout and say, 'I told you so,' or anything like that. He just comes in, puts his bat and helmet away, and sits down. I was like, 'Holy fucking shit, this guy's an animal.' He's got a focus that I've never seen before, and I can't even put a word on it. If I didn't know how much he loves the game, I'd almost call it grim."

On June 9, the night before the A's come to town for a three-game interleague series against the Braves, Hudson is sitting on a couch in the living room of his three-story house in the Buckhead section of Atlanta, watching baseball on TV. While his wife, Kim, who gave birth to their first son in mid-April, is getting their three children ready for a trip to a nearby restaurant, Hudson is hoping to see a replay of Zito's first career big-league hit the previous night in Washington. When it comes, showing Zito line an opposite-field single into left field, Hudson leaps from his seat, raises his arms, and goes nuts. "A fuckin' bullet!" he whoops. "Not just a knock, a fuckin' bullet! Oh, man, I wish I was in that dugout for that, 'cause you know he called for the ball, and if I got my hands on that ball before he did, I'd have had me some fun with that." The following night, there's plenty of fun of another kind. After the A's beat the Braves in the series opener, Hudson has two limos show up at Turner Field and whisks a pack of his current and former teammates to a local club, where he's rented out the VIP section. "If you think about it, I might not see some of these guys for a long time after they leave here," Hudson says over the thumping bass inside the club. "Shoot, we won't play the A's in interleague again 'til 2008, so I'm soakin' as much of this in as I can. . . . I miss the hell out of these guys. Especially Z." If you ask anyone on the A's what they most miss about Hudson, his sense of humor is usually either the first or the second thing that's mentioned. The other is his competitive fire, but that fire burns only slightly hotter than his desire to fuck with a teammate, and Braves catcher Eddie Perez found that out the hard way.

A Hudson staple is talking hotel employees into giving him a teammate's room key and hiding in wait of a big scare. Late in the 2004 season, for example, Hudson and Zito jumped out from behind a hotel shower curtain while hotshot A's rookie Nick Swisher was taking care of some bathroom business. "I went from pissin' to shittin' my pants in about two seconds," Swisher says. "Welcome to the big leagues." In the case of Perez, Hudson even got a camera crew involved. Wearing the black cossack and the ghost mask made famous by the movie *Scream*, Hudson was hiding in a closet with a sound man when Perez, thinking he was being trailed by cameras as the subject of a day-in-the-life piece, arrived at his room. "He's like, 'Here's what a big-league closet looks like,'" Hudson says, "and I bounce out screaming at him. I absolutely crushed him, man. He fuckin' flipped out. Screamin' like a little girl on Halloween. It was one of my best 'gets' ever. An all-timer."

That this prank happened while Hudson was on the disabled list—yet another oblique strain knocked him out from June 16 to July 16—speaks volumes about his comfort level in Atlanta. Injured players often talk about feeling disconnected from their teams, but there was Hudson, the new guy, using his down time to rattle one of the team's elder statesmen. Lonely? Hardly. He showed Mulder around when the Cards visited Atlanta in April, and he spent most of both teams' batting practice during the series against Oakland in front of the A's dugout, but he's not hurting for buddies among the Braves.

"In spring training, he came in and he was professional, but he also mingles with the guys and laughs," says Atlanta's ageless Julio Franco, a twenty-year vet. "You need to bring your personality out so people can get to know you. They need to know what you're about: what you like, what you dislike. So unless you open up your personality and let them know, it'll be very hard to let people find out who you are. Huddy let us see who he is right away. He's a great teammate." Hudson wants to be more than a teammate, though. Teams often develop the personality of the top dogs, and during Oakland's visit to Atlanta, he says that Chipper Jones and John Smoltz are the laid-back leaders of the Braves. "It was real quiet when I got here," he recalls. "Freaky quiet. Like, 'Who died?' quiet. They don't even allow music in the clubhouse, man. Totally different atmosphere than in Oakland, that's for sure." And that's part of why Hudson wants to be a top dog with his new team, too. He likes to bark. "There's a lot of superstitions here," he says. "They've won thirteen division titles in a row, and the rules now are the same rules that were in place when it all started, so I'm not gonna fight that. Like the radio thing. You want to hear music here, you have to MP3 it. But I'm workin' on that. And honestly, when I first got here I felt like we could use a little more life in general. A little more fire. That's what I'd like to bring to this team."

Braves second baseman Marcus Giles says Hudson's impact is already being felt. "I think it's changing for the better since he got here," Giles explains. "You could say it's kind of like a college atmosphere, where maybe we'll get a little more of that rah-rah. It's not that that's going to win games single-handedly, but if you're excited and you're into the game even when you're sitting, you'll be ready when your name is called to go into the game." Hudson agrees that there's been an upswing in energy, but he's quick to credit the Braves' infusion of youth. Atlanta was ravaged by injuries early in the year, forcing the club to bring waves of rookies into the fold. "It's not just because of me," Hudson says. "It's a combination of a lot of guys coming up with a lot of passion, and the guys who've been here a while wanting to give that passion back. I mean, let's have some fun. Let's not be so corporate. Let's smile and laugh and carry on. And it's starting to get more like that. It's not like you're gonna walk in tomorrow and hear music blarin' with a bunch of guys poundin' beers, but you're gonna have some fun."

Though things have gone well for all three of the disbanded Big Three in the second half of 2005, Mulder in early September says communication has been sparse. "I texted Huddy after Derrek Lee hit a homer off him [August 22]," he says. "Lee had gone deep off me, like, ten days earlier [August 11]. Other than that, there hasn't been much." Says Zito, "It's been a long time. I called Mulder in August from the airport on an off day and we talked for about five minutes. I don't remember the last time I talked to Huddy." Adds Hudson, "I called all my friends in August when I got a new cell number, but that's been about it."

Mulder blames geography. "Being in three different time zones is the reason we don't talk as much. Usually, the time you think to call one of them is when you're on your way to the park or after a game. But if I want to call Zito on my way to the park in St. Louis, it might be too early to call him the day after a night game in Oakland. And if I want to call him after a game in St. Louis, he's probably on the field in Oakland. It's the same thing, in reverse, with Huddy. When I'm on my way to the park, he's an hour ahead in Atlanta, so he's already at the park. And when my game is over, it's too late to call him at home because he's got a wife and three kids."

The hope is that there will be reunions during the playoffs, and as of September 15 it looks good. Mulder's Cardinals wrap up the

NL Central, the A's had pulled back into a tie with the Angels atop the AL West the same night, and the Braves are six games up in the NL East with fifteen games to play. "Wouldn't it be somethin' if we played the Cardinals in the NLCS," Hudson muses, "and the winner played the A's in the World Series?" Should the former happen, Mulder says he hopes to square off with Hudson, and that it's prettier than when they matched up on April 29, when they combined to give up ten earned runs in thirteen innings and, when facing each other, looked nothing like the stud college hitters they both were. "We were both awful. On the mound and at the plate," he says.

The Braves end up winning their division, but the A's do not. Another round of injuries to Crosby and Harden take care of that, and Zito goes 2–3 with a 6.50 ERA down the stretch in September. "That's probably the most disappointed I've ever been in baseball," he says in late October. "Overall, I felt like I had a good year (14–13, 3.86), but the way it ended left me bitter. I needed to come up big, which I always pride myself on doing, and I didn't. It's fucked up, because I really wanted this team to be rewarded for coming back from so far down the way we did."

The Cardinals make quick work of the San Diego Padres in the first round of the playoffs, with Mulder cruising to victory in his only start of the series, but Hudson's season dies in one of the most incredible games in playoff history—and an all-too-familiar finish. Having lost the opener of Atlanta's division series against the Houston Astros, Hudson is asked to come back for game four—with the Braves a loss from elimination in the five-game series—on three days' rest. He responds with seven brilliant innings, after which Atlanta leads, 6–1. But the first two Astros batters of the eighth reach base, and Hudson is replaced by Kyle Farnsworth, who has taken the closer's job from Kolb. What follows is hard to believe. Farnsworth gives up a grand slam later in the eighth and a game-tying solo homer with two out in the ninth. Nine innings after that, the Astros homer again for an epic eighteen-inning victory. "Amazin', ain't it?" Hudson says dejectedly, his 14–9 record and 3.52 ERA in his first year in the NL of no consolation. "That took 'sucks' to a whole new level."

The Astros bring Mulder's season to an ugly end, too. He'd pitched well (seven innings, one earned run) in losing game two of the NLCS, but he gets an early hook in the decisive game six after giving up three runs in 4⅔ innings. "At least I got to see what the second round of the playoffs is like," he says with gallows humor. Like Hudson and Zito, Mulder finds little comfort in his solid regular season (16–8, 3.64). "I've said it a million times," Mulder says. "You don't play to win games. You play to win championships. World championships. I really thought this team was capable of doing it. Maybe next year."

Hudson, Mulder, and Zito enter the off-season knowing that barring trades, they'll be scattered across the country again in 2006. Hudson is signed with Atlanta through 2008. Mulder's 2006 contract option has vested during the 2005 season, so he's looking forward to playing in the Cardinals' first season at the new Busch Stadium. "We haven't talked about an extension, but I definitely like it there," he says while in Southern California for a golf tournament in December. "As the year went by, I got more and more comfortable, and it's a great organization and a great city, so, yeah, I could see being here a while." Zito's 2006 option with Oakland has vested, too, and although his name pops up in a trade rumors weekly during the off-season, A's GM Billy Beane sends a message to Zito through a mutual acquaintance in early December: "Tell him not to worry."

Should Mulder and Zito not re-up with the Cards and the A's, they'll be two of the top free agents on the market after the '06 season. Zito has long said he'd like to play in New York, but he's open to anything should things not work out in Oakland, so when a preposterous notion is thrown at him, he doesn't wave it off as casually as you might expect. What if Atlanta, eager to re-create the magic that was the Braves' terrific early-'90s trio of Maddux-Glavine-Smoltz, went after Mulder and Zito and reunited the Big Three? "Oh my God, dude, would that be insane, or what?" Zito says. "Wow, man. I guess that really could happen, huh? I mean, stranger things have happened. I don't think it will, but wow. That would turn the book into a movie, easy." And who might star in that movie? "Matt McConaughey as Huddy, no doubt. He's fiery and small, and he looks sweet with a shaved head," he says. "Mulder? Maybe that dude from *J.A.G.* or Pierce Brosnan. Someone all pimp with perfect hair. And I'd play me. I gotta play me, bro. That'd keep me in the Screen Actors Guild another year, right?"

ACKNOWLEDGMENTS

A lot of people helped to make this book possible, but Erik "Hilly" Hiljus probably deserves the most credit. It was Erik, a member of Oakland's starting rotation when I began working the A's beat in 2001, who essentially vouched for me as a "solid dude" among his teammates. That led to my friendship with Barry Zito, and it was that friendship that afforded me a certain level of trust within the clubhouse. Without that trust, Barry, Tim Hudson, and Mark Mulder would not have allowed me into their worlds, much less their heads. So thank you, Hilly, for being such a "solid dude" yourself and refusing to take the us-versus-them attitude that so many professional athletes apply to the media. And thanks to Barry, Tim, and Mark for following suit—and for being so incredibly generous with your time, knowledge, and honesty during such a trying season. If a book is only as good as its subject(s), I got lucky. It was a pleasure working with all three of you.

The 2004 A's as a whole were a sportswriter's dream. Not a ton of ego in that clubhouse, and when I asked for extra time, I usually got it. Aside from Tim, Mark, and Barry, the guys who helped me the most were Rich Harden, Damian Miller, Curt Young, and Eric Byrnes. Eric Chavez, Jermaine Dye, manager Ken Macha, first base coach Brad Fischer, and infield coach Ron Washington were a big help at times, too. So were a handful of coaches, players, and former players who were *not* part of the 2004 A's, including Rick Peterson, Cory Lidle, Art Howe, Frank Menechino, Jim Palmer, Ray Fosse, Miguel Tejada, Jason Giambi, David Justice, Johnny Damon, and Carlos Peña.

Baseball is a numbers game, and I'm not a numbers guy. So I'd be a fool not to thank the A's PR staff as a whole and Mike Selleck, the team's baseball information manager, in particular. Mike went above and beyond the call and did the dirty work that helped my numbers stay clean. Debbie Gallas, the team's media services coordinator, and Mickey Morabito, the team's traveling secretary, smoothed my path at times, too. And then there's Billy Beane, Oakland's general manager and a far cooler guy than a lot of people take the time to realize. In agreeing to write my foreword, Billy basically gave me the kind of credibility in the publishing world that Hilly gave me in the A's clubhouse.

Working a baseball beat is a grind. Writing a book while working a baseball beat is borderline insanity. Thus, I was crazy like Sybil during the season, my moods ranging from bubbly to brooding and happy to hateful, often in the same hour. But my fellow full-time traveling A's beat writers—Susan Slusser of the *San Francisco Chronicle*, Josh Suchon of the *Oakland Tribune*, Chris Haft of the *San Jose Mercury*, and Rick Hurd of the *Contra Costa Times*—not only put up with me, they lent me a hand when they could. Technically, we're all competitors. Thankfully, we're also friends (most of us, anyway). Slusser, whose tenacity and smarts make her twice the reporter I'll ever be, was unfailingly gracious with her whatever-you-need attitude toward my endeavor, and she routinely propped me up with encouragement when my tank was on "E." Suchon offered countless good suggestions along the way, but his first was the most significant. While he was covering the San Francisco Giants in the spring of 2003, I mentioned to him that I was thinking about writing a book about Zito, who had just won his Cy Young Award. He said a book on the Big Three would be better. He was right. Haft, a former colleague of mine at MLB.com, made more subtle contributions. He suggested things here and there, but what he did more than anything was listen. In press boxes, in dugouts, in clubhouses, in bars, in restaurants. He let me verbalize the things I was struggling to organize in my head, and that he never once grabbed me by the neck and screamed "Shut up about your damn book, already!" is astounding. Hurd and Jeff Fletcher, a very funny man who covers the A's and the Giants for the *Santa Rosa Press Democrat*, did their share of listening to me prattle on, too, and there were writers in other markets who chipped in where they could. Two of them are former A's beat writers: Howard Bryant of the *Boston Herald* and Mark Saxon of the *Orange County Register*. Others include John Schlegel, Gary Washburn, and Mark Feinsand of MLB.com, Scott Miller of CBSSportsline.com, Mike Silver of *Sports Illustrated*, Tyler Bleszinski of athleticsnation.com, and Carl Stewart of the *Oakland Tribune*. Interns Willem "Chachi" Suyderhoud and Mark Thoma were huge helps, too. And while I feel strange lumping him in with the other scribes because he's one of the greatest friends anyone could hope to have, it was Doug Miller of MLB.com who provided the most—and the best—feedback. If I forgot anyone, please forgive me.

Indirectly, Doug also hooked me up with my agent, Jessica Papin of Dystel & Goderich Literary Management in New York City. As a first-time author, I was clueless about "the process," but Jessica was a patient and expert guide in leading me to another mentor of sorts with similar qualities: Stephen Power at John Wiley & Sons. Stephen's passion for publishing is equaled by his passion for baseball, and his ability to "see the big picture" helped me immeasurably.

And finally, thanks to the family members who contributed in ways large and small. To Hal, for teaching me the concept of delayed gratification. To Mark and Dan, for taking an interest in what I do; it means more than you know. To Cathy, for the many contributions you've made over the years that went unthanked. To Marcia and Nolan, for giving me strength and inspiration. To Emily and NeeNee, for your ungodly amount of help at home. To Jackie and Natalie, for reminding me how joyous life can and should be. To Grama, for more than I could possibly list here. And finally, to Kelli, for being everything I'm not, everything I need, and more than I probably deserve. Your unselfishness is nothing short of heroic. I love you all.

CAREER GAME LOGS FOR THE BIG THREE

TIM HUDSON

1999

Date	Opponent	Score	Dec	IP	H	R	ER	BB	SO	HR
June 8	at San Diego	3–5	—	5.0	7	3	3	4	11	1
June 13	Los Angeles	9–3	W	7.0	7	2	1	2	8	0
June 19	at Detroit	13–1	W	7.0	9	1	1	1	5	0
June 24	at Texas	2–5	L	6.0	5	5	5	4	4	0
June 30	Seattle	14–5	W	7.0	7	0	0	3	5	0
July 5	Texas	4–2	W	7.0	5	1	1	4	7	0
July 10	at Arizona	2–0	W	8.1	3	0	0	2	9	0
July 17	San Francisco	2–7	—	7.0	5	2	2	4	6	0
July 22	at Seattle	4–5 (10)	—	5.2	5	3	3	2	1	1
July 27	at Minnesota	2–3	—	7.0	4	2	2	3	9	0
August 3	Baltimore	12–2	W	7.0	7	2	2	3	6	0
August 8	Chicago	7–5	—	4.2	7	4	4	3	4	1
August 14	at Toronto	13–5	W	6.0	9	3	3	2	5	0
August 19	at Boston	6–2	W	8.0	4	2	1	2	7	1
August 24	Cleveland	11–10	—	6.1	6	9	8	6	6	1
August 30	at New York	4–7	—	5.0	4	4	4	3	7	1
September 4	Detroit	2–1	W	9.0	4	1	1	4	8	1
September 10	at Tampa Bay	7–2	W	7.2	6	0	0	0	11	0
September 17	Kansas City	3–9	L	4.0	7	6	4	2	3	0
September 22	Minnesota	4–5	—	6.2	6	3	1	2	5	0
September 28	at Anaheim	9–3	W	5.0	4	3	3	6	5	1
Totals			**11–2**	**136.1**	**121**	**56**	**49**	**62**	**132**	**8**

2000

Date	Opponent	Score	Dec	IP	H	R	ER	BB	SO	HR
April 4	Detroit	3–1	W	7.0	1	0	0	3	8	0
April 10	Cleveland	4–9	—	5.0	5	4	4	6	2	0
April 15	at Boston	2–14	L	1.2	6	7	7	4	1	0
April 20	at Cleveland	5–9	L	2.1	5	4	4	1	3	2
April 25	Toronto	11–2	W	7.0	2	1	1	2	8	1
April 30	at Minnesota	8–2	W	7.2	6	2	2	1	10	0
May 6	at Texas	10–11	—	6.0	9	6	4	4	3	1
May 11	Seattle	7–6	W	7.0	7	6	6	3	7	3
May 16	Kansas City	7–8	—	5.0	6	4	3	6	7	0
May 21	Minnesota	13–4	W	7.0	4	0	0	4	6	0
May 27	at Baltimore	4–0	W	7.1	1	0	0	4	5	0
June 3	San Francisco	9–7	—	6.0	7	5	5	1	6	3
June 9	at Los Angeles	3–1	—	6.1	4	1	1	4	8	1
June 14	at Minnesota	9–6	W	8.0	3	1	1	3	7	1
June 20	Baltimore	8–5	W	8.0	8	5	5	0	3	3
June 27	Texas	7–6	W	5.0	3	3	3	2	4	1
July 2	at Anaheim	10–3	W	7.0	6	2	2	2	6	0
July 7	Arizona	5–4 (11)	—	6.1	6	4	4	4	5	0
July 21	Anaheim	3–12	L	5.1	12	9	9	3	4	3
July 26	at Seattle	6–1	W	7.1	7	1	1	4	5	0
July 31	Toronto	6–1	W	8.0	3	1	1	1	5	1
August 6	at Chicago	0–13	L	2.2	7	8	7	4	1	0
August 12	Detroit	9–5	W	6.0	5	4	4	2	3	1
August 18	at Detroit	1–10	L	3.2	7	6	5	2	3	2
August 23	at Cleveland	5–7	L	5.1	8	7	7	1	5	1
August 28	Chicago	3–0	W	9.0	1	0	0	1	8	0
September 3	at Toronto	4–3	W	7.2	8	3	2	0	5	0
September 9	Tampa Bay	10–0	W	9.0	2	0	0	0	4	0
September 16	at Tampa Bay	5–2	W	6.2	6	2	2	4	6	0

Date	Opponent	Score	Dec	IP	H	R	ER	BB	SO	HR
September 21	at Seattle	5–2	W	6.0	5	2	1	3	6	0
September 26	Anaheim	10–3	W	8.0	5	2	2	1	5	0
October 1	Texas	3–0	W	8.0	4	0	0	2	10	0
Totals			**20–6**	**202.1**	**169**	**100**	**93**	**82**	**169**	**24**

2001

Date	Opponent	Score	Dec	IP	H	R	ER	BB	SO	HR
April 2	at Seattle	4–5	—	5.0	3	2	2	6	5	0
April 7	Anaheim	4–2	W	8.0	3	2	2	1	11	1
April 12	Seattle	3–7	L	2.1	6	5	5	4	2	1
April 17	at Anaheim	5–1	W	7.0	6	1	1	1	5	1
April 22	at Texas	2–11	L	5.2	8	7	7	4	3	2
April 28	at New York	6–7	L	6.0	12	7	7	1	3	1
May 3	Toronto	3–2 (15)	—	9.0	4	2	2	3	7	2
May 9	at Toronto	8–5	W	6.2	5	2	2	1	6	0
May 15	New York	3–2 (12)	—	7.0	10	2	2	0	6	0
May 20	Chicago	6–2	W	8.0	4	2	1	1	3	0
May 26	at Minn. (1)	5–4 (10)	—	6.2	4	3	3	5	6	0
May 31	Tampa Bay	10–1	W	8.0	4	1	1	2	7	1
June 6	at Anaheim	4–1	W	7.0	3	1	1	2	5	0
June 12	at San Diego	5–2	W	7.0	6	1	1	1	7	1
June 17	at San Francisco	0–3	L	6.0	4	2	1	5	5	0
June 22	Texas	1–2	L	9.0	5	2	2	0	11	0
June 27	at Seattle	6–3	W	5.2	8	3	3	5	2	0
July 2	Anaheim	1–0	—	8.0	4	0	0	0	6	0
July 7	at Arizona	5–1	W	9.0	8	1	1	0	6	0
July 13	Los Angeles	11–7	W	6.0	5	4	4	2	7	1
July 18	at Minnesota	7–2	W	7.0	4	0	0	1	8	0
July 23	at Kansas City	7–2	W	7.0	5	2	2	2	3	1
July 28	Kansas City	3–9	L	6.1	8	7	6	2	2	0
August 3	at Detroit	2–1	W	9.0	9	1	1	1	5	0
August 8	Boston	6–1	W	8.0	8	1	1	2	5	1
August 14	at Toronto	3–6	—	6.0	6	2	2	1	4	2
August 19	at Chicago	8–7	—	4.2	8	6	4	1	3	1
August 24	Detroit	4–8	L	5.1	12	8	7	2	4	0
August 29	at Baltimore	4–1	W	6.1	2	1	1	6	4	0
September 3	Baltimore	4–2	W	8.0	3	2	2	0	5	0
September 9	Tampa Bay	4–3 (13)	—	8.0	8	3	3	1	8	1
September 19	at Texas	4–10	L	3.0	5	6	4	4	1	1
September 25	Anaheim	9–3	W	7.0	9	3	3	3	5	0
September 30	at Seattle	3–6	L	6.1	10	6	3	0	5	2
October 5	at Anaheim	6–2	W	6.0	7	1	1	1	6	0
Totals			**18–9**	**235.0**	**216**	**100**	**88**	**71**	**181**	**20**

2002

Date	Opponent	Score	Dec	IP	H	R	ER	BB	SO	HR
April 2	Texas	3–2	—	6.1	4	1	1	1	6	0
April 7	at Seattle	6–5	W	6.0	4	1	1	4	5	0
April 12	at Anaheim	5–1	W	7.0	9	1	1	1	5	0
April 17	Seattle	4–7	L	7.0	9	4	4	3	5	1
April 23	New York	1–2	L	9.0	4	2	2	3	6	1
April 28	Chicago	10–0	W	8.0	3	0	0	1	5	0
May 4	at Chicago	2–10	L	6.1	9	9	9	3	3	1
May 9	Boston	1–5	L	7.0	5	4	4	1	5	2
May 14	at Boston	2–6	L	5.1	6	6	5	6	3	0
May 19	at Toronto	0–11	L	7.0	6	5	5	3	3	3
May 24	Tampa Bay	9–8	—	5.1	7	6	6	4	4	1
May 30	at Tampa Bay	3–4 (13)	—	6.0	11	1	1	2	7	1
June 4	Seattle	3–2 (10)	—	6.1	12	2	2	1	5	0
June 9	Houston	7–6	—	7.0	7	1	1	0	6	0
June 14	at San Francisco	3–2	W	7.0	7	1	1	1	6	0
June 20	at Pittsburgh	5–3	W	8.0	5	2	2	0	4	1
June 25	at Seattle	1–7	L	6.0	8	4	4	4	3	0
June 30	San Francisco	7–0	W	9.0	5	0	0	3	1	0
July 5	Kansas City	4–3	—	7.0	6	1	1	5	6	1
July 12	at Baltimore	1–0	W	7.0	8	0	0	1	2	0
July 17	Anaheim	4–10	L	5.1	8	5	3	3	3	1
July 24	at Anaheim	1–5	L	7.0	8	5	5	0	5	0
July 29	Cleveland	6–8	—	6.0	12	5	5	1	5	0
August 3	Detroit	8–4	W	7.0	4	3	2	2	3	1
August 9	at New York	3–2 (16)	—	7.0	6	0	0	0	5	0
August 14	Toronto	4–2	W	7.1	7	2	1	1	2	1
August 19	at Cleveland	8–1	W	8.1	6	1	1	0	6	1
August 24	at Detroit	12–3	W	9.0	8	3	3	3	7	1
August 30	Minnesota	4–2	W	6.1	8	2	2	2	7	1

Date	Opponent	Score	Dec	IP	H	R	ER	BB	SO	HR
September 4	Kansas City	12–11	—	6.2	11	5	2	0	6	0
September 9	at Anaheim	2–1	W	7.1	6	1	1	0	4	1
September 14	Seattle	1–0	W	9.0	4	0	0	2	2	0
September 19	Anaheim	5–3	W	7.1	6	3	3	2	4	0
September 25	at Seattle	2–3	—	7.0	8	1	1	1	3	0
Totals				**15–9**	**238.1**	**237**	**87**	**79**	**62**	**152**	**19**
2003										
April 1	Seattle	5–0	W	8.0	5	0	0	2	4	0
April 6	Anaheim	7–6	—	5.0	6	4	4	6	1	0
April 11	at Anaheim	5–9	L	6.0	11	6	6	1	1	1
April 16	at Seattle	4–1	W	8.0	5	1	1	0	7	0
April 22	Detroit	6–5 (11)	—	7.2	3	3	3	4	6	1
April 27	Cleveland	4–3	—	7.0	7	3	3	4	6	0
May 3	at New York	5–3 (10)	—	8.0	3	1	1	2	4	0
May 9	New York	7–2	W	8.0	5	2	2	1	5	1
May 14	at Detroit	1–2	—	8.0	7	1	1	1	3	1
May 20	Minnesota	4–1	W	8.0	5	1	1	0	5	0
May 25	Kansas City	4–3 (10)	—	7.0	5	3	2	1	4	0
May 30	at Kansas City	6–11	L	3.2	10	9	6	1	1	2
June 4	at Florida	6–5	—	6.0	7	5	3	3	3	0
June 10	Atlanta	4–3 (12)	—	8.0	6	2	2	2	2	0
June 15	Montreal	9–1	W	7.0	6	1	1	1	5	0
June 21	San Francisco	4–6	L	7.0	11	6	5	2	5	2
June 26	at Texas	13–0	W	7.0	3	0	0	0	8	0
July 1	Seattle	3–2 (11)	—	8.0	5	1	1	2	5	0
July 6	Anaheim	6–5	—	6.2	4	1	1	4	5	0
July 11	Baltimore	2–0	W	9.0	3	0	0	1	9	0
July 17	at Minnesota	2–6	L	7.0	11	6	4	1	2	1
July 22	at Kansas City	10–0	W	7.0	1	0	0	1	8	0
July 27	at Anaheim	10–1	W	9.0	4	1	1	2	6	1
August 1	New York	3–2 (10)	—	7.0	4	2	2	3	5	0
August 6	at Detroit	9–3	W	8.0	7	3	3	0	6	2
August 11	Boston	4–0	W	9.0	2	0	0	1	7	0
August 16	Toronto	6–4	W	6.1	2	1	1	3	6	0
August 24	at Toronto	17–2	W	6.0	6	2	0	1	0	0
August 29	Tampa Bay	5–2	W	8.0	6	2	2	1	7	0
September 3	at Baltimore	0–9	L	3.0	8	5	5	0	1	0
September 8	Anaheim	1–3	L	7.2	9	3	3	4	7	1
September 13	at Texas	9–3	W	6.0	7	3	3	2	6	0
September 19	Seattle	1–6	L	6.0	8	4	4	3	7	1
September 24	Texas	5–3	W	7.0	5	2	1	1	5	1
Totals				**16–7**	**240.0**	**197**	**84**	**72**	**61**	**162**	**15**
2004										
April 5	Texas	5–4	—	5.0	6	2	2	3	3	0
April 10	Seattle	2–1	W	9.0	4	1	1	0	2	0
April 16	at Anaheim	3–0	W	7.1	6	0	0	0	7	0
April 21	at Seattle	7–4	W	8.0	8	4	4	1	4	1
April 27	at New York	8–10	—	7.0	5	4	4	3	3	0
May 2	at Tampa Bay	2–8	L	7.0	9	8	6	1	3	1
May 8	Minnesota	2–3 (10)	—	9.0	9	2	2	0	4	1
May 14	at Kansas City	6–2	W	8.0	5	2	2	2	2	0
May 20	Detroit	3–2	W	8.0	10	2	1	1	2	0
May 25	at Boston	2–12	L	4.0	9	5	5	4	2	0
May 30	at Cleveland	3–4	—	8.0	11	2	2	1	3	0
June 5	Toronto	4–0	W	9.0	8	0	0	1	5	0
June 11	Pittsburgh	6–1	W	7.0	5	1	1	2	5	0
June 17	at St. Louis	4–5	—	7.1	8	2	2	3	5	0
June 22	at Anaheim	1–6	L	5.0	7	5	4	3	2	0
August 7	at Minnesota	3–4	L	5.2	8	4	4	1	4	0
August 12	Detroit	3–5	—	5.0	6	2	2	1	6	0
August 17	at Baltimore	11–0	W	9.0	5	0	0	0	4	0
August 23	Baltimore	4–3	W	7.1	8	3	1	2	5	0
August 28	Tampa Bay	5–4	W	7.0	4	4	2	1	4	0
September 3	at Toronto	7–4	W	7.0	8	4	4	2	4	1
September 8	Boston	3–8	L	3.0	6	7	7	5	3	0
September 13	Texas	7–6 (10)	—	8.0	9	4	4	1	8	2
September 18	at Seattle	7–4	W	8.0	8	3	3	1	2	1
September 23	at Texas	4–5	—	7.0	7	2	2	5	2	0
September 28	Seattle	2–7	L	6.0	11	7	7	0	3	1
October 3	Anaheim	3–2	—	7.0	4	2	2	0	6	0
Totals				**12–6**	**188.2**	**194**	**82**	**74**	**44**	**103**	**8**

MARK MULDER

2000

Date	Opponent	Score	Dec	IP	H	R	ER	BB	SO	HR
April 18	at Cleveland	8–5	W	6.0	5	4	4	3	6	2
April 23	Baltimore	3–2 (11)	—	7.0	4	2	2	2	4	0
April 29	at Minnesota	6–2 (10)	—	6.2	8	2	2	4	4	0
May 5	at Texas	16–17	—	4.1	7	7	7	3	4	0
May 10	at Anaheim	7–4	—	7.2	6	2	2	1	6	1
May 15	Kansas City	6–3	W	6.0	6	3	1	0	2	0
May 20	Minnesota	0–3	L	7.0	7	3	1	4	4	0
May 26	at Baltimore	3–8	L	5.1	10	6	6	3	2	4
June 2	San Francisco	5–4	W	5.0	7	3	3	3	4	2
June 7	San Diego	10–4	—	4.1	5	4	4	3	1	1
June 13	at Minnesota	6–5	W	6.0	8	2	2	4	3	0
June 19	Baltimore	13–12 (10)	—	2.1	7	6	6	2	2	1
June 25	Kansas City	4–3	W	7.0	4	1	1	2	4	0
June 30	at Anaheim	0–7	L	5.2	10	6	6	2	0	2
July 5	at Texas	4–9	L	6.2	15	9	2	3	7	0
July 13	at San Francisco	2–4	L	6.0	4	2	2	2	2	1
July 18	at Colorado	3–18	L	4.0	9	10	9	3	2	0
July 23	Anaheim	5–0	W	7.2	6	0	0	2	5	0
July 28	Boston	1–4	L	8.0	6	4	3	3	3	2
August 2	Toronto	5–4	—	6.0	8	2	2	1	2	1
August 10	at New York	6–12	L	3.1	11	10	10	3	1	2
August 15	Cleveland	5–3	W	6.0	5	2	2	3	2	0
August 21	at Detroit	1–3	L	5.2	6	3	3	2	5	0
August 26	New York	6–10	L	2.0	10	6	6	1	1	1
September 1	at Toronto	3–4	—	5.1	9	3	3	4	5	0
September 6	at Boston	6–4	W	6.0	5	2	2	3	2	2
September 12	Minnesota	5–3	W	7.0	3	2	2	3	5	0
Totals			**9–10**	**154.0**	**191**	**106**	**93**	**69**	**88**	**22**

2001

Date	Opponent	Score	Dec	IP	H	R	ER	BB	SO	HR
April 6	Anaheim	4–5	L	5.1	7	5	4	3	4	0
April 11	Seattle	0–3	—	7.0	2	0	0	3	7	0
April 16	at Anaheim	6–3	W	6.0	5	3	3	0	7	1
April 21	at Texas	7–6	W	6.0	9	5	5	5	5	0
April 27	at New York	2–3	L	6.1	8	3	3	1	6	1
May 2	Toronto	6–0	W	9.0	3	0	0	3	7	0
May 8	at Toronto	8–5	W	7.1	8	4	4	0	2	1
May 13	at Boston	4–5	—	7.0	5	2	2	3	5	0
May 19	Chicago	4–3	W	8.2	4	3	3	0	3	1
May 25	at Minnesota	4–2	W	6.2	7	1	1	1	5	0
May 30	Tampa Bay	15–2	W	5.0	9	2	2	0	1	0
June 5	at Anaheim	3–7	L	4.0	11	7	7	3	2	3
June 10	San Francisco	6–2	W	7.2	5	2	2	0	2	0
June 15	at San Francisco	1–3	L	6.0	6	3	3	0	3	2
June 20	Seattle	6–4	—	5.1	6	3	3	1	4	2
June 26	at Seattle	3–7	L	5.1	12	6	5	2	2	0
July 1	at Texas	1–3	L	7.2	6	3	3	0	6	1
July 6	at Arizona	3–0	W	9.0	1	0	0	0	9	0
July 12	Los Angeles	6–0	W	9.0	6	0	0	1	7	0
July 17	Colorado	3–2	W	7.0	7	2	2	2	3	0
July 22	at Kansas City	4–5	—	5.0	11	4	4	1	1	1
July 27	Kansas City	5–0	W	9.0	4	0	0	2	7	0
August 2	at Cleveland	17–4	W	6.0	6	2	1	1	6	0
August 7	Boston	5–2	W	7.1	6	2	2	0	5	0
August 12	New York	4–2	W	9.0	7	2	2	0	7	1
August 18	at Chicago	5–4	—	4.0	6	4	4	3	4	1
August 23	Cleveland	7–9	L	3.2	10	8	8	2	2	1
August 28	at Baltimore	6–2	W	8.0	4	2	2	3	4	0
September 2	at Tampa Bay	3–1	W	9.0	4	1	1	0	8	0
September 8	Tampa Bay	10–4	W	7.0	7	3	3	1	5	0
September 18	at Texas	6–5	W	6.0	6	4	4	2	3	1
September 23	Seattle	7–4	W	7.0	6	1	1	2	4	0
September 28	at Seattle	3–5	L	6.0	9	5	4	3	2	0
October 4	at Anaheim	5–1	W	7.0	1	0	0	3	5	0
Totals			**21–8**	**229.1**	**214**	**92**	**88**	**51**	**153**	**16**

2002

Date	Opponent	Score	Dec	IP	H	R	ER	BB	SO	HR
April 1	Texas	8–3	W	8.0	6	3	3	0	8	1
April 6	at Seattle	8–3	W	6.1	5	3	3	4	4	0
April 11	at Texas	0–7	L	4.0	6	4	4	3	4	1
May 10	Toronto	2–6	L	4.1	8	6	6	1	3	0

Date	Opponent	Score	Dec	IP	H	R	ER	BB	SO	HR
May 17	at Toronto	1–7	L	5.0	7	5	5	2	2	1
May 23	Baltimore	3–11	L	4.2	6	7	4	3	1	2
May 28	at Baltimore	5–2	W	6.0	8	2	1	0	4	0
June 2	at Tampa Bay	4–2	W	5.2	6	2	2	2	5	0
June 7	Houston	5–3	W	7.1	5	3	3	3	8	0
June 12	Milwaukee	8–0	W	9.0	9	0	0	4	6	0
June 18	at Pittsburgh	4–2	W	6.1	5	2	2	2	3	1
June 23	at Cincinnati	5–1	W	6.0	6	1	1	1	4	0
June 28	San Francisco	10–6	W	8.2	9	6	4	1	5	1
July 3	Minnesota	1–2	L	9.0	6	2	2	1	12	0
July 11	at Baltimore	4–1	W	7.0	3	0	0	4	6	0
July 16	at Tampa Bay	2–1	W	7.1	6	1	1	2	6	0
July 21	Texas	3–7 (12)	—	9.0	3	2	2	2	5	1
July 26	at Texas	4–12	L	6.0	6	5	5	2	2	3
July 31	Cleveland	6–4	W	8.0	6	4	4	1	6	0
August 6	at Boston	9–1	W	6.0	5	1	1	4	3	0
August 11	at New York	5–8	L	6.0	11	8	7	1	8	2
August 17	Chicago	9–2	W	8.0	5	2	1	2	4	0
August 22	at Cleveland	9–3	W	7.2	5	3	3	0	2	2
August 27	at Kansas City	6–4	W	7.0	7	4	4	0	5	0
September 1	Minnesota	7–5	—	8.0	5	4	4	4	7	3
September 7	at Minnesota	2–0	W	8.0	7	0	0	0	10	0
September 12	at Anaheim	6–7	—	7.0	5	5	5	3	4	3
September 17	Anaheim	0–1 (10)	—	9.0	5	0	0	0	12	0
September 22	Texas	7–5	W	6.0	8	3	3	2	5	0
September 27	at Texas	3–2	W	7.0	3	0	0	1	5	0
Totals			**19–7**	**207.1**	**182**	**88**	**80**	**55**	**159**	**21**

2003

Date	Opponent	Score	Dec	IP	H	R	ER	BB	SO	HR
April 3	Seattle	6–7 (11)	—	6.0	8	4	4	4	1	0
April 9	at Texas	13–5	W	5.0	9	4	4	2	4	2
April 14	at Seattle	3–4	L	7.0	8	4	4	1	2	1
April 19	Texas	12–2	W	7.0	5	2	2	2	5	2
April 24	Detroit	2–0	W	9.0	3	0	0	1	5	0
April 30	at Chicago	4–1	W	9.0	4	1	1	0	6	0
May 6	Chicago	6–0	W	9.0	5	0	0	2	4	0
May 11	New York	5–2	W	8.0	3	2	2	2	8	1
May 16	at Cleveland	2–3	L	8.0	7	3	3	2	4	1
May 23	Kansas City	4–1	W	9.0	8	1	1	2	6	0
May 29	at Kansas City	6–1	W	7.0	8	1	1	1	2	0
June 3	at Florida	2–13	L	3.2	12	8	8	2	2	1
June 8	at Philadelphia (G#1)	1–7	L	6.0	9	4	4	3	5	
June 13	Montreal	8–4	W	7.0	8	3	3	2	8	1
June 19	Texas	9–2	W	7.0	10	2	2	0	3	0
June 24	at Texas	6–7	L	7.0	8	4	4	1	6	0
June 29	at San Francisco	5–2	W	7.0	6	1	1	2	3	0
July 4	Anaheim	0–1	L	9.0	3	1	1	0	5	0
July 10	Tampa Bay	5–2	W	9.0	5	2	2	1	5	1
July 19	at Minnesota	4–9	L	6.0	7	5	5	2	5	1
July 24	at Seattle	3–0	W	7.0	7	0	0	1	11	0
July 29	Cleveland	6–2	W	7.2	7	2	2	1	11	2
August 3	New York	2–1	W	9.0	5	1	1	2	7	0
August 8	at Chicago	2–3	L	8.0	10	3	3	0	2	1
August 13	Boston	3–7	L	6.1	9	6	5	3	6	1
August 19	at Boston	3–2	—	3.0	6	2	2	1	2	0
Totals			**15–9**	**186.2**	**180**	**66**	**65**	**40**	**128**	**15**

2004

Date	Opponent	Score	Dec	IP	H	R	ER	BB	SO	HR
April 6	Texas	3–1	W	7.0	5	1	1	1	4	0
April 11	Seattle	4–9	—	7.0	6	2	2	2	5	0
April 17	at Anaheim	3–6	L	7.0	5	4	2	2	5	1
April 22	at Seattle	8–2	W	6.0	5	2	2	3	5	0
April 28	at New York	1–5	L	6.0	7	4	4	2	6	1
May 4	New York	8–10	—	6.1	13	7	7	2	3	1
May 9	Minnesota	· 8–4	W	9.0	6	4	3	2	3	2
May 15	at Kansas City	3–1	W	9.0	4	1	1	1	7	1
May 21	Kansas City	7–0	W	9.0	3	0	0	0	6	0
May 27	at Boston	15–2	W	5.2	4	2	2	7	4	0
June 2	Chicago	3–2 (10)	—	7.0	8	2	2	2	5	0
June 7	Cincinnati	13–2	W	7.0	6	2	2	2	4	1
June 13	Pittsburgh	13–3	W	8.0	4	3	3	2	7	2
June 19	at Chicago (NL)	3–4	—	8.0	10	2	2	2	4	0
June 24	at Anaheim	2–1	W	9.0	4	1	1	3	5	0

Date	Opponent	Score	Dec	IP	H	R	ER	BB	SO	HR
June 29	Anaheim	5–4	W	7.0	9	4	4	3	8	0
July 4	at San Francisco	9–6	W	7.0	8	3	3	2	2	0
July 10	at Cleveland	16–7	W	6.2	9	6	6	3	9	0
July 18	Chicago	5–3	W	8.1	3	3	3	2	8	2
July 23	Texas	3–8	L	6.0	10	7	7	1	4	1
July 28	Seattle	3–2	W	9.0	8	2	2	3	3	1
August 3	at New York	13–4	W	7.0	8	4	4	5	3	2
August 8	at Minnesota	6–5 (18)	—	8.0	6	3	3	4	4	1
August 13	Kansas City	3–10	L	7.0	8	7	7	2	5	2
August 18	at Baltimore	5–4	W	8.0	6	4	4	3	0	0
August 24	Baltimore	6–2	W	6.0	4	2	2	3	2	0
August 29	Tampa Bay	9–6	—	6.0	7	4	4	6	3	0
September 4	at Toronto	9–5	—	6.0	10	5	5	2	5	1
September 10	Cleveland	3–4 (12)	—	7.0	6	3	3	4	2	2
September 15	Texas	3–10	L	6.0	11	8	8	2	5	2
September 21	at Texas	4–9	L	4.0	8	9	5	2	2	1
September 26	at Anaheim	2–6	L	3.2	6	4	3	3	2	1
October 1	Anaheim	0–10	L	2.0	6	4	4	0	0	0
Totals			**17–8**	**225.2**	**223**	**119**	**111**	**83**	**140**	**25**

BARRY ZITO

2000

Date	Opponent	Score	Dec	IP	H	R	ER	BB	SO	HR
July 22	Anaheim	10–3	W	5.0	2	1	1	6	6	0
July 27	Boston	4–5 (10)	—	7.0	4	3	3	4	5	1
August 1	Toronto	3–1 (10)	—	7.0	4	1	1	2	3	0
August 8	at New York	3–4	—	6.1	3	2	1	2	4	0
August 13	Detroit	3–5	L	6.0	7	5	5	2	5	2
August 19	at Detroit	3–4	L	6.0	9	4	4	1	5	0
August 24	at Cleveland	11–7	W	6.2	5	3	2	6	8	0
August 29	Chicago	0–3	L	7.0	4	3	3	4	5	1
September 4	at Toronto	10–0	W	6.2	2	0	0	6	4	0
September 10	Tampa Bay	11–0	W	9.0	5	0	0	0	8	0
September 15	at Tampa Bay	17–3	W	6.0	3	2	2	5	4	1
September 20	at Baltimore (D)	0–2	L	7.2	4	2	2	5	4	1
September 25	Anaheim	7–5	W	6.1	7	3	3	1	10	0
September 30	Texas	23–2	W	6.0	5	1	1	1	7	0
Totals			**7–4**	**92.2**	**64**	**30**	**28**	**45**	**78**	**6**

2001

Date	Opponent	Score	Dec	IP	H	R	ER	BB	SO	HR
April 3	at Seattle	5–1	W	7.0	3	0	0	4	5	0
April 8	Anaheim	4–6	L	5.1	9	6	6	1	7	0
April 14	Texas	8–9	—	6.0	8	8	7	2	9	2
April 19	at Texas	9–5	W	6.0	5	2	2	2	10	1
April 24	at Chicago	6–4	W	7.0	7	3	3	3	6	0
April 29	at New York	1–3	L	6.0	5	3	1	2	7	0
May 5	Boston	1–7	L	4.0	8	5	5	1	3	1
May 10	at Toronto	14–8	—	3.0	6	5	5	4	5	2
May 16	New York	4–3 (10)	—	6.0	4	2	2	2	6	1
May 22	at Kansas City	4–1	—	6.2	6	1	0	2	7	0
May 27	at Minnesota	3–9	L	7.0	6	5	5	2	8	0
June 2	Baltimore	0–7	L	5.0	9	5	5	1	2	0
June 7	at Anaheim	4–6	L	5.1	4	4	4	2	1	0
June 13	at San Diego	6–2	—	6.1	4	2	2	5	4	1
June 18	Seattle	4–3	W	7.0	7	3	3	1	2	0
June 23	Texas	5–4	—	7.0	5	3	2	1	6	1
June 28	at Seattle	6–3	—	6.1	7	3	2	1	5	2
July 3	Anaheim	5–2	W	5.0	3	2	2	3	5	1
July 8	at Arizona	2–1	W	6.0	6	1	1	0	10	0
July 14	Los Angeles	3–5 (15)	—	7.0	4	2	2	1	4	0
July 19	at Minnesota	10–12	L	4.2	9	5	5	2	7	0
July 24	Minnesota	7–6	—	2.0	5	6	6	3	3	0
July 29	Kansas City	6–4	—	6.1	1	0	0	2	9	0
August 4	at Detroit	10–1	W	8.0	1	1	1	2	10	1
August 9	Boston	6–0	W	9.0	4	0	0	2	3	0
August 15	at Toronto	2–5	L	6.1	7	5	3	2	3	1
August 20	Cleveland	9–0	W	9.0	4	0	0	2	11	0
August 25	Detroit	6–1	W	6.0	4	1	1	3	7	0
August 30	at Baltimore	15–0	W	6.0	5	0	0	3	3	0
September 4	Baltimore	5–2	W	6.0	2	1	0	2	5	0
September 10	Texas	7–1	W	9.0	4	1	1	2	10	1
September 20	at Texas	7–2	W	6.0	6	2	2	4	5	1

Date	Opponent	Score	Dec	IP	H	R	ER	BB	SO	HR
September 26	Anaheim	3–1	W	6.0	4	1	1	5	9	0
October 2	Texas	9–4	W	6.0	8	3	3	1	5	1
October 7	at Anaheim	6–2	W	5.0	4	1	1	5	3	1
Totals			**17–8**	**214.1**	**184**	**92**	**83**	**80**	**205**	**18**

2002

Date	Opponent	Score	Dec	IP	H	R	ER	BB	SO	HR
April 3	Texas	9–6	—	6.0	5	1	1	3	6	0
April 9	at Texas	5–4 (11)	—	6.2	4	2	2	4	8	1
April 14	at Anaheim	1–4	L	6.0	7	4	4	1	4	1
April 20	Anaheim	8–7	—	4.0	6	5	4	4	3	1
April 25	New York	6–2	W	7.0	5	1	1	2	6	0
April 30	at New York	2–8	L	4.0	6	6	6	4	6	1
May 5	at Chicago	3–2	W	6.0	6	2	2	0	4	1
May 11	Toronto	7–4	W	6.0	5	2	2	1	10	2
May 16	at Boston	5–0	W	8.0	5	0	0	0	6	0
May 21	Baltimore	4–6 (14)	—	6.0	7	4	4	2	5	2
May 26	Tampa Bay	7–0	W	7.0	2	0	0	4	7	0
June 1	at Tampa Bay	8–3	W	8.0	7	1	1	2	11	1
June 6	Seattle	10–4	W	6.1	8	3	3	3	1	1
June 11	Milwaukee	11–2	W	8.0	2	1	1	1	4	1
June 16	at San Francisco	2–1	W	6.2	4	1	1	2	5	1
June 22	at Cincinnati	10–3	W	7.0	3	3	3	1	6	1
June 27	at Seattle	4–7	L	3.0	9	7	7	2	4	1
July 2	Minnesota	4–3	—	8.0	7	3	3	3	3	1
July 7	Kansas City	3–2	W	7.2	6	2	2	1	9	1
July 13	at Baltimore	6–0	W	7.0	3	0	0	3	3	0
July 18	Anaheim	2–0	W	7.1	4	0	0	2	4	0
July 23	at Anaheim	2–1	W	6.1	5	1	1	4	5	0
July 28	at Texas	12–2	W	7.0	5	2	2	3	4	1
August 2	Detroit	1–3	L	6.0	6	3	1	3	3	1
August 8	at Boston	2–4	L	8.0	7	4	4	4	7	1
August 13	Toronto	5–4	W	8.0	4	3	1	1	7	0
August 18	Chicago	7–4	W	5.2	4	3	3	3	5	1
August 23	at Detroit	9–1	W	7.0	4	0	0	2	5	0
August 28	at Kansas City	7–1	W	7.0	4	1	1	2	3	0
September 2	Kansas City	7–6	—	6.0	10	5	2	0	4	2
September 8	at Minnesota	6–0	W	7.0	3	0	0	2	7	0
September 13	Seattle	5–0	W	8.0	2	0	0	1	7	0
September 18	Anaheim	7–4	W	5.1	7	4	4	4	4	0
September 24	at Seattle	7–8	—	6.1	7	4	3	2	2	1
September 29	at Texas	8–7	W	6.0	3	1	1	2	4	0
Totals			**23–5**	**229.1**	**182**	**79**	**70**	**78**	**182**	**24**

2003

Date	Opponent	Score	Dec	IP	H	R	ER	BB	SO	HR
April 2	Seattle	8–3	W	6.0	3	1	1	2	3	0
April 8	at Texas	2–1	W	7.0	4	1	1	4	7	1
April 13	at Anaheim	2–8	L	5.0	8	7	7	4	1	2
April 18	Texas	9–0	W	9.0	6	0	0	1	6	0
April 23	Detroit	1–4	L	7.0	5	2	2	3	2	1
April 29	at Chicago	3–2	W	7.0	4	2	1	3	3	1
May 4	at New York	2–0	W	8.0	4	0	0	3	4	0
May 10	New York	2–5	L	6.0	5	4	4	4	7	2
May 15	at Detroit	11–2	W	6.0	4	2	1	2	5	0
May 21	Minnesota	3–4	—	7.0	5	2	2	3	1	1
May 27	at Minnesota	3–4	L	8.0	3	4	4	2	10	2
June 1	at Kansas City	6–4	—	6.2	7	4	4	1	4	0
June 6	at Philadelphia	7–4	W	6.0	5	2	2	3	3	0
June 12	Atlanta	2–4	L	7.0	5	3	3	2	3	2
June 18	Texas	4–3 (11)	—	6.0	4	1	1	3	4	0
June 23	at Texas	3–1	—	6.0	4	1	1	4	3	0
June 28	at San Francisco	7–8 (10)	—	6.0	10	6	6	2	3	1
July 3	Seattle	5–2	W	7.1	10	2	2	0	5	1
July 8	Tampa Bay	3–9	L	5.1	15	7	7	2	2	0
July 13	Baltimore	1–0	—	8.0	4	0	0	2	2	0
July 18	at Minnesota	2–3	L	8.0	3	3	2	4	9	0
July 23	at Seattle	0–6	L	6.0	3	4	4	6	5	1
July 28	at Anaheim	1–2	—	7.0	4	0	0	0	2	0
August 2	New York	7–10	L	3.0	8	8	3	2	1	2
August 7	at Detroit	2–3	L	8.0	6	3	0	1	3	1
August 12	Boston	5–3	W	5.1	6	3	3	2	4	0
August 17	Toronto	7–3	W	7.0	4	3	3	3	6	0
August 22	at Toronto	3–6	L	5.1	6	5	5	4	3	0

Date	Opponent	Score	Dec	IP	H	R	ER	BB	SO	HR
August 27	Baltimore	6–2	W	8.0	4	2	2	2	3	1
September 2	at Baltimore	2–0	—	8.0	4	0	0	2	7	0
September 7	at Tampa Bay	2–11	L	5.1	6	7	7	3	3	0
September 12	at Texas	9–3	W	7.0	5	3	3	3	8	0
September 17	at Anaheim	2–1	W	8.1	2	1	0	2	6	0
September 22	Texas	7–3	W	6.0	3	1	0	3	4	0
September 27	at Seattle	4–7	—	5.0	7	4	4	1	4	0
Totals			**14–12**	**231.2**	**186**	**98**	**85**	**88**	**146**	**19**

2004

Date	Opponent	Score	Dec	IP	H	R	ER	BB	SO	HR
April 7	Texas	1–2	L	8.0	7	2	2	4	5	0
April 13	at Texas	10–9	W	5.0	11	6	4	2	2	0
April 18	at Anaheim	7–1	W	6.0	4	1	1	1	4	0
April 23	Anaheim	2–12	L	4.0	10	9	9	1	3	2
April 29	at New York	5–7	L	6.0	8	6	6	2	9	4
May 5	New York	3–4	—	6.0	6	2	2	3	6	2
May 11	at Detroit	5–4 (15)	—	7.0	10	4	4	1	5	0
May 16	at Kansas City	6–2	W	6.0	4	2	2	2	3	0
May 22	Kansas City	5–4 (11)	—	7.0	7	4	4	2	7	1
May 28	at Cleveland	0–1	—	8.0	3	0	0	5	7	0
June 3	Toronto	3–2 (11)	—	8.0	5	1	1	2	5	0
June 8	Cincinnati	10–6	W	5.0	8	5	5	1	5	2
June 15	at St. Louis	4–8	—	5.0	7	3	2	5	8	0
June 20	at Chicago (NL)	3–5	L	5.0	7	4	4	3	2	1
June 25	San Francisco	4–6	L	7.0	7	6	1	3	2	2
June 30	Anaheim	4–2	—	7.0	4	2	2	2	4	1
July 6	at Boston	0–11	L	4.0	9	7	6	3	2	1
July 11	at Cleveland	1–4	L	7.0	6	2	2	4	6	1
July 16	Chicago	5–1	W	7.0	4	1	1	1	3	0
July 21	at Seattle	5–6 (10)	—	5.0	9	5	5	3	4	2
July 26	Seattle	14–5	W	6.0	8	5	5	3	3	1
July 31	at Texas	9–4	W	5.2	5	4	4	5	4	2
August 5	at New York	1–5	L	6.2	11	5	4	1	3	0
August 10	Detroit	5–4	W	7.0	5	3	3	1	5	1
August 15	Kansas City	1–6	L	6.2	4	2	2	3	9	0
August 21	at Tampa Bay	5–0	W	8.0	4	0	0	1	6	0
August 26	Baltimore	9–4	W	5.1	4	4	4	4	4	0
September 1	at Chicago	4–5	—	6.2	7	4	4	1	6	0
September 6	Boston	3–8	L	6.1	6	4	4	3	4	2
September 12	Cleveland	1–0	W	7.0	4	0	0	2	10	0
September 17	at Seattle	3–6	—	6.0	4	1	1	1	5	0
September 22	at Texas	3–5	L	5.0	7	5	5	4	6	1
September 27	Seattle	6–5	—	6.2	8	5	5	1	3	1
October 2	Anaheim	4–5	—	7.0	3	2	2	1	3	1
Totals			**11–11**	**213.0**	**216**	**116**	**106**	**81**	**163**	**28**

INDEX

CPSIA information can be obtained at www.ICGtesting.com
Printed in the USA
BVOW031354170312

285368BV00002B/1/P

9 780471 763161